ALL

An Annotated Glossary of Common FORTH Ideograms

by Glen B. Haydon

MVP-FORTH Series

Volume 1

MOUNTAIN VIEW PRESS, INC.

MVP-FORTH SERIES

Glen B. Haydon, General Editor

1. ALL ABOUT FORTH, Glen B. Hayden, 1983

2. MVP-FORTH SOURCE LISTINGS, Glen B. Haydon and Robert E. Kuntze, 1983

3. FLOATING POINT AND MATH, Charles Springer, 1983

4. EXPERT TOOLKIT, Jack Park, 1983

5. FILE MANAGEMENT SYSTEM, Pierre Moreton, 1983

ISBN 0-914699-00-8

First Edition
  First Printing   March 1982
  Second Printing   September 1982
Second Edition
  First Printing   March 1983
  Second Printing   March 1984

MOUNTAIN VIEW PRESS, INC.
PO Box 4656
Mountain View, CA 94040

CONTENTS

PREFACE to the SECOND EDITION

The appearance of the Second Edition of this reference manual marks the beginning of a new series of MVP-FORTH books. It is Volume 1. Volume 2 contains the public domain source listings for the implementation of MVP-FORTH on three different processors. Volume 3 contains selected MVP-FORTH math extensions. Volume 4 contains high level MVP-FORTH floating point extensions.

The acceptance of MVP-FORTH has been most gratifying. The implementation of MVP-FORTH on each system has been stable for six months as Version 1.xx.02. Minor corrections have been made to 5 ideograms, <R/W>, ?STACK, BUFFER, LIST and SET-IO, for the next version, 1.xx.03. It is my intention to maintain MVP-FORTH as a stable, friendly and powerful FORTH dialect. I have three goals: First to make all of the documentation including source listings available and in the public domain; Second, to encourage the spread of portable utilities, tools and sample application programs; and, Third, to help the user make custom changes for specific applications.

FORTH can not be mastered over night. Learning from a reference manual can be difficult. The tutorial, STARTING FORTH, by Leo Brodie, Prentice Hall, 1981, is an excellent adjunct to the learning process. The present and future volumes in the MVP-FORTH Series are designed to help the learning process. However, nothing can replace active use of FORTH on a system.

The format of the Second Edition of this reference manual has been made compatible with the MVP-FORTH Series. The documentation has been updated to MVP-FORTH Version 1.xx.03.

Ideograms have been added for a 16 bit, 8086/8088 system. However, the I-O implementations are included only for the 8080/Z80 CP/M based system. Except for the disk I-O functions, all MVP-FORTH ideograms execute the same functions regardless of the system. High level FORTH programs are portable.

A new section on the inner interpreter has been added. Details of a FORTH system not covered by the glossary are discussed in this section. I appreciate the help and suggestions from Charles H. Moore and Kim Harris in developing this discussion.

I thank those who have taken the time to point out specific difficulties with MVP-FORTH and this manual. I have been able to clarify a number of the discussions. I also thank those who have pointed out the inevitable typographical errors. I hope that the new edition does not add more than it corrects.

Special thanks go to Roy Martens for his continuous support and encouragement in this venture.

I have not always adopted the generous suggestions which have been offered, though the thought and effort that has gone into them is appreciated. I remain fully responsible for the result.

GBH
March,1983

PREFACE

This glossary and MVP-FORTH document and implement a successor to fig-FORTH. The functional definitions conform with the Required Word Set of the FORTH-79 STANDARD. Both the documentation and implementation are released without any restrictions. This effort is dedicated to the future of the FORTH language.

I have tried to reconcile the several public domain versions of FORTH. At first, fig-FORTH was all that was available. Then after rumors that it was going to be withdrawn, I modified the source code to implement the FORTH-79 STANDARD. About 40 ideograms in fig-FORTH needed to be changed and many were dropped, including most of the very necessary primitives. The result was a "pure" FORTH-79 STANDARD implementation and it imposed a most frustrating limitation, especially after one had become used to fig-FORTH where access to everything was available. Then came the book, STARTING FORTH, which was the first instructional text on the use of the language. Though it made reference to FORTH-79, the function of many of its ideograms is based on poly-FORTH, whose implementation is not in the public domain. These differences have been a blow to writing portable user programs.

As a result of my frustrations with these problems,-I have assembled this ANNOTATED GLOSSARY of a living language. In conjunction with this work, I have implemented yet another version of FORTH. This full implementation of FORTH is being distributed by Mountain View Press as MVP-FORTH. The full source code for the implementation is included.

Charles Moore wrote the initial versions of FORTH. A great deal of credit goes to him for his bringing the concepts of the language to life. William Ragsdale has lead the Forth Interest Group in making the language available on some 12 CPU's with the implementation software placed in the public domain. He did not do this alone. However, there are just too many who have contributed to acknowledge them individually, so I acknowledge them all collectively.

I must acknowledge the valuable help of several people in these efforts. Jerry Boutelle adapted his Nautilus Systems Cross-Compiler to generate a FORTH-79 System and gave me many hours of tutorial in understanding the language, collaborated in the implementation of MVP-FORTH, and proofread this manuscript. Robert L. Smith has contributed to my interpretation of the FORTH-79 Standard and carefully reviewed my implementation of the Required Word Set. Klaxon Suralis has read this manuscript letter by letter and made many editorial and substantive suggestions. Roy Martens has given me the added push necessary to bring all of this work together. I have not always heeded the advice I have received and remain fully responsible for the result.

I hope that this exercise in organization will prove useful to others. The job is a never-ending one. I regret that I have not yet incorporated all of the material I have collected, and particularly that from the University of Utrecht and the University of Rochester.

GBH
March 1982

INTRODUCTION

FORTH is a relatively new computer language. Dialects of FORTH are, however, increasing in number. This GLOSSARY has been assembled to include the more common usages in the hope that it will serve as a reference to prevent the various dialects from deviating too much from one another.

I use the word ideogram to characterize the vocabulary used in FORTH and to emphasize the nature of each member of the vocabulary. These ideograms are frequently referred to as FORTH words, but the concepts associated with each ideogram are somewhat different from words in the usual context within the Indo-European cultures. I refer you to my article, "FORTH and the Nature of Ideographic Thought" for a discussion of this usage of ideograms. (1981 Rochester FORTH Standards Conference, available from Mountain View Press, Inc.)

The definition of each ideogram gives precedence to that given by the FORTH STANDARDS TEAM, as given in their publication FORTH-79 which is distributed by the Forth Interest Group, P.O. Box 1105, San Carlos, CA 94070. These definitions have been placed in the public domain. A second source is from the INSTALLATION MANUAL GLOSSARY MODEL which is also distributed by the Forth Interest Group. This publication includes in addition to the GLOSSARY, an implementation of that GLOSSARY which is placed in the public domain with the statement that further distribution must include a notice. The fig-FORTH FOR 8080 ASSEMBLY SOURCE LISTING, also from the Forth Interest Group, has served as the model for the internal structure of MVP-FORTH as it is now implemented. The contributions of the Forth Interest Group have been a major stimulus to the spread of the language.

Other implementations of FORTH have also published glossaries, but often without the details of the actual implementation. Among these one of the early ones is from the National Radio Astronomy Observatory, Tuscon, Arizona, COMPUTER DIVISION INTERNAL REPORT NO. 17, Basic Principles of FORTH Language as Applied to a PDP-11 Computer, by E. D. Rather, C. H. Moore and Jan M. Hollis, March 1974. The Kitt Peak National Observatory, Tuscon, Arizona 85726, published A FORTH PRIMER by W. Richard Stevens, February 1979 (Update 2). In addition, several Universities have implemented FORTH. Among them are the University of Utrecht, the Netherlands, and the University of Rochester, Rochester N. Y. The glossaries associated with these versions of FORTH have been made available without copyright limitations and are in the public domain.

The functional definitions given in STARTING FORTH, by Leo Brodie, Prentice Hall, 1981, are all copyrighted. However, all of those definitions were published before its appearance. Those definitions in this glossary which also appear in STARTING FORTH are indicated for the convenience of those using that instructional material. Unfortunately, there are some conflicts in the function of some ideograms with the FORTH-79 STANDARD. These have been decided in favor of the STANDARD.

All of the FORTH-79 STANDARD Required Word Set is included as faithfully as possible. I have added a number of ideograms which are unique to the implementation, in conjunction with the underlying operating system and several additional utilities which I find helpful. The primitive ideograms used in defining the FORTH-79 STANDARD are also included. The Double Number Word Set has been modified as noted.

1.   The use of parentheses around ideograms to indicate that they are primitives conflicts with the use of parentheses around comments. One cannot refer to such a primitive within a comment without terminating the comment. I have adopted the convention of placing such primitives within angle brackets. For the sake of completeness, both forms are included in the glossary, but only the angle brackets are used in the MVP-FORTH implementation.

2.   I feel that the convention of combining the ideogram 2 with other ideograms is frequently confusing. This ideogram 2 conveys the concept of quantity, such as in 2+, 2* etc. Originally, Charles H. Moore did mean 2 constants with 2CONSTANTS. He was using ratios in his calculations. On the other hand, the ideogram D is combined with other ideograms to indicate that they apply to double precision numbers such as DMAX, DMIN, DNEGATE, etc. I find the ideograms in the FORTH-79 Extension Word Sets headed 11.1 DOUBLE NUMBER WORD SETS, yet using the ideogram, 2, to be confusing. True, it makes little difference in some cases, and the use of synonyms is appropriate; but a DOUBLE NUMBER WORD SET should have the connotation of double numbers associated with them. Thus, I have made the basic definitions of all words in that set start with D, rather than the 2, that some of them now have. There are some systems in which the ideograms beginning with 2 and D will have different implementations. Beware! For those already in the habit of using the original definitions, and for possible applications already written, I have implemented the ideograms as synonyms.

An EDITOR vocabulary is not included in the

ANNOTATED GLOSSARY or in the MVP-FORTH source code; however, two rudimentary editing ideograms are included: PP and CLEAR . They make it possible to enter and load your choice of editors from the published listings. Several good line editors and screen editors are available some of which are in the public domain. For convenience, the line editor from FORTH DIMENSIONS, Vol III, No 3 has been loaded on top of MVP-FORTH. Remember, when using an editor it is necessary to call it up with the appropriate vocabulary name, usually EDITOR.

THE INNER INTERPRETER

The key to FORTH's power lies in the efficiency of its inner interpreter. However, understanding the operations of the inner interpreter is not necessary for effective use of FORTH. Read this section to better appreciate the power of FORTH.

FORTH provides an interface for software to a wide variety of processors. When a common dialect of FORTH is implemented on different processors, all high level FORTH programs are portable among them. The implementation of FORTH's inner interpreter is processor dependent and will be different for each processor. However, the necessary functions can be described in FORTH.

FORTH uses four pointers. In the implementation of FORTH on a given processor, these pointers may be assigned actual registers or memory addresses. The functions of the inner interpreter must be coded for the paticular processor. It is however, possible to make the pointers FORTH variables and to describe the implementation of the functions in high level FORTH. In this manner, FORTH is written in FORTH.

The FORTH implementation described here is known as indirect threaded code. The implementation is different for direct threaded or token threaded FORTH.

The inner interpreter determines the order of execution of FORTH functions. The most common functions are a series of other FORTH functions which are compiled in colon definitions. Such compiled definitions contain a series of addresses to the successive functions to be executed. Colon definitions can nest other colon definitions without limit. Of course the size of memory does impose a limit on the space in the dictionary for new definitions. The inner interpreter is able to find its way through all levels of nesting.

All processors have a "program counter". In our virtual FORTH system we make the program counter a variable (PC). Our implementation of FORTH uses two stacks. We use a pointer to the top of each of these stacks: the data stack pointer, (SP), and a return stack pointer, (RP). The data stack is used for temporary storage of data and for operations on data. The return stack is used to keep track of the order of nested functions for the inner interpreter. We make the data stack the same as the processors hardware stack. We must keep up with two other FORTH pointers: the interpreter pointer, (IP), and the current word pointer, (W). IP points to the next word to be interpreted. W points to the word currently being executed. The key to the function of FORTH lies in the interaction among these pointers.

We define the pointers as variables in our virtual system.

```
VARIABLE   PC          Program counter
VARIABLE   SP          Data Stack Pointer
VARIABLE   RP          Return Stack Pointer
VARIABLE   IP          Interpreter Pointer
VARIABLE   W           Current Word pointer
```

Ultimately, operation of FORTH is contained in a group of code instructions which are actually implemented in machine language. In our virtual machine we describe their function in high level FORTH.

For a top down description of our inner interpreter we can begin with just colon definitions. The dictionary header of each colon definition includes a code field. The appropriate function is innitiated by an indirect jump to a group of machine instructions being pointed to by the code field. This group of machine instructions, in fact all machine instructions, end with a jump to the next group of machine instructions to be executed. The interpreter pointer keeps track of that location. The machine instructions for a colon definition, parse a series of addresses contained in the definition's parameter field. These addresses point to the successive functions which make up a colon definition. The last function must terminate the colon definition.

For the bottom up description we begin with NEXT which terminates machine code instructions. It gets the next address value from the IP and moves it to the PC.

This function is factored into two parts:

```
: NEXT1   W @ @     PC ! ;
```

The address pointed to by W is moved to the PC. The new address in the PC becomes the address of the next opcode for the system.

Note: Some implementations of FORTH may increment the address in W at this point, however, it is not necessary.

NEXT then uses NEXT1.

```
: NEXT    IP @ @     W !
          2 IP +!    NEXT1 ;
```

NEXT fetches the address currently being pointed to by IP and stores it in W. The address in IP is incremented 2 bytes to set it to the next address. Finally, the function of

NEXT1 places the address pointed to by W into the system's PC.

The header for each entry in the FORTH dictionary contains a code field. The code field points to a function written in machine code for the system's hardware, whence its name. The code segment pointed to by the code field instructs the program in it's handling of the information at the beginning of the parameter field.

The code field for a colon definition points to a machine code segment often given the label DOCOL. This label is not a FORTH ideogram and is not directly accessible in most FORTH implementations. DOCOL's function must interpret the series of code field addresses which follow.

DOCOL may be factored. The factor, DOCOL1, illustrates the use of a variable as a stack pointer. Remember, a stack pointer points to the current value on the top of a stack. When a value is added to the top of a stack, i.e., pushed, the stack pointer must be moved to the new address before the value is stored there. Also, after a value is removed from a stack, i.e., popped, the stack pointer must be moved to the previous value on the stack.

DOCOL1 saves the contents of IP on the return stack.

: DOCOL1   -2 RP +!   IP @   RP @ ! ;

RP is first decremented 2 bytes, one stack cell, in preparation for pushing a new value. Then the current address in IP is fetched and placed in the new cell on the return stack.

Then the function at DOCOL can be defined.

: DOCOL   DOCOL1   W @ 2+ IP !   NEXT ;

After storing the current value in IP on the return stack, the value in W is fetched and incremented by 2 to point to the next word to be interpreted. It is then stored in IP and NEXT is executed.

Note: In actual implementations, the value in W may be incremented in two steps which may occur at different points.

A colon definition is terminated by executing EXIT in most FORTH's vocabularies. Rather than continuing through the address cells in the parameter field of a colon definition, the top of the return stack is popped to IP before NEXT is executed.

```
: EXIT   RP @ @    IP !   2 RP +!
  NEXT   ;
```

The value currently pointed to by RP is fetched and stored in IP.   RP must now be changed to point to the next value on the return stack.   Then NEXT is executed.   In fig-FORTH, the ideogram, ;S, was used.

In the following discussion we will need to push and pop values to our virtual data stack.   The data stack in our descriptive FORTH, might be thought of as the accumulator of our virtual system.   We therefore define a PUSH and POP. These are not a part of FORTH's standard vocabulary.   By factoring these functions, the subsequent discussion is much simplified.

```
: PUSH   -2 SP +!  SP @ ! ;
```

Move SP to point to a new value, fetch the address of the new location and store the value.

```
: POP   SP @ @   -2 SP +! ;
```

Fetch the value on the top of the data stack and then move SP to the previous value.

It is possible to interrupt the normal sequence of the inner interpreter and execute the address on the top of the data stack by EXECUTE:

```
: EXECUTE   POP  W !   NEXT1 ;
```

The value currently on the top of the stack is moved to W.   The opcode pointed to by this address is then executed by NEXT1. If the location pointed to by the address on the top of the stack is not machine code, the results are completely unpredictable.

Execution of a variable places it's parameter field address on the data stack.   The function pointed to by the code field address of a variable, is often given the label DOVAR. The label is not an ideogram in most FORTH implementations.

```
: DOVAR   W @   2+   PUSH   NEXT ;
```

The address in W is incremented 2 bytes and is pushed to the data stack.   NEXT is then executed.   This function places the address of an integer variable on the top of the stack.   It is the address of the beginning of the parameter field.

Execution of a constant places it's value on the data

stack. The function pointed to by the code field address of a constant, is often given the label D O C O N. The label is not an ideogram in most F O R T H implementations.

```
: D O C O N    W a 2+  a   PUSH   NEXT  ;
```

The address in W is incremented 2 bytes, it's contents is fetched and pushed on the top of the data stack. N E X T is then executed. This function places the contents of the parameter field on the top of the data stack. It is the value of the constant.

Execution of a user variable places it's address on the data stack. User variables are accessed as an offset relative to the beginning of the user table. This is accomplished by a code routine which is often labeled D O U S E.

```
: D O U S E    W a 2+ a      UP  +
               ( Add base of user table.)
               PUSH    NEXT  ;
```

The contents of the cell following that pointed to by W is fetched. UP is a constant (it may be a variable in some systems) which is the address of the base of the user table. The values are added and pushed on the data stack. It is the actual user variable address. N E X T is then executed.

One of the most unusual capabilities of F O R T H is the ability to write new defining ideograms. A defining ideogram is used to compile new entries into the dictionary with a new and unique function. That function is usually defined in high level F O R T H following the ideogram D O E S> . A short code operation is called to initiate the high level definitions. The defining ideogram's definition is a standard colon definition. It is then used to define new ideograms.

The defining ideogram uses a call, or a jump to a subroutine which places the address for the return function on the top of the hardware stack. Remember, in our system the hardware stack and the data stack are the same. The called subroutine will place a newly defined ideogram's parameter address on the data stack and then execute the code field addresses for the functions which follow D O E S> in the defining ideogram. The subroutine which is called is often given the label D O D O E S, but it is not included in the F O R T H vocabulary.

This F O R T H operation is one of the most difficult to understand. It might help to construct a diagram showing the memory image of each of three words: D O E S>, a new defining word, and a new word being defined with it. Then trace the operation of each word.

```
: DODOES   DOCOL1
     ( Push IP on the return stack )
  POP  IP !
     ( Store the call's return address)
  W @ 2+  PUSH
     ( Push the address of the next cell)
  NEXT  ;
```

DOCOL1 saves the current interpreter pointer on the return
stack. Remember, a call routine including the call to DODOES
will leave the address of the cell following the call on the
systems hardware stack and we have made that the data stack.
We pop the return address and store it in IP. We then fetch the
address in W, increment it by 2 and push it onto the data stack.
Finally, we execute NEXT.

     In addition to these several labels pointed to by the
code field of entries in the dictionary, several other machine
instructions are useful. They include a method of including a
value in a colon definition which is to be pushed on the data
stack, and two branch routines.

     In colon definitions a series of code field addresses
is usually compiled. However, it is occasionally desirable to
compile an integer value which is to be placed on the stack at
run time. This requires that the preceeding code field address
places the contents of the next address on the data stack and
then skip to the next address in the parameter field. This
function is accomplished with the FORTH ideogram LIT .

```
: LIT    IP @ @  PUSH  2 IP +!
  NEXT  ;
```

The value pointed to by the address in IP is fetched and pushed
onto the data stack. IP is incremented 2 bytes to skip to the
next code field address before going to NEXT.

     Structures such as IF ... ELSE ... THEN and BEGIN ...
UNTIL require conditional and unconditional branches. They
require a change in the interpretive pointer for the next
execution. These can be accomplished with the designation of
an absolute jump or a relative jump from the occurance of the
code. The relative jump is more common.

     The unconditional branch is easiest and often given
the label BRAN.

```
: BRAN   IP @ @
  IP @
  +   IP !
  NEXT  ;
```

Fetch the contents of address pointed to by W. It is the offset. Then fetch the address itself and add them. This will be the address to which to jump. Store it in IP and execute NEXT.

The conditional branch is often given the label ZBRAN.

```
: ZBRAN  0=
    IF   BRAN
    ELSE   2  IP  +!
    THEN
    NEXT  ;
```

If the value on the stack is 0, set the flag left on the stack or else reset it. Then if the flag is set, i.e., value was a zero, execute BRAN. If the flag is reset, then skip the cell containing the offset value and start execution with the next cell.

Finally, we need an address to place in the code field for a code definition using the assembler. This is simple. Remember that the code field address is a pointer to machine code. The machine code begins at the next address. This is accomplished by CODE in FORTH.

After CREATE in the definition of CODE, the sequence, HERE DUP 2- ! , places the next address in the code field address of the new ideogram. This address is the beginning of the parameter field which contains machine code. It must end with a jump to NEXT.

This discussion has attempted to use FORTH to describe those function which must be implemented in machine code to fit the actual processor. A way of thinking of this has been to assume a virtual processor which runs FORTH. In many cases, I think that you will find that the functions are only made difficult by trying to describe them in English. The language, FORTH, provides a compact and precise way of describing a function. Including both the English and FORTH descriptions might also help learning FORTH.

All of the words in the FORTH-79 STANDARD Required Word Set are included with the functions as defined by the Standards Team. The Required Word Set can be cross-compiled alone to make a "pure" implementation of the FORTH-79 STANDARD which includes none of the primitives or extensions. To my reading, the STANDARD implies that all added vocabulary must be written in "pure" FORTH-79, including the Double Number Word Set, the Reference Word Set, and all application programs. Such a "pure" FORTH-79 STANDARD should be used to comply with those requirements.

I find the STANDARD's requirements frustrating, and the MVP-FORTH is not strictly standard, though all of the individual functional definitions are met. MVP-FORTH has been cross-compiled to include all of the primitives and selected FORTH-79 Extensions, Reference Word Set, and the additional utilities. Source for the implementation of all but a few obsolete ideograms are included in the glossary and the full implementation source is included in the MVP-FORTH product. The "pure" version is simply cross-compiled with all non STANDARD ideograms left headerless.

The glossary of FORTH ideograms is organized in order of the ASCII codes used in the ideograms. Where the definition of the ideogram is used in FORTH-79, that definition is given. Thence, as necessary, definitions are taken from the FORTH-79 EXTENSION WORD SET, referred to as FORTH-79(E); the FORTH-79 REFERENCE WORD SET, referred to as FORTH-79(R); fig-FORTH; and finally a few of my own writing. Those words which have a function defined in STARTING FORTH are indicated, and though most of these words have the same function, not all of them do. It should be noted that none of the words defined in STARTING FORTH are original with that publication.

For groupings of the ideograms by function, copies of the FORTH-79 and fig-FORTH handy reference cards are included in the appendix.

Each entry in the glossary includes the following information:

1. The entry, stack notation before and after implementation, the attributes, the assigned serial number where available, and a designation with regard to its use:

MVP-FORTH

These entries include the entire FORTH-79 STANDARD Required Word Set, as well as most of those necessary to implement them. Together, they are included in the source for the cross-compiler and the assembly source listings. This combination constitutes the MVP-FORTH nucleus. Everything except the Required Word Set may be compiled as headerless ideograms to produce a "pure" FORTH-79.

MVP-FORTH - DISK I-O

These entries for the system disk access routines are also included in the MVP-FORTH nucleus. However, they will not be the same for all implementations.

MVP-FORTH - UTILITY

These entries include a selection of utilities. Their source is included as a set of screens which may be loaded with the MVP-FORTH nucleus to provide a convenient MVP-FORTH Development System.

MVP-FORTH - SUPPLEMENTAL

These entries include those additional definitions necessary to implement some of the older ideograms and the vocabulary used in STARTING FORTH. Note that some STARTING FORTH functions conflict with FORTH-79 STANDARD functions. These will not function according to STARTING FORTH usage. For example, many students have lost much time trying to make the examples of .S run with fig-FORTH or FORTH-79 systems. This is just not possible.

NOT USED

These entries are included for reference only. Should one wish to use them in their implementation, he will have to add them. In many cases, the necessary implementation is given.

2. The form of the use of the ideogram where appropriate.

3. The pronunciation of the ideogram where appropriate.

4. The functional definition cited is from the first reference listed. It is followed by other common sources which define the function. Some of the secondary sources may be in conflict with the first one.

5. The implementation may be given in high level FORTH, or in assembly language for the Cross-Compiler. Note that unless otherwise indicated all numerical values are given in hex and that some labels refer to words only available in the Cross-

Compiler. The actual implementation in MVP-FORTH may differ, but the functional definition will be adhered to.

6. The source usage lists some the occurrences of that ideogram in other definitions included in the source for MVP-FORTH Version 1.xx.03. MVP-FORTH utilizes indirect threaded code and follows the example in fig-FORTH. See the section on the inner interpreter for a description of these routines in high level FORTH. Efforts have been made to make the implementation functionally correct, not efficient or elegant. Though some of the FORTH-79 STANDARD functions are particularly inefficient, the stated functions have been carefully adhered to. As use develops, more efficient implementation of the ideograms will be utilized. Implementations of FORTH in direct threaded code may run faster. Use of the cross compiler will facilitate investigations of new implementations; however, in all cases the functional definitions should remain as given here. Use new ideograms to do new things.

7. The example may be an important or representative definition from the source code, a reasonable use, or in a few cases a contrived use. With each example is a short discussion of the example.

8. The comment tries to put that ideogram in some sort of perspective.

9. Occasional notes have been added at points of particular concern or where caution must be used.

The specialized use of terms and notations conforms with those of FORTH-79, A Publication of the FORTH Standards Team, October 1980, and distributed by the FORTH Interest Group. That publication with the exception of the glossaries, is included in Appendix A, for your convenience. The contributions of the Team to the evolution of FORTH are recognized and acknowledged.

Store n at address.

Pronounced: store

Defined in: FORTH-79, fig-FORTH, STARTING FORTH

Implementation:

8080:

```
CODE  !   H POP  D POP  E M MOV  H INX
   D M MOV  NEXT JMP  END-CODE
```

Source usage: Many

Example: CAUTION - May corrupt or crash your system.

HEX 13 4AC2 ! DECIMAL

   You are in HEX and the single precision integer 13 is stored in the memory cell beginning at address 4AC2.

Comment: This is one of the most dangerous words in FORTH. It performs no bounds checking and will quite happily overwrite your dictionary, FORTH nucleus, or operating system. A store to an incorrect address may crash your system right away, or it may work like a time bomb, spitting out mysterious gibberish hours later. The responsibility for its correct use lies entirely with you, the user. You had better have adequate back up of all of your work.

   Almost every FORTH implementation has this operator. The byte order is unspecified in FORTH-79. In some CPUs, the byte order is reversed from others.

!CSP   ---   NOT USED

Save the stack position in CSP. Used as part of the compiler security.

Defined in: fig-FORTH

Implementation:

```
: !CSP   SP@  CSP ! ;
```

Source usage: None.

Example:

!CSP

The current position of the stack pointer is saved in the user variable CSP. The stack itself is left unchanged.

Comment: This ideogram conspires with ?CSP to trap malformed colon definitions at compile time. It is used in fig-FORTH; error checking is not standardized and may vary widely among implementations. Although the fig-FORTH approach is used here, this ideogram is next to useless; MVP-FORTH omits it, spelling out "SP@ CSP !" as required.

!L   n   seg   addr   ---   MVP-FORTH

Store the value n in segment seg at address addr. Used in 8086/8088 systems.

Defined in: MVP-FORTH

Implementation:

8086/8088

CODE !L   BX POP   DS POP   AX POP   [BX], AX MOV
     BX, CS MOV   DS, BX MOV   NEXT JMP   END-CODE

Source usage: None.

Example:

HEX
4182 2000 0 !L
DECIMAL

Store the 16-bit value, 4182, in segment 2000, address 0.

Comment: The ideogram is used with the 8086/8088, 16 bit CPU. This CPU utilizes segments for the extended addressing. In MVP-FORTH for the 8086/8088, all segments begin at the same location.

ud1   ---   ud2   158   MVP-FORTH

Generate from an unsigned double-number ud1, the next ASCII character which is placed in an output string. The result ud2 is the quotient after division by BASE and is maintained for further processing. Used between <# and #>.

Pronounced: sharp

Defined in: FORTH-79, fig-FORTH, STARTING FORTH

Implementation:

```
: #   BASE @ M/MOD   ROT  9  OVER  <
    IF  7  +  THEN
        30  +  HOLD  ;
```

Source usage: #S

Example:

43 0 <# # # # #> TYPE

The value 43 is extended to unsigned double precision by placing a zero on top. Using the current value of BASE, the numeric conversion ideograms then extract the three low-order digits, "043", passing them as an ASCII string to TYPE.

Comment: The fig-FORTH definition of "#", used herein, complies with FORTH-79. The number is unsigned. If the value is to be signed, additional treatment is required.

#>   ud --- addr n   190   MVP-FORTH

End pictured numeric output conversion. Drop ud , leaving the text address, and character count, suitable for TYPE.

Pronounced: sharp-greater

Defined in: FORTH-79, fig-FORTH, STARTING FORTH

Implementation:

```
: #>   DDROP  HLD  @  PAD  OVER  -  ;
```

Source usage: D.R

Example:

43 0 <# # # # #> TYPE

The value 43 is extended to unsigned double precision by placing a zero on top. Using the current value of BASE, the numeric conversion ideograms then extract the three low-order digits, "043", passing them as an ASCII string to TYPE.

Comment: This ideogram is one of a group which must be used together in formatting the output of numbers. # #< #S <#

#BUFF   --- n   MVP-FORTH
#BUF

A constant returning the number of disk buffers allocated.   For
the disk I-O routines to work correctly #BUFF must be greater
than 1.   Note that some implementations use only one F.

Defined in: fig-FORTH(8080)

Implementation:

NBUF   CONSTANT   #BUFF

Source usage: SAVE-BUFFERS   CHANGE

Example:

: SAVE-BUFFERS   #BUFF   1+   0
   DO 0 BUFFER DROP LOOP ;

   There is one pass through the loop for each buffer.

Comment: This constant simplifies the disk I/O code.   Not
all implementations have it.   In MVP-FORTH, its value may be
altered and then CHANGE will dynamically reconfigure memory
to include the new number of buffers.

#S   ud --- 0 0   209   MVP-FORTH

Convert all digits of an unsigned 32-bit number ud, adding each
to the pictured numeric output text, until remainder is zero.   A
single zero is added to the output string if the number was
initially zero.   Use only between <# and #>.

Pronounced: sharp-s

Defined in: FORTH-79, fig-FORTH, STARTING FORTH

Implementation:

: #S   BEGIN   #   DDUP   OR   NOT   UNTIL   ;

Source usage: D.R

Example:

43   0   <# #S #> TYPE

The value 43 is extended to unsigned double precision by placing a zero on top.   Using the current value of base, the numeric conversion ideograms then extract the three low-order digits, "043", passing them as an ASCII string to TYPE.

Comment: This ideogram is one of a group which must be used together in formatting the output of numbers.   #   #<   #S   <#   HOLD   SIGN

'   --- addr   I, 171   MVP-FORTH

If executing, leave the parameter field address of the next word accepted from the input stream.   If compiling, compile this address as a literal;   later execution will place this value on the stack.   An error condition exists if not found after a search of the CONTEXT and FORTH vocabularies.   Within a colon-definition ' <name> is identical to [' <name>] LITERAL .

Form: '   <name>

Pronounced: tick

Defined in: FORTH-79,   fig-FORTH, STARTING FORTH

Implementation:

: '   -FIND   NOT
          ABORT" NOT FOUND"
   DROP   [COMPILE] LITERAL   ;   IMMEDIATE

Source usage: .SL   .SR   CHANGE   COLD   CONFIGURE   FREEZE

Example:

' MAX-DRV   @   .

Find the parameter field address of the constant, MAX-DRV, fetch and print that constant's value.

Comment: This FORTH-79 version searches only FORTH after CONTEXT. The fig-FORTH implementation, however, searched CURRENT as well. This difference between the two implementations is subtle, yet pervasive.

CAUTION: STARTING FORTH users: do not EXECUTE the parameter field address returned by this implementation until you use CFA to convert it to the code field address. Otherwise, you will crash the system.

'-FIND   --- addr   U   MVP-FORTH

A user variable containing the address to be executed by -FIND.

Defined in: MVP-FORTH

Implementation:

16 USER '-FIND

Source usage: -FIND

Example:

'-FIND @ 2+ NFA ID.

   Type the name of the function currently assigned to -FIND, assuming it is not headerless.

Comment: By vectoring the -FIND function, it is possible to dynamically change the implementation of that function. Thus it is not necessary to recompile the source to make such changes.

'?TERMINAL   --- f   MVP-FORTH

A user variable containing the compilation address to be executed by ?TERMINAL.

Defined in: MVP-FORTH

Implementation:

18 USER '?TERMINAL

Source usage: ?TERMINAL
         Example:

: ?TERMINAL   '?TERMINAL @ EXECUTE ;

The example is taken from the source for ?TERMINAL. It vectors the run-time function to the code field address stored at '?TERMINAL.

Comment: Unfortunately, hardware differences do not permit all implementations of this ideogram to be exactly the same. Thus it is not fully portable among all implementations of MVP-FORTH. However, the differences are minor, and can be adjusted to easily.

'ABORT   --- addr   U   MVP-FORTH

A user variable containing the compilation address to be executed by ABORT.

Defined in: MVP-FORTH

Implementation:

1A   USER   'ABORT

Source usage: ABORT

Example:

'ABORT @   2+   NFA ID.

Type the name of the function currently assigned to ABORT, assuming it is not headerless.

Comment: By vectoring the ABORT function, it is possible to dynamically change the implementation of that function. Thus it is not necessary to recompile the source to make such changes.

'BLOCK   --- addr   U   MVP-FORTH

A user variable containing the compilation address to be executed by BLOCK.

Defined in: MVP-FORTH

Implementation:

1C   USER   'BLOCK

Source usage: BLOCK

Example:

'BLOCK @ 2+ NFA ID.

   Type the name of the function currently assigned to BLOCK,
assuming it is not headerless.

Comment: By vectoring the BLOCK function, it is possible to
dynamically change the implementation of that function. Thus
it is not necessary to recompile the source to make such
changes.

'CR   --- addr   U   MVP-FORTH

A user variable containing the compilation address to be
executed by CR.

Defined in: MVP-FORTH

Implementation:

1E USER 'CR

Source usage: CR

Example:

'CR @ 2+ NFA ID.

   Type the name of the function currently assigned to CR,
assuming it is not headerless.

Comment: By vectoring the CR function, it is possible to
dynamically change the implementation of that function. Thus
it is not necessary to recompile the source to make such
changes.

'EMIT   --- addr   U   MVP-FORTH

A user variable containing the compilation address to be
executed by EMIT.

Defined in: MVP-FORTH

Implementation:

20 USER 'EMIT

Source usage: EMIT

Example:

'EMIT @ 2+ NFA ID.

   Type the name of the function currently assigned to EMIT, assuming it is not headerless.

Comment: By vectoring the EMIT function, it is possible to dynamically change the implementation of that function. Thus it is not necessary to recompile the source to make such changes. 'EMIT is particularly useful for redirecting terminal output to the printer.

'EXPECT   ---   MVP-FORTH

A user variable containing the compilation address to be executed by EXPECT.

Defined in: MVP-FORTH

Implementation:

22   USER 'EXPECT

Source usage: EXPECT

Example:

: EXPECT 'EXPECT @ EXECUTE ;

   This example is taken from the source code for EXPECT. It vectors the run-time function to the code field address stored at 'EXPECT.

Comment: With the development of some application, it is desirable to change EXPECT. This is easily done by vectoring.

'INTERPRET   --- addr   U MVP-FORTH

A user variable containing the compilation address to be executed by INTERPRET.

Defined in: MVP-FORTH

Implementation:

24   USER 'INTERPRET

Source usage: INTERPRET

Example:

'INTERPRET @ 2+ NFA ID.

   Type the name of the function currently assigned to
INTERPRET, assuming it is not headerless.

Comment: By vectoring the INTERPRET function, it is possible
to dynamically change the implementation of that function.
Thus it is not necessary to recompile the source to make such
changes.

'KEY   --- addr   U   MVP-FORTH

A user variable containing the compilation address to be
executed by KEY.

Defined in: MVP-FORTH

Implementation:

26 USER 'KEY

Source usage: KEY

Example:

'KEY @ 2+ NFA ID.

   Type the name of the function currently assigned to KEY,
assuming it is not headerless.

Comment: By vectoring the KEY function, it is possible to
dynamically change the implementation of that function. Thus
it is not necessary to recompile the source to make such
changes.

'LOAD   --- addr   U   MVP-FORTH

A user variable containing the compilation address to be
executed by LOAD.

Defined in: MVP-FORTH

Implementation:

28 USER 'LOAD

Source usage: LOAD

Example:

'LOAD @ 2+ NFA ID.

   Type the name of the function currently assigned to LOAD,
assuming it is not headerless.

Comment: By vectoring the LOAD function, it is possible to
dynamically change the implementation of that function. Thus
it is not necessary to recompile the source to make such
changes.

'NUMBER   --- addr   U   MVP-FORTH

A user variable containing the compilation address to be
executed by NUMBER.

Defined in: MVP-FORTH

Implementation:

2A USER 'NUMBER

Source usage: NUMBER

Example:

'NUMBER @ 2+ NFA ID.

   Type the name of the function currently assigned to NUMBER,
assuming it is not headerless.

Comment: By vectoring the NUMBER function, it is possible to
dynamically change the implementation of that function. Thus
it is not necessary to recompile the source to make such
changes.

'PAGE   --- addr   U   MVP-FORTH

A user variable containing the compilation address to be
executed by PAGE.

Defined in: MVP-FORTH

Implementation:

2C USER 'PAGE

Source usage: PAGE

Example:

`'PAGE @ 2+ NFA ID.`

Type the name of the function currently assigned to PAGE, assuming it is not headerless.

Comment: By vectoring the PAGE function, it is possible to dynamically change the implementation of that function.   Thus it is not necessary to recompile the source to make such changes.

`'R/W      --- addr                    U  MVP-FORTH`

A user variable containing the compilation address to be executed by R/W.

Defined in: MVP-FORTH

Implementation:

`2E   USER  'R/W`

Source usage: R/W

Example:

`'R/W @ 2+ NFA ID.`

Type the name of the function currently assigned to R/W, assuming it is not headerless.

Comment: By vectoring the R/W function, it is possible to dynamically change the implementation of that function.   Thus it is not necessary to recompile the source to make such changes.

`'S        --- addr            MVP-FORTH - SUPPLEMENTAL`

Place the address of the top of the stack on the top of the stack.

Defined in: STARTING FORTH

Implementation:

`: 'S   SP@  ;`

Source usage: None.

Example:

'S   U.

The address of the top of the stack is pushed onto the stack and then printed leaving the stack unchanged.

Comment: This ideogram is an alias for SP@ and is defined here only for the convenience of those working with STARTING FORTH.   Usually it is more useful to use DEPTH.

'STREAM   ---   addr   MVP-FORTH

Returns the address of the next character in the input stream.

Defined by: MVP-FORTH

Implementation:

```
: 'STREAM    BLK   @   ?DUP
     IF   BLOCK   ELSE   TIB   @   THEN
              >IN   @   +   ;
```

Source usage: ." <WORD> ABORT"

Example:

```
: ."      'STREAM   C@   22   =
              IF   1   >IN   +!
     ELSE   22   STATE   @
              IF   COMPILE   <.">   THEN
     WORD   DUP   C@   1+   OVER   +   C@   22   =   NOT
     ?STREAM   STATE   @
              IF   C@   1+   ALLOT
     ELSE   COUNT   TYPE
        THEN
     THEN   ;     IMMEDIATE
```

This example is taken from the MVP-FORTH source code.

Comment: This ideogram provides a useful factor to return the current address if the input stream.

'T&SCALC   ---   addr   U   MVP-FORTH - DISK I-O

A user variable containing the compilation address to be executed by T&SCALC.

Defined in: MVP-FORTH

Implementation:

30   USER   'T&SCALC

Source usage: T&SCALC

Example:

'T&SCALC   @   2+   NFA   ID.

   Type the name of the function currently assigned to
T&SCALC, assuming it is not headerless.

Comment: By vectoring the T&SCALC function, it is possible to
dynamically change the implementation of that function.   Thus
it is not necessary to recompile the source to make such
changes.

'TITLE   ---   addr   MVP-FORTH - UTILITY

A variable holding the compilation address executed by TRIAD
to place a message at the bottom of each printed page.

Defined in: MVP-FORTH

Implementation:

VARIABLE   'TITLE   ' TITLE   CFA   'TITLE   !

Source usage: None.

Example:

FIND   CR   'TITLE   !

Set the vector so that TRIAD will print no message text at the
bottom of the page.

Comment: By defining special message ideograms, any text may
be inserted at the bottom of each page of copy.   The code for a
form-feed could be included with the title if desired.   The
ideogram TITLE supplies the default message.

'VOCABULARY   ---   MVP-FORTH

A user variable containing the compilation address to be
executed by VOCABULARY.

Defined in: MVP-FORTH

Implementation:

32   USER   'VOCABULARY

Source usage: VOCABULARY

Example:

' <VOCABULARYFIG>   CFA   'VOCABULARY   !

   The example will change the function of VOCABULARY in MVP-FORTH from the FORTH-79 STANDARD to fig-FORTH.

Comment: The function of the ideogram, VOCABULARY, as defined in the FORTH-79 STANDARD, is more restrictive than in fig-FORTH.   Although it is non-STANDARD, many users prefer the latter function.   Others, have new functions for VOCABULARY. Vectoring makes it possible to change functions easily.

'WORD   --- addr   U   MVP-FORTH

A user variable containing the compilation address to be executed by WORD.

Defined in: MVP-FORTH

Implementation:

34   USER   'WORD

Source usage: WORD

Example:

'WORD @ 2+   NFA   ID.

   Type the name of the function currently assigned to WORD, assuming it is not headerless.

Comment: By vectoring the WORD function, it is possible to dynamically change the implementation of that function.   Thus it is not necessary to recompile the source to make such changes.

(---   I, 122   MVP-FORTH

Accept and ignore comment characters from the input stream, until the next right parenthesis. As a word, the left

parenthesis must be followed by one blank.   It may be freely
used while executing or compiling.   An error condition exists
if the input stream is exhausted before the right parenthesis.

Form   (xxx ...)

Pronounced: paren   close-paren

Defined in: FORTH-79, fig-FORTH, STARTING FORTH

Implementation:

: (-1 >IN +! 29 WORD C@ 1+ HERE +
    C@ 29 = NOT ?STREAM ;
    IMMEDIATE

Source usage: None.

Example:

(THIS IS A COMMENT)

   Upon executing this ideogram, the interpreter skips through
the input stream until a close-paren (right parenthesis) is
found.   The enclosed comment is in effect, one big ignored
ideogram.

Comment: This ideogram is common in all versions of FORTH.
Customarily, the first line of every source screen is used for a
comment, holding a screen title, author's initials, and the date
of last modification.   Unlike other languages', FORTH's
parentheses may not be nested.

(.")   ---   C   NOT USED

The run-time procedure, compiled by ." which transmits the
following in-line text to the selected output device.

Defined in: fig-FORTH

Implementation:

The function of this ideogram has been assigned to <.">.

Comment: This ideogram, because of the close-paren, plays
havoc with FORTH comments.   Thus, <."> has been assigned its
function in MVP- FORTH.

(+LOOP)   n ---   C   NOT USED

The run-time procedure compiled by +LOOP, which increments
the loop index by n and tests for loop completion. See +LOOP.

Defined in: fig-FORTH

Implementation:

The function of this ideogram has been assigned to <+LOOP>.

Comment: This ideogram, because of the close-paren, plays
havoc with FORTH comments. Thus, <+LOOP> has been
assigned its function in MVP- FORTH.

(;CODE)   ---   C   NOT USED

The run-time procedure, compiled by ;CODE, that rewrites the
code field of the most recently defined word to point to the
following machine code sequence.

Defined in: fig-FORTH

Implementation:

The function of this ideogram has been assigned to <;CODE:>

Comment: This ideogram, because of the close-paren, plays
havoc with FORTH comments. Thus, <;CODE> has been
assigned its function in MVP- FORTH.

(ABORT)   ---   NOT USED

Executes after an error when WARNING is -1. This word
normally executes ABORT, but may be altered (with care) to a
user's alternative procedure.

Defined in: fig-FORTH

Implementation:

The function of this ideogram has been dropped in MVP-FORTH.

Comment: This ideogram, because of the close-paren, plays
havoc with FORTH comments. Thus, <ABORT> has been
assigned this function and is vectored from ABORT through
'ABORT.

(DO)   ---   C   NOT USED

The run-time procedure compiled by DO which moves the loop control parameters to the return stack. See DO.

Defined in: fig-FORTH

Implementation:

The function of this ideogram has been assigned to <DO>.

Comment: This ideogram, because of the close-paren, plays havoc with FORTH comments. Thus, <DO> has been assigned its function in MVP-FORTH.

(FIND)   NOT USED
          addr1   addr2   ---   pfa   b   tf   (ok)
          addr1   addr2   ---   ff   (bad)

Searches the dictionary starting at the name field address addr2, matching to the text at addr1. Returns parameter field address, length byte of name field and boolean true for a good match. If no match is found, only a boolean false is left.

Defined in: fig-FORTH

Implementation:

The function of this ideogram has been assigned to <FIND>.

Comment: This ideogram, because of the close-paren, plays havoc with FORTH comments. Thus, <FIND> has been assigned its function in MVP-FORTH.

(LINE)   n1   n2   ---   addr   count   NOT USED

Convert the line number n1 and the screen n2 to the disc buffer address containing the data. A count of 64 indicates the full line text length.

Defined in: fig-FORTH

Implementation

The function of this ideogram has been assigned to <LINE>.

Comment: This ideogram, because of the close-paren, plays havoc with FORTH comments. Thus, <LINE> has been assigned its function in MVP-FORTH.

(LOOP)   ---   C   NOT USED

The run-time procedure compiled by LOOP which increments the loop index and tests for loop completion. See LOOP.

Defined in: fig-FORTH

Implementation:

The function of this ideogram has been assigned to <LOOP>.

Comment: This ideogram, because of the close-paren, plays havoc with FORTH comments. Thus, <LOOP> has been assigned its function in MVP- FORTH.

(NUMBER)   d1   addr1   ---   d2   addr2   NOT USED

Convert the ASCII text beginning at addr1+1 with regard to BASE. The new value is accumulated into double number d1, being left as d2. addr2 is the address of the first unconvertable digit. Used by NUMBER.

Defined in: fig-FORTH

Implementation:

   This ideogram is not implemented in MVP-FORTH.

Comment: This ideogram is obsolete and has been completely dropped. The FORTH-79 STANDARD now uses CONVERT for its function. Note that STARTING FORTH also allows the use of >BINARY.

*   n1 n2 --- n3   138   MVP-FORTH

Leave the arithmetic product of n1 times n2.

Pronounced: times

Defined in: FORTH-79, fig-FORTH, STARTING FORTH

Implementation:

: *   U*   DROP ;

Source usage: Many.

Example:

3   -6   *   .

The two single precision signed integers are placed on the stack, and then multiplied together leaving a single precision signed value on the stack which is then printed.

Comment: Should an overflow occur, it will go undetected. The result returned is always the low-order 16 bits of a 32-bit signed product. It will also work for unsigned numbers with the overflow ignored.

---

*/   n1   n2   n3   ---   n4   220   MVP-FORTH

Multiply n1 by n2, divide the result by n3 and leave the quotient   n4.   n4   is rounded toward zero.   The product of n1   times   n2   is maintained as an intermediate 32-bit value for greater precision than the otherwise equivalent sequence: n1   n2   *   n3   /   .

Pronounced: times-divide

Defined in: FORTH-79, fig-FORTH, STARTING FORTH

Implementation:

: */   */MOD   SWAP   DROP   ;

Source usage: None.

Example:

13   5   3   */   .

This computes five-thirds of thirteen, rounding the result toward zero, and types the result: 21.

Comment: This ideogram is useful for scaling and rounding.   In many cases, its 32-bit intermediate precision and use of ratios eliminate the need for floating point arithmetic.

---

*/MOD   n1   n2   n3   ---   n4   n5   192   MVP-FORTH

Multiply   n1   by   n2 ,   divide the result by   n3   and leave the remainder   n4   and quotient   n5.   A 32-bit intermediate product is used as for   */ .   The remainder has the same sign as   n1 .

Pronounced: times-divide-mod

Defined in: FORTH-79, fig-FORTH, STARTING FORTH

Implementation:

: */MOD   >R   M*   R>   M/ ;

Source usage: */

Example:

13   5   3   */MOD   .   .

As with */ above, this computes five-thirds of thirteen, yielding 21. However, the remainder 2 is preserved and typed after the quotient. It could have been used to round the quotient up to 22.

Comment: This ideogram is useful for scaling and rounding. In many cases, its 32-bit intermediate precision and use of ratios eliminate the need for floating point arithmetic.

+   n1   n2   ---   n3   121   MVP-FORTH

Leave the arithmetic sum of n1 plus n2 .

Pronounced: plus

Defined in: FORTH-79, fig-FORTH, STARTING FORTH

Implementation:

8080:

CODE +   D POP   H POP   D DAD
     HPUSH   JMP   END-CODE

Source usage: Many.

Example:

2   3   +   .

Two integers are placed on the stack, added together, and then printed.

Comment: Note that carry and overflow conditions go undetected. Because of the twos-complement arithmetic, the ideogram works for both signed and unsigned numbers.

Add n to the 16-bit value at the address, by the convention
given for + .

Pronounced: plus-store

Defined in: FORTH-79, fig-FORTH, STARTING FORTH

Implementation:

8080:

```
CODE +!   H POP   D POP   M A MOV   E ADD
   A M MOV   H INX   M A MOV   D ADC   A M MOV
   NEXT JMP   END-CODE
```

Source usage: Many.

Example: CAUTION: May corrupt or crash your system.

HEX 1 4CD2 +! DECIMAL

   Increments the 16-bit cell at memory location 4CD2 by 1.

Comment: Particularly useful for incrementing/ decrementing
counters in memory. Carry and overflow are ignored. Note:
Since this ideogram will write to any location in machine
address space, take care not to corrupt your dictionary,
nucleus, or operating system.

+-   n1 n2   --- n3   MVP-FORTH

Apply the sign of n2 to n1, which is left as n3.

Defined in: fig-FORTH

Implementation:

: +-   0< IF   NEGATE   THEN   ;

Source usage: M/ ABS

Example:

-4 -2 +- .

   Since the -2 on top is less than zero, the -4 underneath is
negated, leaving the result of 4, which is printed.

Comment: Simplifies the implementation of some signed

multiplication and division operations.

+BUF   addr1   ---   addr2   f   MVP-FORTH

Advance the disc buffer address addr1 to the address of the next
buffer addr2. Boolean f is false when addr2 is the buffer
presently pointed to by the variable PREV.

Defined in: fig-FORTH

Implementation: (HDBT equals 404H - buffers size plus 4)

: +BUF   HDBT   +   DUP   LIMIT   =
    IF   DROP   FIRST   THEN
    DUP   PREV   @   -   ;

Source usage: BLOCK   BUFFER

Example:

: BUFFER   USE   @   DUP   >R
    BEGIN   +BUF   UNTIL
    USE   !   R@   @   0<
    IF   R@   2+   R@   @   7FFF   AND   0   R/W   THEN
    R@   !   R@   PREV   !   R>   2+   ;

    This example is taken from the system source code. Note
that +BUF is cyclic; when its value reaches LIMIT, it
short-circuits around to the start of the buffer area.

Comment: This ideogram, used in the implementation of the
FORTH-79 ideograms, BLOCK and BUFFER, may be available to
the programmer.

+LOOP   n   ---   I, C, 141 MVP-FORTH

Add the signed increment n to the loop index using the
convention for +, and compare the total to the limit. Return
execution to the corresponding DO until the new index is equal
to or greater than the limit (n>0) or until the new index is less
than the limit (n<0). Upon the exiting from the loop, discard
the loop control parameters, continuing execution ahead.
Index and limit are signed integers in the range -32768 ...32767
.

(Comment: It is a historical precedent that the limit for n<0
is irregular. Further consideration of the characteristic is
likely.)

Pronounced: plus-loop

Defined in: FORTH-79, fig-FORTH, STARTING FORTH

Implementation:

```
: +LOOP   3  ?PAIRS  COMPILE  <+LOOP>
    HERE  -  ,  ;      IMMEDIATE
```

Source usage: None.

Example:

```
: TEST   10 1 DO  I . 3 +LOOP ;
```

Executing TEST will cause the values 1 4 7 to be printed.

Comment: This ideogram works with DO to form a nestable control structure. LEAVE may be used to terminate the loop before the index has run its full course. Various FORTH implementations react differently to an index which changes sign over its range.

Note that when the value of n1 is <0   the loop is decreasing which means that the first value before the DO is less than the second. Also note that in such a decreasing loop the loop will be executed when the index is equal to the limit. This is different from the usual ascending loop which terminates when the index equals the limit. Furthermore, because of the signed values, the index cannot be used as an address when crossing the extremes of signed numbers.

+ORIGIN   n --- addr   NOT USED

Leave the memory address relative by n to the origin parameter area. n is the minimum address unit, either byte or word. This definition is used to access or modify the boot-up parameters at the origin area.

Defined in: fig-FORTH

Implementation:

```
: +ORIGIN   ORIGIN + ;
```

(This implementation would only be applicable in fig-FORTH. It is of no use in MVP-FORTH.)

Source usage: None.

Example:

VOC-LINK @ 20 +ORIGIN !

This example would only apply to a fig-FORTH implementation. The current value in the user variable VOC-LINK is fetched and stored in its corresponding location in the bootup parameter area of memory.

Comment: During a cold start, the user variables such as VOC-LINK must be initialized. Their initial values are fetched from an area of "boot up parameters", located near the bottom of the system at a fixed offset from the origin. Since the origin may vary among implementations, the proper absolute addresses are calculated from an offset and a base location. Instead of +ORIGIN, MVP-FORTH uses the constant INIT-USER to locate the start of this area.

,   n ---   143   MVP-FORTH

Allot two bytes in the dictionary, storing n there.

Pronounced: comma

Defined in: FORTH-79, fig-FORTH, STARTING FORTH

Implementation:

: , HERE ! 2 ALLOT ;

Source usage: Many.

Example:

: LITERAL STATE @
 IF COMPILE LIT , THEN ; IMMEDIATE

This example from the MVP-FORTH source code uses comma to place a literal value in-line with compiled code.

Comment: This ideogram is useful for initializing arrays of integers at compile time.

-        n1 n2 --- n3   134   MVP-FORTH

Subtract n2 from n1 and leave the difference n3.

Pronounced: minus

Defined in: FORTH-79, fig-FORTH, STARTING FORTH

Implementation:

8080:

CODE -   D POP   H POP   SSUB CALL
    HPUSH JMP   END-CODE

Source usage: Many.

Example:

23   -12   -   .

In this example, -12 is subtracted from 23, yielding the
result, 35 , which is printed.

Comment: A basic arithmetic operator.   As usual, borrow and
overflow conditions are ignored.

-->   ---   NOT USED

Continue interpretation with the next disk screen.

Pronounced: next-block

Defined in: FORTH-79(R), fig-FORTH

Implementation:

: -->   ?LOADING   0 >IN   !   B/SCR   BLK   @
    OVER   MOD   -   BLK   +!   ;

Source usage: None.

Example:

(On line 8 of Screen # 102:)

    -->

Assume the ideogram appears on line 8 of screen 102:
Loading of screen 102 proceeds normally until it is
encountered.   The input stream is then diverted to the start of
screen 103, bypassing lines 9-15 of screen 102.

Comment: This is one of several ways of loading a series of
screens.   In any case one should not end a screen with the
next screen number followed by LOAD.   This can produce a
heavy load on the return stack.   By using -->, the input stream
from that screen is terminated and started at the beginning of

the next sequential screen. It has a difficulty when a series of screens being loaded needs to be interrupted to insert an additional screen. The interrupting screen must be edited first. It is better to use THRU, or better still, a load screen with a list which can be commented.

-DUP   NOT USED

```
n  ---  n          (if zero)
n  ---  n  n       (if non-zero)
```

Reproduce n only if it is non-zero. This is usually used to copy a value just before IF, to eliminate the need for an ELSE part to drop it.

Defined in: fig-FORTH

Implementation:

```
: -DUP   ?DUP ;
```

Source usage: None.

Example:

```
: TEST   -DUP  IF  ." NON-ZERO RETURN CODE: " .
              THEN ;
```

Frequently, as in the above example, a non-zero value will require some sort of processing, while no action will be needed for zero. In this kind of situation, using -DUP or better ?DUP, in front of IF will save coding the additional clause " ELSE DROP ."

Comment: This ideogram is obsolete, being replaced by FORTH-79's ?DUP. Although -DUP may be included for fig-FORTH compatibility, its use is discouraged.

-FIND   MVP-FORTH

```
---  pfa  b  tf   (if found)
---  ff           (if not found)
```

Accepts the next word (delimited by blanks) in the input stream to HERE and searches the CONTEXT and then the FORTH vocabularies for a matching entry. If found, the dictionary entry's parameter field address, its length byte, and a boolean true is left. Otherwise, only a boolean false is left.

Defined in: MVP-FORTH, fig-FORTH

Implementation:

: -FIND   '-FIND @ EXECUTE ;

Source usage: ' FIND   INTERPRET   [COMPILE]

Example:

-FIND   JUNK

   Search the dictionary for the ideogram JUNK. Presumably,
the word is not in the dictionary and the flag value of 0 is left
on the stack.

Comment: Both -FIND and FIND are used. The difference is
that -FIND leaves a parameter field address and length byte,
while FIND leaves only a code field address on the stack.
They are otherwise the same. Note: the null character used
to terminate the terminal and disk buffers is defined as an
ideogram in the dictionary (See X). This may
occasionally produce bewildering error messages or unexpected
results when you use the ideograms: -FIND , ' , [COMPILE] ,
FORGET , or others which search the dictionary or define new
words. In MVP- FORTH, -FIND is vectored to <-FIND>.

-TEXT   MVP-FORTH - SUPPLEMENTAL
            addr1 n1 add2   ---   n2

Compare two strings over the length n1 beginning at addr1
and addr2 . Return zero if the strings are equal. If
unequal, return n2 , the difference between the last character
compared: addr1(i) - addr2(i).

Pronounced: dash-text

Defined in: FORTH-79(R), STARTING FORTH

Implementation:

: -TEXT   DDUP + SWAP
   DO DROP 2+ DUP 2- @ I @ - DUP
      IF DUP ABS / LEAVE THEN
   2 /LOOP
   SWAP DROP ;

Source usage: None.

Example:

HEX 4EC2 6 100 BLOCK -TEXT DECIMAL

44   ALL ABOUT FORTH

See if the first six bytes beginning at memory address 4EC2 compare with the first six bytes in BLOCK number 100H which is brought into a memory buffer placing its beginning address on the stack. A flag is left on the stack according to the test.

Comment: An ideogram which appears in slightly different forms in many editors. This version compares two byte pairs at a time. Thus, the length n1 must be even.

-TRAILING   148   MVP-FORTH
                    addr   n1   ---   addr   n2

Adjust the character count   n1   of a text string beginning at addr   to exclude trailing blanks,   i.e., the characters at the addr+n2 to addr+n1-1 are blanks.   An error condition exists if n1 is negative.

Pronounced: dash-trailing

Defined in: FORTH-79, fig-FORTH, STARTING FORTH

Implementation:

```
: -TRAILING    DUP  0
    DO   DDUP  +  1  -  C@  BL  -
       IF  LEAVE  ELSE  1  -  THEN
    LOOP  ;
```

Source usage: .LINE

Example:

PAD   COUNT   -TRAILING   TYPE

   Print the text beginning at PAD plus 1 for the count at the byte whose address is PAD, but drop all trailing spaces from the length.

Comment: This ideogram saves time in typing output, but if some spacing is necessary for formatting it should not be used.

.   n   ---   193   MVP-FORTH

Display n converted according to BASE in a free-field format with one trailing blank.   Display only a negative sign.

Pronounced: dot

Defined in: FORTH-79, fig-FORTH, STARTING FORTH

Implementation:

```
: .   S->D   D. ;
```

Source usage: Many.

Example:

```
43 .
```

   Place the value 43 on the stack and then print it.

Comment: Printing a value removes it from the stack.   In
most implementations, a stack underflow check is not performed
until after a number is printed, in which case the number is
garbage.

```
."              ---                    I, 133   MVP-FORTH
```

Interpreted or used in a colon-definition. Accept the
following text from the input stream, terminated by " (double-
quote).   If executing, transmit this text to the selected output
device.   If compiling, compile so that later execution will
transmit the text to the selected output device.   At least 127
characters are allowed in the text.   If the input stream is
exhausted before the terminating double-quote, an error
condition exists.

Form: ." cccc"

Pronounced: dot-quote

Defined in: FORTH-79, fig-FORTH, STARTING FORTH

Implementation:

```
: ."   'STREAM C@  22  =
   IF 1 >IN +!
   ELSE 22 STATE @
      IF COMPILE <."> THEN
      WORD DUP C@ 1+ OVER + C@
      22 = NOT ?STREAM STATE @
      IF C@ 1+ ALLOT
      ELSE COUNT TYPE
      THEN
   THEN ;  IMMEDIATE
```

Source usage: Many.

Example:

." PRINT THIS"

   Entering this source will cause the contents between the
double quotes to be printed, in this case - PRINT THIS.

Comment: This ideogram generally does the same thing among
the various versions of FORTH. However, not all versions
will print one or more blank spaces, and in some versions the
buffer size may be different.

.INDEX   n   ---   MVP-FORTH - UTILITY

Print line 0 on screen n.

Defined in: MVP-FORTH

Implementation:

: .INDEX
    USE @ SWAP PAD USE !
    OFFSET @ + 8 * T&SCALC SET-IO
    SEC-READ
    PAD C/L -TRAILING TYPE
    USE ! ;

Source usage: None.

Example:

20 .INDEX

Print line zero of screen 20.

Comment: This ideogram does the work inside INDEX. Since
it bypasses FORTH's buffer management and reads only the first
sector of each screen, it runs significantly faster than
conventional versions of INDEX. This illustrates how
nontransportable, nonstandard programs can sometimes run
circles around their FORTH-79 equivalents.

.LINE   line scr ---   MVP-FORTH

Print on the terminal device, a line of text fron the disk by its
line and screen number. Trailing blanks are suppressed.

Defined in: fig-FORTH

Implementation:

: .LINE   <LINE> -TRAILING   TYPE ;

Source usage: LIST

Example:

10 12 .LINE

   Print the contents of line number 10 on screen 12.

Comment: A way to print any line on any screen. Using this
ideogram, LOAD could be modified to list the 0 line of each
screen, along with the screen number, before it is loaded to
indicate the progress in loading a long series of screens and as
one way to indicate the location of an error during loading.

.R   n1 n2 ---   MVP-FORTH

Print n1 right aligned in a field of n2 characters,
according to BASE . If n2 is less than 1, no leading
blanks are supplied.

Defined in: FORTH-79(R), fig-FORTH

Implementation:

: .R   >R S->D   R>   D.R ;

Source usage: LIST

Example:

3456 10 .R

   Print the value 3456 right justified within a field of 10
spaces.

Comment: Although not available in all versions of FORTH,
this ideogram is easy to implement and quite useful in formatted
output.

.S   ---   MVP-FORTH - UTILITY
.SL
.SR
.SS

These ideograms work in concert to implement nondestructive
stack display. .S will print the values on the stack in

ascending or descending order, according to the flag in the constant .SS. The flag is set by .SL and .SR.

Defined in: MVP-FORTH, STARTING FORTH

Implementation:

```
0  CONSTANT  .SS

: .SL    0  '  .SS  !  ;

: .SR   -1  '  .SS  !  ;

: .S     CR DEPTH
   IF  .SS  IF  SP@  S0  2-
   ELSE  SP@  S0  SWAP  THEN
   DO  I @  0  D.  2  .SS  +-  +LOOP
   ELSE  ."  EMPTY STACK  "  THEN  CR  ;
```

Source usage: None.

Example:

```
1 2 3 4  .SR  .S  .SL  .S
```

Print the current values on the stack, forwards and backwards. Use the way you like best.

Comment: Some users concieve the printed list of values to proceed from the top most value to the bottom of the stack. Other users seem to work the other way. Try .S with both and determine which is most meaningful to you.

/   n1 n2 --- n3   178   MVP-FORTH

Divide n1 by n2 and leave the quotient n3. n3 is rounded toward zero.

Pronounced: divide

Defined in: FORTH-79, fig-FORTH, STARTING FORTH

Implementation:

```
: /  /MOD  SWAP  DROP  ;
```

Source usage: Many.

Example:

```
25  2  /  .
```

The two values are entered on the stack and the first is divided by the second leaving the quotient on the stack and dropping the remainder. The quotient is then printed: 12 .

Comment: Signed numbers are used with this operator. Note that division by 0 is not usually checked and the result will be unpredictable or perhaps in some implementations, an infinite loop.

/LOOP   n ---   I, C   MVP-FORTH

A DO-LOOP terminating word. The loop index is incremented by the unsigned magnitude of n. Until the resultant index exceeds the limit, execution returns to just after the corresponding DO, otherwise, the index and limit are discarded. Magnitude logic is used.

Note: The above definition is taken from the FORTH-79 STANDARD, Reference Word Set. However, to be consistant with the other loop functions, it has been implemented to increment until the resultant equals or exceeds the limit.

Pronounced   up-loop

Defined in: FORTH-79(R), STARTING FORTH

Implementation:

```
: /LOOP   3  ?PAIRS   COMPILE  </LOOP>
     HERE   -  ,  ;    IMMEDIATE
```

Source usage: TYPE EXPECT

Example:

```
: TEST   10  1  DO  I  .  3  /LOOP  ;
```

This ideogram must be used in a colon definition. In this example, to 9 from 1 print the value of the index and increment the index by 3. The values will be 1   4   7 .

Comment: Another variation for DO-LOOP control structures. This ideogram will avoid problems should the range cross from a positive to negative value as do some addresses or block numbers.

/MOD   n1 n2 --- n3 n4   198   MVP-FORTH

Divide n1 by n2 and leave the remainder n3 and quotient n4.   n3 has the same sign as n1.

Pronounced: divide-mod

Defined in: FORTH-79, fig-FORTH, STARTING FORTH

Implementation:

: /MOD   >R   S->D   R>   M/   ;

Source usage: <T&SCALC>   WHERE

Example:

25 3 /MOD . .

   Enter the two values on the stack and divide the first by the
second leaving the quotient on top. Then print the quotient
followed by the remainder.

Comment: A convenient arithmetic operator which allows full
precision and rounding in integer arithmetic. Note: Signed
numbers are used and division by zero is not usually trapped,
yielding unpredictable results or perhaps an infinite loop.

0   --- 0   MVP-FORTH

The value is defined as an ideogram.

Defined in: fig-FORTH, STARTING FORTH

Implementation:

0 CONSTANT 0

Source usage: Many.

Example:

0

   Places the value of 0 on the stack. However, since it is an
ideogram the value is taken from the name of the constant and
not converted to the value according the the present value of
BASE.

Comment: By defining common values as ideograms in the
FORTH dictionary, search time is decreased for the text
interpreter. Also, a reference to a constant compiles just 2
bytes, while a literal would require twice that. Note that not
all implementations of FORTH take advantage of this

capability.

0<   n --- flag   144   MVP-FORTH

True if n is less than zero (negative).

Pronounced: zero-less

Defined in: FORTH-79, fig-FORTH, STARTING FORTH

Implementation:

8080:

```
CODE 0<   H POP  H DAD  O H LXI
     CS  IF  H INX  THEN
     HPUSH JMP  END-CODE
```

Source usage: Many.

Example:

45   0<

   Place the value 45 on the stack and after the operation leave a
0 flag on the stack because the test fails.   The value, 45, is
lost.

Comment: One of several logical operators.   Logical operators
destroy the values being tested.

0=   n --- flag   180   MVP-FORTH

True if n is zero.

Pronounced: zero-equals

Defined in: FORTH-79, fig-FORTH, STARTING FORTH

Implementation:

: 0=   NOT ;

Source usage: FORGET

Example:

45   0=

   Place the value 45 on the stack and test it for being equal to

0. Since it is not, a 0 flag is left on the stack. The value, 45, is lost.

Comment: One of several logical operators. Logical operators destroy the values being tested.

0>   n --- flag   118   MVP-FORTH

True if n is greater than zero.

Pronounced: zero-greater

Defined in: FORTH-79, STARTING FORTH

Implementation:

: 0>   0 > ;

Source usage: PICK   FILL

Example:

45 0>

   Place the value 45 on the stack and test it for being greater than 0. Since it is, leave the flag of value 1 on the stack. The value, 45, is lost.

Comment: One of several logical operators. Logical operators destroy the values being tested.

0BRANCH   f ---   C   MVP-FORTH

   The run-time procedure to conditionally branch. If f is false (zero), the following in-line parameter is added to the interpretive pointer to branch ahead or back. Compiled by IF, UNTIL, and WHILE.

Defined in: fig-FORTH

Implementation:

8080:

CODE 0BRANCH   H POP L A MOV H ORA   BRAN1 JZ
   B INX B INX   NEXT JMP   END-CODE
Source usage: UNTIL   IF

Example:

: IF   COMPILE   OBRANCH   HERE   0 , 2 ;
IMMEDIATE

This example comes from the MVP-FORTH source code.

Comment: The compilation address of OBRANCH functions as a
conditional branching opcode for the address interpreter.   An
in-line branch displacement must follow any compiled instance
of this ideogram. These displacements are automatically
generated by the IF ... ELSE ... THEN, BEGIN ... WHILE ...
REPEAT and BEGIN ... UNTIL constructs. Additional user
defined constructs such as a CASE may be implemented by using
OBRANCH and BRANCH within new immediate compiling
ideograms.

CAUTION: Executing OBRANCH directly from the terminal or
screen will crash your system.

1   ---   1   MVP-FORTH

A common integer defined as a constant.

Defined in: fig-FORTH, STARTING FORTH

Implementation:

1 CONSTANT 1

Source usage: Many.

Example:

1

   Causes the value of 1 to be placed on the stack without having
to perform the number conversion.

Comment: By defining this value as a FORTH ideogram,
dictionary search time and memory space are saved.

1+   n --- n+1   107   MVP-FORTH

Increment n by one, according to the operation for +.

Pronounced: one-plus

Defined in: FORTH-79, fig-FORTH, STARTING FORTH

Implementation:

`: 1+   1 + ;`

or 8080:

`CODE 1+   H POP   H INX   HPUSH JMP   END-CODE`

Source usage: Many.

Example:

`45   1+`

   Enter the value 45 on the stack and then increment it by 1 leaving the value of 46 on the stack.

Comment: A required word in FORTH-79, which can be defined in high level FORTH for portability, or in code for maximum speed.

`1-`   n --- n-1   105   MVP-FORTH

Decrement   n   by one, according to the operation -.

Pronounced: one-minus

Defined in: FORTH-79, STARTING FORTH

Implementation:

`: 1-   1 - ;`

or 8080:

`CODE 1-   H POP   H DCX   HPUSH JMP   END-CODE`

Source usage: Many.

Example:

`45   1-`

   Enter the value 45 on to the stack and then decrement the value by one.

Comment: A required word in FORTH-79, which can be defined in high level FORTH for portability, or in code for maximum speed.

A common integer value defined as a constant.

Defined in: fig-FORTH, STARTING FORTH

Implementation:

2 CONSTANT 2

Source usage: Many.

Example:

2

   Causes the value of 2 to be placed on the stack without using
the number conversion routines. Since the ideogram is
actually in the dictionary, the value can be placed on the stack
even when in BINARY.

Comment: The value is used often enough that some gain is
made at interpret time by not having to search the dictionary
and then CONVERT.

2 !   d addr   ---   MVP-FORTH - SUPPLEMENTAL

Store d in 4 consecutive bytes beginning at addr, as for a double
number.

Pronounced: two-store

Defined in: FORTH-79(E), STARTING FORTH

Implementation:

: 2!   D! ;

Source usage: None.

Example: CAUTION: May corrupt or crash your system.

HEX 33.33   4AC2 2! DECIMAL

   Enter the double precision value on the stack taking four
bytes. Then remove these four bytes from the stack and store
them in four bytes beginning at memory address 4AC2. The
actual byte order within each cell is implementation dependent.

Comment: This ideogram is included in the extended double
number word set of FORTH-79. However, the ideogram D! is

a better mnemonic because it avoids conflict in interpretation
with the quantity 2. Thus D! is used in MVP-FORTH and 2! may
be added as an alias.

2*   n1 -- n2   MVP-FORTH

Leave 2*(n1).

Pronounced: two-times

Defined in: FORTH-79(R), STARTING FORTH

Implementation:

8080:

CODE 2*   H POP H DAD HPUSH JMP END-CODE

Source usage: Many.

Example:

45 2*

   Enter the value of 45 on the stack and then double it.

Comment: A useful operation whose definition is provided in the
reference vocabulary of FORTH-79. Note that the carry and
overflow are ignored.

2+   n --- n+2   135   MVP-FORTH

Increment n by two, according to the operation for + .

Pronounced: two-plus

Defined in: FORTH-79, fig-FORTH, STARTING FORTH

Implementation:

: 2+   2 + ;

or 8080:

CODE 2+   H POP H INX H INX
      HPUSH JMP END-CODE

Source usage: Many.

Example:

45   2+

Enter the value of 45 on the stack and then increment it by 2.

Comment: A required word in FORTH-79, which can be defined in high level FORTH for portability, or in code for maximum speed.

2-   n --- n-2   129   MVP-FORTH

Decrement n by two, according to the operation for - .

Pronounced: two-minus

Defined in: FORTH-79, STARTING FORTH

Implementation:

: 2-   2 - ;

or 8080:

CODE 2-   H POP   H DCX   H DCX
       HPUSH JMP   END-CODE

Source usage: Many.

Example:

45   2-

Enter the value 45 on the stack and then decrement it by 2 .

Comment: A required word in FORTH-79, which can be defined in high level FORTH for portability, or in code for maximum speed.

2/   n1 --- n2   MVP-FORTH - SUPPLEMENTAL

Leave (n1)/2.

Pronounced: two-divide

Defined in: FORTH-79(R), STARTING FORTH

Implementation :

: 2/   2 / ;

Source usage: BYE   DEPTH

Example:

45   2/

   Enter the value of 45 on the stack, halve it and drop the
remainder.

Comment: A useful operation whose definition is provided in the
reference vocabulary of FORTH-79. The result is always
rounded toward zero.

2@   addr   ---   d   MVP-FORTH - SUPPLEMENTAL

Leave on the stack the contents of the four consecutive bytes
beginning at addr, as for a double number.

Pronounced: two-fetch

Defined in: FORTH-79(E), STARTING FORTH

Implementation:

: 2@   D@ ;

Source usage: None.

Example:

4AC2 2@

   This would retrieve the double precision value, 3333, which
we put at this address in the example under 2!.

Comment: This ideogram is included in the extended double
number word set of FORTH-79. However, the ideogram D@
is a better mnemonic because it avoids conflict in
interpretation with the quantity 2. Thus, D@ is used in MVP-
FORTH and 2@ may be added as an alias.

2CONSTANT   d   ---   MVP-FORTH - SUPPLEMENTAL

A defining word used to create a dictionary entry for <name>,
leaving d in its parameter field. When <name> is later
executed, d will be left on the stack.

Pronounced: two-constant

Form: d 2CONSTANT <name>

Defined in: FORTH-79(E), STARTING FORTH

Implementation:

: 2CONSTANT   DCONSTANT ;

Source usage: None.

Example:

33.33   2CONSTANT   NEW-VALUE

Enter the value 33.33 which will be a double precision number and store it in an ideogram named NEW-VALUE. NEW-VALUE will then cause the 33.33 to be placed on the stack. NOTE: The decimal point location is not preserved in a double precision integer.

Comment: This ideogram is included in the extended double number word set of FORTH-79. However, the ideogram DCONSTANT is a better mnemonic because it avoids conflict in interpretation with the quantity 2.   Thus, DCONSTANT is used in MVP-FORTH and 2CONSTANT may be added as an alias.

2DROP   d ---   MVP-FORTH - SUPPLEMENTAL

Drop the top double number on the stack.

Pronounced: two-drop

Defined in: FORTH-79(E), STARTING FORTH

Implementation:

: 2DROP   DDROP ;

Source usage: None.

Example:

2DROP

This ideogram will cause the top four bytes on the stack to be removed which would drop a double precision number or any other pair of single quantities.

Comment: This ideogram is included in the extended double number   word   set   of   FORTH-79. However,   the   ideogram DDROP is a better mnemonic because it avoids conflict in interpretation with the quantity 2. Thus, DDROP is used in MVP-FORTH and 2DROP may be added as an alias.

2DUP   d --- d d   MVP-FORTH - SUPPLEMENTAL

Duplicate the top double number on the stack.

Pronounced: two-dup

Defined in: FORTH-79(E), STARTING FORTH

Implementation:

: 2DUP   DDUP ;

Source usage: None.

Example:

33.33   2DUP

Place the double precision number on the stack taking 4 bytes and make a copy of it using the next four bytes. NOTE: The decimal point location is not maintained in the double precision integer.

Comment: This ideogram is included in the extended double number word set of FORTH-79. However, the ideogram DDUP is a better mnemonic because it avoids conflict in interpretation with the quantity 2. Thus, DDUP is used in MVP-FORTH and 2DUP may be added as an alias.

2OVER   MVP-FORTH - SUPPLEMENTAL
        d1 d2 --- d1 d2 d1

Leave a copy of the second double number on the stack.

Pronounced: two-over

Defined in: FORTH-79(E), STARTING FORTH

Implementation:

: 2OVER   DOVER ;

Source usage: None.

Example:

33.33   44.44   2OVER

Place the two double precision numbers on the stack and then add on a copy of the first one. NOTE: the decimal point location is not maintained in double precision integers.

Comment: This ideogram is included in the extended double number word set of FORTH-79. However, the ideogram DOVER is a better mnemonic because it avoids conflict in interpretation with the quantity 2. Thus, DOVER is used in MVP-FORTH and 2OVER may be added as an alias.

2SWAP   MVP-FORTH - SUPPLEMENTAL

          d1   d2   ---   d2   d1

Exchange the top two double numbers on the stack.

Pronounced: two-swap

Defined in: FORTH-79(E), STARTING FORTH

Implementation:

: 2SWAP   DSWAP ;

Source usage: None.

Example:

33.33   44.44   2SWAP

Place two double precision numbers on the stack and then exchange their positions. The decimal point location is not maintained in the double precision integer.

Comment: This ideogram is included in the extended double number word set of FORTH-79. However, the ideogram DSWAP is a better mnemonic because it avoids conflict in interpretation with the quantity 2. Thus, DSWAP is used in MVP-FORTH and 2SWAP may be added as an alias.

2VARIABLE   ---   MVP-FORTH - SUPPLEMENTAL

A defining word used to create a dictionary entry of <name> and assign 4 bytes for storage in the parameter field. When <name> is later executed, it will leave the address of the first byte of its parameter field on the stack.

Form: 2VARIABLE   <name>

Defined in: FORTH-79(E), STARTING FORTH

Implementation:

: 2VARIABLE   DVARIABLE ;

Source usage: None.

Example:

2VARIABLE   NEW-VARIABLE

   Make a new ideogram referring to a double precision variable.
Its value is not initialized.

Comment: This ideogram is included in the extended double
number word set of FORTH-79. However, the ideogram
DVARIABLE is a better mnemonic because it avoids conflict in
interpretation with the quantity 2.   Thus, DVARIABLE is used
in MVP-FORTH and 2VARIABLE may be added as an alias.

79-STANDARD   ---   119   MVP-FORTH

Execute assuring that a FORTH-79 Standard system is
available, otherwise an error condition exists.

Defined in: FORTH-79

Implementation:

: 79-STANDARD ;

Source usage: None.

Example:

79-STANDARD

   This ideogram does nothing in this implementation, but also
does not create an error - the word is in the vocabulary.

Comment: A required ideogram in the standard, but it is
unspecified how the error condition is to be generated.

:   ---   116   MVP-FORTH

A defining word which selects the CONTEXT vocabulary to be
identical to CURRENT.   Create a dictionary entry for <name>
in CURRENT, and set compile mode.   Words thus defined are
called 'colon-definitions'. The compilation addresses of
subsequent words from the input stream which are not immediate

words are stored into the dictionary to be executed when <name> is later executed. IMMEDIATE words are executed as encountered. If a word is not found after a search of the CONTEXT and FORTH vocabularies, conversion compilation of a literal number is attempted, with regard to the current BASE; that failing, an error condition exists.

Form: : <name> ... ;

Pronounced: colon

Defined in: FORTH-79, fig-FORTH, STARTING FORTH

Implementation:

8080:

```
: :  SP@  CSP  !  CURRENT  @  CONTEXT  !
   CREATE  SMUDGE    ]  ;CODE
   RPP LHLD   H DCX   B M MOV   H DCX   C M MOV
   RPP SHLD   D INX   E C MOV   D B MOV
   NEXT JMP   END-CODE
```

Source usage: None.

Example:

: TEST ;

   Creates a new ideogram in the dictionary which in this case does nothing.

Comment: This is one of the most used ideograms in FORTH. The implementations of this ideogram vary according to which vocabularies are searched and in what order. The MVP-FORTH definition is taken from FORTH-79 which implies that after the CONTEXT is searched, even if it is a daughter vocabulary, the search skips immediately to FORTH.

;   ---   I, C, 196   MVP-FORTH

Terminate a colon-definition and stop compilation. If compiling from mass storage and the input stream is exhausted before encountering ; an error condition exists.

Pronounced: semi-colon

Defined in: FORTH-79, fig-FORTH, STARTING FORTH

Implementation:

```
: ;   ?CSP  COMPILE  EXIT  SMUDGE
   [COMPILE]  [  ;   IMMEDIATE
```

Source usage: None.

Example:

```
: TEST  ;
```

Used to end the colon definition which in this case does nothing.

Comment: In this implementation, the FORTH-79 error condition aborts with an "INPUT STREAM EXHAUSTED" message.

;CODE   ---   C, I, 206 NOT USED

Used in the form:

```
        : <name>  ...  ;CODE
```

Stop compilation and terminate a defining word <name>. ASSEMBLER becomes the CONTEXT vocabulary. When <name> is executed in the form:

```
        <name>  <namex>
```

to define the new <namex>, the execution address of <namex> will contain the address of the code sequence following the ;CODE in <name>. Execution of any <namex> will cause this machine code sequence to be executed.

Pronounced: semi-colon-code

Defined in: FORTH-79 ASSEMBLER WORD SET, fig-FORTH

Implementation:

8080:

```
: ;CODE  ?CSP  COMPILE  <;CODE>
   [COMPILE]  [  [COMPILE]  ASSEMBLER
   IMMEDIATE
```

Source usage: None.

Example:

```
: USER    CONSTANT  ;CODE  D  NX  XCHG   M E MOV
    O D MVI  UP LHLD   D DAD   HPUSH JMP   END-CODE
```

In this example, after the USER variable is given a name in a colon definition, we switch to the ASSEMBLER which is not included in this implementation but is referenced by the CROSS-COMPILER. This begins the specification of the run-time activity for USER variables.

Comment: This ideogram functions like DOES>, except that the generated offspring's code address is redirected to usable machine code rather than to a call to the subroutine, DODOES. It should be included as part of an ASSEMBLER vocabulary.

;S   ---   NOT USED

Stop interpretation of a screen. ;S is also the run-time word compiled at the end of a colon-definition which returns execution to the calling procedure.

Defined in: FORTH-79(R), fig-FORTH

Implementation:

8080:

```
CODE ;S    RPP LHLD   M C MOV   H INX
    M B MOV   H INX   RPP SHLD   NEXT JMP   END-CODE
```

Source usage: None.

Example:

```
: ;   COMPILE  ;S  [COMPILE]  [  ;  IMMEDIATE
```

This simplified implementation of semicolon compiles the ideogram and sets the execution mode. No error checking or unsmudging is performed.

Comment: This ideogram is now obsolete, having been replaced by EXIT.

<   n1 n2 --- flag   139   MVP-FORTH

True if n1 is less than n2.

Pronounced: less-than

Defined in: FORTH-79, fig-FORTH, STARTING FORTH

Implementation:

8080:

```
CODE <    D POP   H POP   D A MOV   H XRA   0>=
    IF   SSUB   CALL
    THEN   H INR   H DCR   0>=
    IF   0 H LXI   HPUSH JMP
    THEN   1 H LXI   HPUSH JMP   END-CODE
```

Source usage: Many.

Example:

        45   47   <

Enter two integers on the stack and then test to see if the first is less than the second. In this example it is and the value of the flag on the stack is set to 1. The test destroys both operands.

Comment: The limits for this signed comparison are strictly defined in FORTH-79: −32768 32767 < must return true and −32768 and 0 must be distinguished.

<#   d1   ---   d1   169   MVP-FORTH

Initialize pictured numeric output. The ideograms <#, #, #S, HOLD, SIGN, and #> can be used to specify the conversion of a double-precision number into an ASCII character string stored in right-to-left order.

Pronounced: less-sharp

Defined in: FORTH-79, fig-FORTH, STARTING FORTH
            Implementation:

: <#   PAD   HLD   !   ;

Source usage: D.R

Example:

45.   <#   #S   #>   TYPE

Enter the double precision value 45. on the stack, then format the value for printing it and finally print it.

Comment: In FORTH-79 there is no specification as to where

the pictured number will be stored. Also, implementations
vary on how the sign of negative numbers is handled.

<+LOOP>   n ---   C   MVP-FORTH

The run-time procedure compiled by +LOOP, which increments
the loop index by n and tests for loop completion.   See +LOOP.

Defined in: MVP-FORTH

Implementation:

8080:

CODE <+LOOP>   D POP   G<LOOP> JMP   END-CODE

Source usage: +LOOP

Example:

: +LOOP   3 ?PAIRS   COMPILE <+LOOP>
    HERE - , ;   IMMEDIATE

    The example illustrates the use of this run time procedure.

Comment: Although dangerous and almost totally useless for
applications, this ideogram is available to the programmer.
Like BRANCH and 0BRANCH, it expects an in-line branching
displacement.

<-FIND>   MVP-FORTH
         --- pfa b tf   (if found)
         --- ff   (if not found)

Accepts the next word (delimited by blanks) in the input stream
to HERE and searches the CONTEXT and then the FORTH
vocabularies for a matching entry. If found, the dictionary
entry's parameter field address, its length byte, and a boolean
true is left. Otherwise, only a boolean false is left.

Defined in: MVP-FORTH

Implementation:

: <-FIND>   BL WORD CONTEXT @ @ <FIND> ;

Source usage: None.

Example:

<-FIND> JUNK

Search the dictionary for the ideogram JUNK. Presumably, the ideogram is not in the dictionary and the flag value of 0 is left on the stack.

Comment: This ideogram is vectored from -FIND via the user variable '-FIND. Note: the null character used to terminate the terminal and disk buffers is defined as an ideogram in the dictionary (see X). This may occasionally produce bewildering error messages or unexpected results when you use the ideograms: -FIND, ' , [COMPILE] , FORGET , or others which search the dictionary or define new words.

<."> 　　　　　 --- 　　　　　　　　　　 C 　 MVP-FORTH

A run-time procedure, compiled by ." which transmits the folowing in- line text to the selected output device.

Defined in: MVP-FORTH

Implementation:

```
: <."> R@ COUNT DUP 1+ R> + >R TYPE ;
```

Source usage: ."

Example: CAUTION: Execution outside a colon definition will crash the system.

```
: ." BLK @
  IF BLK @ BLOCK ELSE TIB @ THEN
  >IN @ + C@ 22 = NOT
  IF 22 STATE @
    IF <."> WORD C@ 1+ ALLOT
    ELSE WORD COUNT TYPE THEN
  ELSE 1 >IN +! THEN ;
```

This example is an alternate implementation of .".

Comment: This synonym for fig-FORTH's (."), is used in MVP-FORTH in order to avoid confusion with comments within parentheses.

</LOOP> 　　　 u 　--- 　　　　　　　　　　 C 　 MVP-FORTH

The run-time procedure compiled by /LOOP, which increments

the loop index by u and tests for loop completion.   See
/LOOP .

Defined in: MVP-FORTH

Implementation:

8080:

```
CODE </LOOP>    D POP  RPP LHLD   M A MOV   E ADD
        A M MOV   A E MOV   H INX   M A MOV   D ADC
        A M MOV   H INX   D INR   D DCR   A D MOV
        0</LOOP>  JC   E A MOV   M SUB   D A MOV
        H INX   M SBB   BRAN1 JC   1</LOOP> JMP
     HERE LABEL 0</LOOP>   H INX
     HERE LABEL 1</LOOP>   H INX   RPP SHLD
        B INX   B INX   NEXT JMP   END-CODE
```

Source usage: /LOOP

Example:

```
: /LOOP   3   ?PAIRS   COMPILE   </LOOP>
    HERE   -  ,  ;  IMMEDIATE
```

    The example illustrates the use of this run-time procedure.

Comment: Although dangerous and almost totally useless for
applications, this ideogram is available to the programmer.
Like BRANCH and 0BRANCH, it expects an inline branching
displacement. It differs from <+LOOP> in that the index is
unsigned which is desirable for address looping.

<;CODE>   ---   C   MVP-FORTH

The run-time procedure, compiled by ;CODE, that rewrites the
code field of the most recently defined word to point to the
following machine code sequence.

Defined in: MVP-FORTH

Implementation:

```
: <;CODE>   R>   LATEST   PFA   2   -   !   ;
```

Source usage: DOES>

Example: CAUTION: Execution outside a colon definition
will crash the system.

```
HEX
: DOES>    ?CSP  COMPILE  <;CODE>  CD  C,
    COMPILE  [  HERE  4  +  ,  ]  ;
DECIMAL
```

This is the only use of this word. It provides the necessary
function for the revised DOES> as used in FORTH-79. Note
that the literal hex value CD, is the 8080 specific op-code
which is compiled at this point.

Comment: This ideogram is needed by DOES>, and therefore
appears even in systems which lack an assembler vocabulary and
the ideogram, ;CODE . The functional definition differs from
that given by fig-FORTH. The latter includes two extra bytes
between the code field address and the parameter field address
of every DOES> word. The FORTH-79 function makes the
format of all compiled definitions more consistent.

<<CMOVE>   addr1   addr2   u   ---   MVP-FORTH

The primitive code routine for <CMOVE. It can move up to
65535 bytes. Nothing is moved if u = 0.

Defined in: MVP-FORTH

Implementation:

8080:

```
CODE <<CMOVE>
        C L MOV   B H MOV   B POP   D POP   XTHL
        B DAD   H DCX   XCHG   B DAD   H DCX   XCHG
    BEGIN   B A MOV   C ORA   0<<CMOVE> JZ
        M A MOV   H DCX   D STAX   D DCX   B DCX
    0=  UNTIL
    HERE LABEL 0<<CMOVE>   B POP
    NEXT JMP   END-CODE
```

Source usage: <CMOVE

Example:

```
: <CMOVE    DUP  1  <
    IF   DDROP   DROP   ELSE   <<CMOVE>  THEN  ;
```

This example is from the MVP-FORTH source code.

Comment: This is the primitive for the <CMOVE function which

proceeds within the bytes from high memory towards low memory.

<?TERMINAL>   ---   f   MVP-FORTH

The run-time procedure which perform a test of the terminal
keyboard for actuation of the break key.   A true flag indicates
actuation.   This definition is installation dependent.

Defined in: MVP-FORTH

Implementation:

8080

CODE <?TERMINAL>   0 H LXI PQTER JMP END-CODE

8086/8088 (IBM)

CODE <?TERMINAL>   DS PUSH   BX PUSH
      BX, # 40 MOV   DS, BX MOV   BX, # 1A MOV
      CX, [BX] MOV   AX, CX MOV   BX, # 1C MOV
      AX, [BX] SUB   [BX], CX MOV   AQTER1 JZ
      AX, [BX] MOV   BX, AX MOV   AX, [BX] MOV
      AH, AH SUB
   HERE LABEL AQTER1 BX POP   DS POP
      APUSH JMP END-CODE

Source usage: ?TERMINAL

Example:

' <?TERMINAL> CFA '?TERMINAL !

    The example illustrates assigning the run-time code field
address to a user variable for vectoring.   It is taken for the
source code.

Comment: This installation dependent function can not be
made the same for all implementations of MVP-FORTH.   The
implementation for the IBM is more complicated than some.   It
is necessary to probe the type-ahead input buffer and modify it.
Since the character struck would otherwise be lost, its ASCII
value is left as the true flag.   The system flag is
automatically cleared.   Under the 8080 CP/M implementation
there is no type-ahead buffer.   The flag must be cleared with
KEY DROP.

The run-time procedure used with A B O R T " .

Defined in: MVP-FORTH

Implementation:

```
: <ABORT">
  IF   WHERE  CR  R@  COUNT  TYPE
     SP!  QUIT
  ELSE  R>  DUP  C@  +  1+  >R
  THEN  ;
```

Source usage: ABORT"

Example:

```
: ABORT"  ?COMP  COMPILE  <ABORT">  'STREAM
    C@  22  =
  IF  1  >IN  +!  0  C,
  ELSE  22  WORD  DUP  C@  1+  SWAP  OVER
    +  C@  22  =  NOT  ?STREAM  ALLOT
  THEN  ;  IMMEDIATE
```

  This example is taken from the MVP-FORTH source code.

Comment: This ideogram takes an inline string which is set up
by the immediate compiling ideogram ABORT". Although
dangerous and almost totally useless for applications, it is
available to the programmer.

Clear the data and return stacks, setting execution mode.
Return control to the terminal.

Defined in: MVP-FORTH

Implementation:

```
: <ABORT>  SP!  ?STACK
  [COMPILE]  FORTH  DEFINITIONS  QUIT  ;
```

Source usage: None.

Example:

<ABORT>

This simple ideogram will clear the stack and return to
FORTH definitions so that you can begin again. Your
definitions are not forgotten.

Comment: This ideogram is vectored from ABORT via variable
'ABORT. In some versions of FORTH, this ideogram also
includes a statement of the name of the version and other
information, while in FORTH-79, no indication is made.

`<BLOCK>`   n --- addr   MVP-FORTH

Leave the address of the first byte in block n . If the block
is not already in memory, it is transferred from mass storage
into whichever memory buffer has been least recently accessed.
If the block occupying that buffer has been UPDATEd (i.e.
modified), it is rewritten onto mass storage before block n
is read into the buffer. n is an unsigned number. If
correct mass storage read or write is not possible, an error
condition exists. Only data within the latest block
referenced by `<BLOCK>` is valid by byte address, due to
sharing of the block buffers.

Defined in: MVP-FORTH

Implementation:

```
: <BLOCK>   OFFSET  @  +  >R  PREV  @  DUP  @
   R@  -  2*
   IF
      BEGIN  +BUF  NOT
         IF  DROP  R@  BUFFER
            DUP  R@  1  R/W  2  -
         THEN
         DUP  @  R@  -  2*  NOT
      UNTIL
      DUP  PREV  !
   THEN  R>  DROP  2+  ;
```

Source usage: None.

Example:

45 `<BLOCK>`

Entering the desired block number followed by the ideogram
leaves the address of the beginning of that block on the top of
the stack. If it is not already in a buffer, the block will be
read in from disk.

Comment: This ideogram is vectored from BLOCK via user

variable 'BLOCK. It is a useful ideogram which speeds access to disk information when it is not modified. The MVP-FORTH has fixed a problem in some earlier implementations of fig-FORTH, which sometimes failed to update the last two lines of a source screen on disk.

<BUILDS   ---   C   NOT USED

Used in conjunction with DOES> in defining words. When <name> executes, <BUILDS creates a dictionary entry for the new <namex>. The sequence of words between <BUILDS and DOES> establishes a parameter field for <namex>. When <namex> is later executed, the sequence of words following DOES> will be executed, with the parameter field address of <namex> on the data stack.

Form: : <name>   <BUILDS ... DOES> ... ;
             <name>   <namex>

Defined in: FORTH-79(R), fig-FORTH

Implementation:

: <BUILDS   CREATE   ;

Source usage: None.

Example:

: CONSTANT   <BUILDS   , DOES> @   ;

This example illustrates a high level implementation of CONSTANT. The built-in implementation utilizing ;CODE and assembly language will run faster.

Comment: Because the word is so well established and has some beauty of construct in conjunction with DOES>, it may be defined as an alias of CREATE. The definition is modified from that in fig-FORTH and older programs and may not always work.

<CMOVE   addr1 addr2 n   ---   MVP-FORTH

Copy n bytes beginning at addr1 to addr2. The move proceeds within the bytes from high memory toward low memory.

Pronounced: reverse-c-move

Defined in: FORTH-79(R), STARTING FORTH

Implementation:

```
: <CMOVE    DUP 1 <
   IF  DDROP  DROP
   ELSE  <<CMOVE>  THEN   ;
```

Source usage: None.

Example:

```
HEX  4AC3  4AC4  20  <CMOVE    DECIMAL
```

With the normal CMOVE the data from 4AC4 up would be written over with the value in 4AC3 and the information would be lost.   Instead, <CMOVE shifts 32 bytes one position to the right.

Comment: This ideogram works exactly like <CMOVE>, except when its source and destination fields overlap.   The ideogram BMOVE, a better solution, intelligently chooses the action so that overlapping fields hold no surprises for the programmer.

<CMOVE>   addr1 addr2 u   ---   MVP-FORTH

The primitive code routine for CMOVE and MOVE.   Up to 65,535 bytes may be moved.   Nothing is moved when u = 0.

Defined in: MVP-FORTH

Implementation:

8080:

```
CODE <CMOVE>
      C L MOV   B H MOV   B POP   D POP
      XTHL   0<CMOVE> JMP
      BEGIN    M A MOV   H INX   D STAX
        D INX   B DCX
   HERE LABEL 0<CMOVE>  B A MOV   C ORA   0=
      UNTIL   B POP   NEXT JMP   END-CODE
```

Source usage: CMOVE   MOVE

Example:

```
: CMOVE    DUP 1 <
   IF DROP DROP DROP
   ELSE <CMOVE>
   THEN  ;
```

The example uses this procedure which remains available to the programmer.

Comment: This version of a byte move utility was developed early and was at one time used in the definition of FILL by taking advantage of its overwriting property. In MVP-FORTH, it is not used in this way. There really is little reason to use it instead of BMOVE, which moves bytes without over writing them - an intelligent CMOVE.

<CR>   ---   MVP-FORTH

Cause a carriage-return and line-feed to occur at the current output device, as configured by CP/M. The user variable OUT is reset to zero.

Defined in: MVP-FORTH

Implementation:

8080:

```
CODE <CR>   4A D LXI   UP LHLD   D DAD   0 M MVI
   H INX  0 M MVI  PCR JMP   END-CODE
```

Source usage: None.

Example:

<CR> <CR> ." HELLO"

The two ideograms cause the display to advance two lines and then print HELLO at the left margin of the display.

Comment: This ideogram is vectored from CR via user variable 'CR. Placing the ideogram, <CR>, in the input stream is not equivalent to pressing the "Return" key on the terminal keyboard.

<DO>   n1 n2 ---   C   MVP-FORTH

The run-time procedure compiled by DO which moves the loop control parameters to the return stack. See DO.

Defined in: MVP-FORTH after fig-FORTH

Implementation:

8080:

```
CODE <DO>    RPP LHLD   H DCX   H DCX   H DCX
   H DCX   RPP SHLD   D POP   E M MOV   H INX
   D M MOV   D POP   H INX   E M MOV   H INX
   D M MOV   NEXT JMP   END-CODE
```

Source usage: DO

Example:

: DO   COMPILE   <DO>   HERE   3   ;   IMMEDIATE

The example uses the run time procedure. It remains available to the programmer.

Comment: This ideogram <DO> has been used as the primitive in MVP-FORTH in place of (DO) which is used in fig-FORTH. The change was made to avoid use of parentheses.

<EMIT>   c   ---   MVP-FORTH

Transmit a character to the currently defined output port according to the configuration of CP/M. The user variable OUT is increased by one.

Defined in: FORTH-79, fig-FORTH, STARTING FORTH

Implementation:

8080:

```
CODE <EMIT>   H POP B PUSH   L C MOV   CPOUT CALL
   B POP   4A   D LXI   UP LHLD   D DAD   M E MOV
   H INX   M D MOV   D INX   D M MOV   H DCX
   E M MOV   NEXT JMP   END-CODE
```

Source usage: None.

Example:

65   <EMIT>

Entering the decimal value 65 followed by this ideogram will cause the character A to be printed.

Comment: This ideogram is vectored from EMIT via the user variable 'EMIT.

The run-time routine executed by E X P E C T. It transfers
characters from the terminal beginning at addr, upward, until a
"return" or the count of n has been received. Take no
action for n less than or equal to zero.   One or two nulls are
added at the end of the text.

Defined in: FORTH-79, fig-FORTH, STARTING FORTH

Implementation:

```
: <EXPECT>     OVER   +   OVER
    DO   KEY   DUP  8  =   OVER  7F  =   OR
      IF   DROP   DUP   I  =   DUP   R>   2-   +   >R
          IF  BELL
          ELSE  BSOUT   DUP  EMIT   20   EMIT   THEN
      ELSE  DUP  OD  =
          IF   LEAVE   DROP   BL   0
          ELSE  DUP   THEN   I  C!   0   I   1+   !
      THEN   EMIT
    1   /LOOP   DROP   ;
```

Source usage: EXPECT

Example:

' <EXPECT>   CFA   'EXPECT   !

    Store the code field address of the run-time routine
<EXPECT> in the user variable 'EXPECT.   It is then ready to be
vectored by EXPECT.

Comment: Because EXPECT has features which may be
installation dependent, it has been vectored. This ideogram
is the run-time routine which includes some features, such as
backspace handling.

<FILL>   addr   n   b   ---   MVP-FORTH

A primitive for FILL which executes the actual function if
selected.

Defined in: MVP-FORTH

Implementation:

8080:

```
CODE <FILL>    C L MOV   B H MOV   D POP
     B POP  XTHL  XCHG
   HERE LABEL O<FILL>     B A MOV   C ORA
     1<FILL> JZ   L A MOV   D STAX   D INX
     B DCX   O<FILL> JMP
   HERE LABEL 1<FILL>   B POP
     NEXT JMP   END-CODE
```

Source usage: FILL

Example:

```
: FILL    OVER   O>
  IF  <FILL>  ELSE  DROP   DROP   DROP   THEN   ;
```

   The example illustrates the use of the ideogram in taking no
action if zero bytes are to be moved.

Comment: This implementation of <FILL> utilizes its own
code and not the high level CMOVE.

<FIND>   MVP-FORTH
        addr1 addr2   ---   pfa b tf   (ok)
        addr1 addr2   ---   ff   (bad)

Searches the dictionary starting at the name field address
addr2, matching to the text at addr1.   Returns parameter field
address, length byte of name field and boolean true for a good
match. If no match is found, only a boolean false is left.

Defined in: MVP-FORTH after fig-FORTH

Implementation:

8080:

```
CODE <FIND>   D POP
   HERE LABEL O<FIND>    H POP   H PUSH   D LDAX
     M XRA  03F ANI  4<FIND> JNZ
   HERE LABEL 1<FIND>    H INX   D INX   D LDAX
     M XRA   A ADD  3<FIND> JNZ  1<FIND> JNC
     5 H LXI   D DAD   XTHL
   HERE LABEL 2<FIND>    D DCX   D LDAX   A ORA
     2<FIND> JP   A E MOV   O D MVI
     1 H LXI   DPUSH JMP
   HERE LABEL 3<FIND>    5<FIND> JC
   HERE LABEL 4<FIND>    D INX   D LDAX
```

```
         A  ORA   4<FIND>  JP
    HERE  LABEL  5<FIND>      D  INX   XCHG   M  E  MOV
      H  INX   M  D  MOV   D  A  MOV   E  ORA
      0<FIND>  JNZ   H  POP   0  H  LXI
      HPUSH  JMP   END-CODE
```

Source usage: <-FIND> FORGET

Example:

: -FIND   BL   WORD   CONTEXT   @   @   <FIND>   ;

   This example comes from the MVP-FORTH implementation
source code.

Comment: This is the primitive used in MVP-FORTH in place
of (FIND) in order to avoid confusion with comments. It
provides a means of searching the dictionary without using the
input stream.

<INTERPRET>   ---   MVP-FORTH

Begin interpretation at the character indexed by the contents of
>IN relative to the block number contained in BLK, continuing
until the input stream is exhausted. If BLK contains zero,
interpret characters from the terminal input buffer.

Defined in: MVP-FORTH

Implementation:

: <INTERPRET>
    BEGIN -FIND
      IF   STATE   @   <
           IF   CFA   ,   ELSE   CFA   EXECUTE   THEN
      ELSE   HERE   NUMBER   DPL   @   1+
           IF   [COMPILE]   DLITERAL
           ELSE   DROP   [COMPILE]   LITERAL
           THEN
      THEN   ?STACK
    AGAIN ;

Source usage: None.

Example:

: <LOAD>   BLK   @   >R   >IN   @   >R   0   >IN   !
    BLK   !   <INTERPRET> R>   >IN   !
    R>   BLK   !   ;

   This   example   is   modified   from   the   MVP-FORTH

                   ALL ABOUT FORTH   81
```
```

implementation.

Comment: This ideogram is vectored from INTERPRET via the user variable 'INTERPRET. It is used to interpret text source in MVP-FORTH. The sequence " STATE @ < " is sneaky. It returns a true flag only if the compilation mode is set and the ideogram located by -FIND is not immediate. <INTERPRET> is then written as an infinite loop which exits implicitly at the end of an input line or disk screen.

<KEY>   ---   char   MVP-FORTH

Leave the ASCII value of the next available character from the current input device, according to the configuration of CP/M.

Defined in: MVP-FORTH

Implementation:

8080:

CODE <KEY> PKEY JMP END-CODE

Source usage: None.

Example:

<KEY>

Execution of this ideogram causes the program to wait for any single input from the keyboard and upon receiving it places the ASCII value of the input on the stack.

Comment: This ideogram is vectored from KEY via user variable 'KEY. It provides a way of finding out the ASCII value of characters without reference to a chart. It may also be used in selecting from a menu requiring only a single character input or for a wait until any character is input from the terminal. The internal details of <KEY> are installation dependent.

<LINE>   n1   n2   ---   addr   count   MVP-FORTH

Convert the line number n1 and the screen n2 to the disc buffer address containing the data. A count of 64 indicates the full line text length.

Defined in: MVP-FORTH

Implementation

`: <LINE>   BLOCK   SWAP   C/L   *   +   C/L ;`

Source usage: .LINE

Example:

`: .LINE   <LINE>  -TRAILING   TYPE  ;`

This simple example comes from the MVP-FORTH source code.

Comment: This primitive is useful in a variety of manipulations among lines on various screens and to identify lines for searching with -TEXT and MATCH, for example.

<LOAD>   n ---   MVP-FORTH

Begin interpretation of screen n by making it the input stream; preserve the locators of the present input stream (from >IN and BLK). If interpretation is not terminated explicitly it will be terminated when the input stream is exhausted. Control then returns to the input stream containing LOAD , determined by the input stream locators >IN and BLK .

Defined in: MVP-FORTH

Implementation:

```
: <LOAD>   ?DUP NOT
  ABORT" UNLOADABLE"
  BLK  @  >R  >IN  @  >R
  0  >IN  !  BLK  !  INTERPRET
  R>  >IN  !  R>  BLK  ! ;
```

Source usage: None.

Example:

45 <LOAD>

This example will start loading the contents of Screen 45.

Comment: This ideogram is vectored from LOAD via user variable 'LOAD. Screens which end with several blank lines will load faster if the ideogram, EXIT, appears following the last definition or operation. Also, one can avoid loading a whole screen without erasing the undesired contents by terminating the desired source with the ideogram. This technique is not sanctioned by FORTH-79 and is implementation dependent. Note: this implementation does not permit loading block zero.

<LOOP>   ---   C   MVP-FORTH

The run-time procedure compiled by LOOP which increments the loop index and tests for loop completion. See LOOP.

Defined in: MVP-FORTH

Implementation:

8080:

```
CODE <LOOP>    1 D LXI
    HERE LABEL 0<LOOP>    RPP LHLD   B PUSH
      M  A MOV   E ADD   A  M MOV
      A  C MOV   H INX   M  A MOV   D ADC   A B MOV
      M  A MOV   3<LOOP> JM   D ANA   4<LOOP> JP
    HERE LABEL 1<LOOP>    H INX   H INX
    HERE LABEL 2<LOOP>    H INX   RPP SHLD   B POP
      B INX   B INX   NEXT JMP
    HERE LABEL 3<LOOP>    D ORA   1<LOOP> JP
    HERE LABEL 4<LOOP>    B M MOV   C A MOV   H INX
      M SUB   H INX   B A MOV   M SBB   B A MOV
      8<LOOP> JM   A ANA   6<LOOP> JM
    HERE LABEL 5<LOOP>    D A MOV   A ANA
      2<LOOP> JP   B POP   BRAN1 JMP
    HERE LABEL 6<LOOP>    M A MOV   A ANA
      5<LOOP> JM
    HERE LABEL 7<LOOP>    D A MOV   A ANA
      2<LOOP> JM   B POP   BRAN1 JMP
    HERE LABEL 8<LOOP>    B A MOV   A ANA
      7<LOOP> JM   6<LOOP> JMP   END-CODE
```

Source usage: LOOP

Example:

: LOOP   3   ?PAIRS   COMPILE   <LOOP>   HERE   - , ;
IMMEDIATE

   This example from the MVP-FORTH source code illustrates the only use of <LOOP> which, though dangerous, remains available to the programmer.

Comment: This is a primitive similar to (LOOP) in fig-FORTH but renamed to avoid confusion with comments and modified to conform with the requirements of FORTH-79.   Any compiled instance of <LOOP> must be followed by an in-line branching

displacement.   This is the main use of this primitive though
it is available to the programmer.

<NUMBER>   addr   ---   d   MVP-FORTH

Convert the count and character string at   addr , to a signed
32-bit integer, using the current base.   If numeric conversion
is not possible, an error condition exists.   The string may
contain a preceding negative sign.

Defined in: MVP-FORTH

Implementation:

```
: <NUMBER>   0   0   ROT   DUP   1+   C@
    AMINUS   =   DUP   >R   +   -1   DPL   !
    CONVERT   DUP   C@   BL   >
    IF   DUP   C@   ADOT   =   NOT
      ABORT" NOT RECOGNIZED"   0   DPL   !
      CONVERT   DUP   C@   BL   >
      ABORT" NOT RECOGNIZED"
    THEN   DROP   R>
    IF   DNEGATE   THEN   ;
```

(AMINUS is the ASCII value of   " - ")
(ADOT   is the ASCII value of   " . ")
(These are compiled as literals by the cross-compiler.)

Source usage: None.

Example:

```
: INPUT   ." INPUT AN INTEGER --- "
    QUERY   BL   WORD   <NUMBER>   DROP ;
```

  This definition provides for a prompt and then a pause for the
operator to input the requested integer.   Then the input
character stream is parsed, converted to a double precision
value and reduced to a single precision value left on the stack.

Comment: The version and implementation of this ideogram in
MVP-FORTH conforms with that in the FORTH-79 reference
word set and fig-FORTH.   It will recognize two non-numeric
characters: a decimal point and a leading negative sign.   The
position of the decimal point is recorded in the user variable
DPL.   This feature enables a user program to scale or adjust
the converted value as desired.   It will give an error message
if any other special character is used.   Note that the
definition given in STARTING FORTH is different.

Clear the terminal screen or perform an action suitable to the output device currently active.

Defined in: MVP-FORTH

Implementation:

: <PAGE> 1B EMIT 45 EMIT ;

(Note: This is the CLEAR SCREEN sequence for the Heath/Zenith Z19 terminal. In the distibution version of MVP-FORTH, a fail safe implementation produces a carriage return rather than the expected function. Since this is a vectored function, the user can add his own CLEAR SCREEN sequence.)

Source usage: None.

Example:

<PAGE>

  Entering this ideogram will clear the terminal screen.

Comment: This ideogram is vectored from PAGE via user variable 'PAGE. It allows one to start with a clear screen and the cursor at home. Note that inspite of a common operating system such as CP/M, not all terminals will use this code to clear the screen. This ideogram can be redefined in high level FORTH for the particular terminal and the new code field address placed in 'PAGE.

<R/W>   addr blk f ---   MVP-FORTH - DISK I-O

The fig-FORTH standard disk read-write linkage. addr specifies the source or destination buffer address, (not necessarily the FORTH buffer), blk is the sequential number of the referenced block; and f is a flag for f = 0 write and f = 1 read. <R/W> determines the location on mass storage, performs the read-write and performs any error checking.

Defined in: MVP-FORTH

Implementation:

: <R/W>   USE @ >R ROT USE ! SWAP MAX-DRV 0
      DO I DR-DEN DENSITY !
          DUP BPDRV - -1 >

```
        IF  BPDRV  -  I  1+  MAX-DRV  =
          IF  R>  R>  DDROP  R>  USE  !
            1  ABORT" BLOCK OUT OF RANGE"  THEN
          ELSE  I  DRIVE  !  SET-DRIVE  LEAVE
          THEN
      LOOP  SPBLK  *  SPBLK  0
      DO    DDUP  T&SCALC  SET-IO
        IF  SEC-READ
        ELSE  SEC-WRITE
        THEN  1+  HDBT  4  -  SPBLK  /  USE  +!
      LOOP
      DDROP  R>  USE  !  ;
```

Note: HDBT is a cross compiler equate for 1028, the block size plus header and trailer.

Source usage: None.

Example:

```
: BUFFER     USE  @  DUP  >R
    BEGIN   +BUF  UNTIL
    USE  !  R@  @  0<
    IF  R@  2+  R@  @  7FFF  AND  0  <R/W>  THEN
    R@  !  R@  PREV  !  R>  2+  ;
```

   This definition is modified from the MVP-FORTH source code. It is one of the principal uses of the ideogram, <R/W>.

Comment: This   ideogram   is   a   primitive   in   many implementations of FORTH. If it is available, it is possible to read and write from disk to any area in memory such as a special buffer, without going through the regular block buffers. Of course such a procedure is installation dependent and prohibited by FORTH-79.

<T&SCALC>   n ---   MVP-FORTH - DISK I-O

Track & Sector and drive calculation for disk IO. n is the total sector displacement. The corresponding track, and sector numbers are calculated. The track number is stored in TRACK; the sector number is stored in SEC.

Defined in: MVP-FORTH

Implementation:

```
: <T&SCALC>    SPT  /MOD  TRACK  !
               1+  SEC  !  ;
```

Note: Most CP/M systems start counting sectors at 1.

However, a few start at sector 0. It is a simple patch to add a
no-op, NOOP, to FORTH and replace the code field address of
1+ in <T&SCALC> with the code field address of NOOP.

Source usage: None.

Example:

```
: <R/W>    USE  @  >R  ROT  USE ! SWAP  MAX-DRV   0
    DO I  DR-DEN  DENSITY  !
       DUP  BPDRV  -  -1  >
       IF  BPDRV  -  I  1+  MAX-DRV  =
          IF  R>  R>  DDROP  R>  USE  !
             1  ABORT" BLOCK OUT OF RANGE"  THEN
       ELSE  I  DRIVE  !  SET-DRIVE  LEAVE
       THEN
    LOOP   SPBLK  *  SPBLK  0
    DO   DDUP  T&SCALC  SET-IO
       IF  SEC-READ
       ELSE  SEC-WRITE
       THEN  1+  HDBT  4  -  SPBLK  /  USE  +!
    LOOP
    DDROP  R>  USE ! ;
```

This example is modified from the MVP-FORTH
implementation.

Comment: This is a revised implementation from that in fig-
FORTH; it takes into account the number of sectors which are
present on each disk in making the calculation.

<VOCABULARY79>   ---   208   MVP-FORTH

The run-time routine for a defining word to create (in the
CURRENT vocabulary) a dictionary entry for <name>, which
specifies a new ordered list of word definitions. Subsequent
execution of <name> will make it the CONTEXT vocabulary.
When <name> becomes the CURRENT vocabulary (see
DEFINITIONS), new definitions will be created in that list.
In lieu of any further specifications, new vocabularies 'chain'
to FORTH. That is, when a dictionary search through a
vocabulary is exhausted, FORTH will be searched.

Form: VOCABULARY <name>

Defined in: FORTH-79, STARTING FORTH

Implementation:

```
: <VOCABULARY79>
    CREATE   A081  ,  '  FORTH  ,
```

```
     HERE  VOC-LINK  @  ,  VOC-LINK  !
     DOES>  2+  CONTEXT  !  ;
```

Source usage: 'VOCABULARY

Example:

```
  '  <VOCABULARY79>  CFA  'VOCABULARY  !
```

The example places the code field address of the run-time
ideogram in the user variable for use by VOCABULARY.

Comment: The implementation produces the correct run-time
procedure according to the function described in the FORTH-79
STANDARD. Note that the implementation has been changed
from that in early versions of MVP-FORTH. Chaining of
vocabularies is not possible with this implementation.

<VOCABULARYFIG>   ---   MVP-FORTH

The run-time routine for a defining word to create a vocabulary
definition <name>. Subsequent use of <name> will make it the
CONTEXT vocabulary which is searched first by INTERPRET.
The sequence " <name> DEFINITIONS" will also make <name>
the CURRENT vocabulary into which new definitions are placed.
In fig- FORTH, <name> will be so chained as to include all
definitions of the vocabulary in which <name> is itself defined.
All vocabularies ultimately chain to FORTH. By convention,
vocabulary names are to be declared IMMEDIATE. See VOC-
LINK.

Form: <VOCABULARYFIG> <name>

Defined in: fig-FORTH

Implementation:

```
: <VOCABULARYFIG>
    CREATE  A081  ,  CURRENT  @  CFA  ,
    HERE  VOC-LINK  @  ,  VOC-LINK  !
    DOES>  2+  CONTEXT  !  ;
```

Source usage: None.

Example:

```
' <VOCABULARYFIG>  CFA  'VOCABULARY  !
```

The example will change the function of VOCABULARY in
the distribution version of MVP-FORTH to that used by fig-

FORTH. This is not allowed in the FORTH-79 STANDARD.

Comment: The function of VOCABULARY defined by the
FORTH-79 STANDARD is restrictive. Many users have found
that of fig-FORTH much better. Other have developed other
functions for VOCABULARY. By vectoring VOCABULARY, it
is possible for a user to use a function of his own design as
well.

<WORD>	char --- addr	MVP-FORTH

Receive characters from the input stream until the non-zero
delimiting character is encountered or the input stream is
exhausted, ignoring leading delimiters. The characters are
stored as a packed string with the character count in the first
character position. The actual delimiter encountered (char
or null) is stored at the end of the text but not included in the
count. If the input stream was exhausted as WORD is
called, then a zero length will result. The address of the
beginning of the is packed string is left on the stack.

Defined in: MVP-FORTH

Implementation:

```
: <WORD>    'STREAM
   SWAP  ENCLOSE  DDUP  >
   IF  DDROP  DDROP  0  HERE  !
   ELSE  >IN  +!  OVER  -  DUP  >R
      HERE  C!  +  HERE  1+  R>  DUP  FF  >
      ABORT" INPUT > 255"  1+  CMOVE
   THEN  HERE  ;
```

Source usage: None.

Example:

```
: INPUT    ." Input an integer -- "
   QUERY  BL  <WORD>  NUMBER  DROP  ;
```

The definition provides for a prompt and then a pause for the
operator to input the requested integer. Then the input
character stream is parsed with this ideogram, converted to a
double precision value and reduced to a single precision value
left on the stack.

Comment: This ideogram is vectored from WORD via user
variable 'WORD. In MVP-FORTH, <WORD> leaves the
address of the initial count on top of the stack. As in fig-
FORTH, the string is stored at HERE.

=   n1   n2   ---   flag   173   MVP-FORTH

True if n1 is equal to n2 .

Pronounced: equals

Defined in: FORTH-79, fig-FORTH, STARTING FORTH

Implementation:

: =   - NOT ;

Source usage: Used many times in the source code.

Example:

45   45   =

   The two values are placed on the stack and the test made.   In
this case the values are equal and a 1 is left on the stack as a
true flag.

Comment: A common operator to all versions of FORTH.   The
comparison destroys both comparands.

>   n1   n2   ---   flag   102   MVP-FORTH

True if n1 is greater than n2 .

Pronounced: greater-than

Defined in: FORTH-79, fig-FORTH, STARTING FORTH

          Implementation:

: >   SWAP < ;

Source usage: 0>   <WORD>   MIN

Example:

45   46   >

   The two values are placed on the stack and the test is made.
In this case the test is false and a 0 flag is left on the stack.

Comment: A common logical operator in all versions of
FORTH.   The comparison destroys both comparands.

          d1   addr1   ---   d2   addr2

Same as   CONVERT.

Pronounced: to-binary

          Defined in: STARTING FORTH

Implementation:

: >BINARY   CONVERT ;

Source usage: None.

Example:

: TEST   BL   WORD   0   0   ROT   >BINARY   DROP ;

    A definition which provides a simple demonstration of the
conversion of a WORD to a double precision binary value.

Comment: Some   FORTH   implementations   hash   the   name
ideograms in order to save space. In so doing the FORTH-79
CONVERT,   normally   used,   may   conflict   with   CONTEXT,
therefore the need of an alias.

>IN   ---   addr   U, 201   MVP-FORTH

Leave the address of a variable which contains the present
character offset within the input stream.   0..1023

Pronounced: to-in

Defined in: FORTH-79

Implementation:

36   USER   >IN

Source usage: 'STREAM (<LOAD> <WORD>
    ABORT" QUERY   WHERE

Example:

: QUERY   TIB @ 50 EXPECT 0 >IN ! ;

    The value of the user variable, >IN, is set to 0 after
EXPECT.

Comment: This ideogram replaces IN in the earlier fig-FORTH. Together with BLK, it determines the location of the next character from the input stream.

>R   n ---   C, 200   MVP-FORTH

Transfer n to the return stack. Every >R must be balanced by a R> in the same control structure nesting level of a colon-definition.

Pronounced: to-r

Defined in: FORTH-79, fig-FORTH, STARTING FORTH

Implementation:

```
CODE  >R    D POP   RPP LHLD   H DCX   H DCX
      RPP SHLD   E M MOV   H INX   D M MOV
      NEXT JMP   END-CODE
```

Source usage: Many.

        Example:

```
: TEST   45  47  >R  1+  R>  ;
```

A contrived example: place two values on the stack and then increment the value immediately below the top of the stack.

Comment: CAUTION: This ideogram must be used with care to avoid crashing the system. Within its limitations, it is useful for accessing buried numbers. PICK and ROLL, however, offer a less dangerous alternative.

>TYPE   addr n ---   MVP-FORTH - SUPPLEMENTAL

Same as TYPE except that the output string is moved to the pad prior to output. Used in multiprogrammed systems to output strings from disk blocks.

Defined in: STARTING FORTH

Implementation:

```
: >TYPE    ." Used in multiprogrammed systems only "
    QUIT ;   IMMEDIATE
```

Source usage: None.

Example:

PAD   COUNT   >TYPE

In this implementation you are informed that the ideogram is not available for use.

Comment: This ideogram needs to be implemented only in multiuser systems.

?   addr   ---   194   MVP-FORTH

Display the number at address, using the format of "." .

Pronounced: question-mark

Defined in: FORTH-79, fig-FORTH, STARTING FORTH

Implementation:

: ?   @ . ;

Source usage: None.

Example:

HEX   4AC2   ?   DECIMAL

Place an address on the stack and the value contained in the sixteen bits beginning with that address is printed.

Comment: Provides a quick way of finding the current value at a given address anywhere in memory. It is most useful in developing and debugging programs.

?COMP   ---   MVP-FORTH

Issue an error message if not compiling.

Defined in: fig-FORTH

Implementation:

: ?COMP   STATE @ NOT
    ABORT" COMPILE ONLY " ;

Source usage: ABORT" COMPILE BEGIN THEN
                      [COMPILE]

Example:

```
: BEGIN   ?COMP   HERE  1  ;
```

Ensure that you are compiling as in this definition.

Comment: An ideogram used by fig-FORTH and some other implementations. It is an error-handling function which, in MVP-FORTH, types its message from an in-line ABORT" string.

?CONFIGURE   ---   MVP-FORTH

Display the current configuration for all available disk drives. The density code for each drive is given as an integer from 0 through 6, with the following interpretation:

```
0 - 5"  Single Sided, Single Density   (5-SSSD)
1 - 8"  Single Sided, Single Density   (8-SSSD)
2 - 8"  Double Sided, Single Density   (8-DSSD)
3 - 8"  Single Sided, Double Density   (8-SSDD)
4 - 8"  Double Sided, Double Density   (8-DSDD)
5 - 8"  Single Sided, Extended Density  (8-SSEXT)
6 - 8"  Double Sided, Extended Density  (8-DSEXT)
```

The number of drives available is determined by the value of the constant MAX-DRV, which may be altered.

Defined in: MVP-FORTH

Implementation:

```
: ?CONFIGURE   CR CR MAX-DRV .
    ." DRIVES WITH DENSITIES: "
  MAX-DRV 0 DO  I  DR-DEN  2 SPACES  .  LOOP
  CR CR  ." DENSITY CODE "
  CR ." 0 - 5-SSSD"      CR ." 1 - 8-SSSD"
  CR ." 2 - 8-DSSD"      CR ." 3 - 8-SSDD"
  CR ." 4 - 8-DSDD"      CR ." 5 - 8-SSEXT"
  CR ." 6 - 8-DSEXT"
          CR  ;
```

Source usage: CONFIGURE

Example:

?CONFIGURE

Display current physical drive parameters, without changing their settings. Stacks and dictionary remain unaffected.

Comment: ?CONFIGURE displays the contents of the array, DEN, for drives numbered 0 through MAX-DRV less one. To change these values from the terminal, use CONFIGURE. The density codes refer to the order of items in the arrays SEC/TR and BLK/DRV. They can be easily examined with DUMP and modified as necessary.

?CSP   ---   MVP-FORTH

Issue error message if stack position differs from value saved in CSP.

Defined in: fig-FORTH

Implementation:

```
: ?CSP   SP@  CSP  @  -
    ABORT" DEFINITION NOT FINISHED " ;
```

Source usage: ;   DOES>

Example:

```
: ;   ?CSP  COMPILE  ;S  SMUDGE  [COMPILE]  [ ;
IMMEDIATE
```

In this definition from the MVP-FORTH source code, the ideogram does the error checking.

Comment: An ideogram used by fig-FORTH and some other implementations. It is an error-handling function which, in MVP-FORTH, types its message from an in-line ABORT" string.

?DUP   n --- n (n)   184   MVP-FORTH

Duplicate n if it is non-zero.

Pronounced: query-dup

Defined in: FORTH-79, STARTING FORTH

Implementation:

```
: ?DUP   DUP  IF  DUP  THEN  ;
```

Source usage: FORGET SPACES TYPE

Example:

```
: INFORM   DISK-ERROR @ ?DUP
    IF ." DISK ERROR CODE " . THEN ;
```

The message is printed only when the value is non-zero.

Comment: This is the current ideogram for the now obsolete one -DUP . It saves having to DROP the value from the stack should a test, as for IF , turn out false.

?ERROR   f n ---   NOT USED

Issue an error message number n , if the boolean flag is true.

Defined in: fig-FORTH

Implementation:

This ideogram is not implemented because the messages are not handled from the disk as in fig-FORTH.

Comment: Used to select an error message from disk in fig-FORTH if WARNING is set to 1, or the message number if WARNING is set to zero. Other implementations of FORTH handle error messages in different ways.

?EXEC   ---   NOT USED

Issue an error message if not executing.

Defined in: fig-FORTH

Implementation:

(This ideogram is not implemented in MVP-FORTH.)

Comment: Not a FORTH-79 ideogram. Used in fig-FORTH and may be present in other implementations of FORTH.

?LOADING   ---   MVP-FORTH

Issue an error message if not loading.

Defined in: fig-FORTH

Implementation:

```
: ?LOADING   BLK @  NOT
```

```
ABORT" LOADING ONLY " ;
```

Source usage: None.

Example:

```
: --> ?LOADING  0  >IN  !  B/SCR  @  OVER
   MOD  -  BLK  +!  ;  IMMEDIATE
```

   This fig-FORTH definition illustrates the use of the
ideogram. It will not work in MVP-FORTH, and there are
better ways to load multiple screens (See THRU).

Comment: Not a FORTH-79 STANDARD ideogram. Used in
fig-FORTH and may be present in other implementations of
FORTH.

?PAIRS   n1 n2 ---   MVP-FORTH

Issue an error message if n1 does not equal n2. The message
indicates that compiled conditionals do not match.

Defined in: fig-FORTH

Implementation:

```
: ?PAIRS   -
   ABORT" CONDITIONALS NOT PAIRED " ;
```

Source usage: +LOOP /LOOP AGAIN
    ELSE THEN UNTIL

Example:

```
: AGAIN   1 ?PAIRS
   COMPILE  BRANCH  HERE  -  ,  ;
```

   In a correct colon definition, " 1 ?PAIRS " will encounter the
value 1 left on the stack by the corresponding BEGIN. This
ensures the proper nesting in practically all cases.

Comment: Not a FORTH-79 STANDARD ideogram. Used in
fig-FORTH and may be present in other implementations of
FORTH.

?STACK   ---   MVP-FORTH

Issue an error message if the stack is out of bounds. This
definition may be installation dependent.

Defined in: fig-FORTH

Implementation:

```
: ?STACK    SP@ 2+  SO  SWAP  U<
    ABORT" STACK OUT OF BOUNDS "    SP@  HERE  80
+   U<
    ABORT" FULL STACK " ;
```

Note: In some MVP-FORTH implementation the value 2+ has been left out.

Source usage: <ABORT> INTERPRET

Example:

```
: INTERPRET
    BEGIN  -FIND
        IF  STATE  @  <
            IF  2-  ,  ELSE  2-  EXECUTE  THEN  ?STACK
        ELSE HERE  NUMBER  DPL  @  1+
            IF  [COMPILE] DLITERAL
            ELSE  DROP  [COMPILE] LITERAL
            THEN  ?STACK
        THEN
    AGAIN  ;
```

This definition from an early version of the source illustrates this ideogram. Note that stack checking is an expensive operation best reserved for outermost loops and recursive definitions.

Comment: Not a FORTH-79 STANDARD ideogram. Used in fig-FORTH and may be present in other implementations of FORTH. STARTING FORTH uses this ideogram with a different function.

?STREAM   f ---   MVP-FORTH

Issue an error message if the flag is true indicating that the input stream is exhausted.

Defined in: MVP-FORTH

Implementation:

```
: ?STREAM    ABORT" INPUT STREAM EXHAUSTED" ;
```

Source usage: (." ABORT"

Example:

```
: (    -1  >IN  +!  29  WORD  C@  1+
   HERE  +  C@  29  =  NOT
   ?STREAM  ;  IMMEDIATE
```

The example comes from the MVP-FORTH source code.

Comment: This ideogram signals an error condition, and is available for the programmer.

?TERMINAL   --- f   MVP-FORTH

Perform a test of the terminal keyboard for actuation of the break key. A true flag indicates actuation. This definition is installation dependent.

Defined in: fig-FORTH

Implementation

```
: ?TERMINAL  '?TERMINAL  @  EXECUTE  ;
```

Source usage: LIST

Example:

```
: TEST   1000  1  DO  I  .  ?TERMINAL
   IF  LEAVE  THEN  LOOP  ;
```

   With this definition, TEST , will start printing numbers which can be interrupted any time by hitting any key in the MVP-FORTH implementation.

Comment: Not a FORTH-79 STANDARD ideogram. Used in fig-FORTH and may be present in other implementation of FORTH. It is a convenient test in a definition which permits interrupting a loop by entering something from the keyboard. There is nothing like it when a paper in the printer hangs up. It is, however not defined in most versions of FORTH, because of its installation dependency which would limit portability. However, it is usually a simple matter to modify a program according to the installation requirements. In the IBM implementation, a true flag is the ASCII value of the character struck.

@   addr --- n   199   MVP-FORTH

Leave on the stack the number contained at addr.

Pronounced: fetch

Defined in: FORTH-79, fig-FORTH, STARTING FORTH

Implementation:

8080:

```
CODE @   H POP   M E MOV   H INX   M D MOV
     D PUSH   NEXT JMP   END-CODE
```

Source usage: Many.

Example:

HEX 4AC2 @ .   DECIMAL

   Place the address on the stack, fetch the value at that
address and then print it.

Comment: A common and frequently used FORTH ideogram
present in almost all implementations.

@L   seg addr --- n   MVP-FORTH

In an 8086/8088 system, leave on the stack the number contained
in   seg at addr.

Defined in: MVP-FORTH

Implementation:

8086/8088 (IBM)

```
CODE @L   BX POP   DS POP   AX, [BX] MOV
     BX, CS MOV   DS, BX MOV   APUSH JMP   END-CODE
```

Source usage: None.

Example:

HEX
40 17 C@ .
DECIMAL

   The example examines the " caps lock " key flag on the IBM
Personal Computer and print its value.

Comment: The function of this ideogram allows one to examine
parts of memory outside the segments used by FORTH.

ALL ABOUT FORTH   101

Clear the data and return stacks, setting execution mode.
Return control to the terminal.

Defined in: FORTH-79, fig-FORTH

Implementation:

: ABORT   'ABORT @ EXECUTE ;

Source usage: COLD

Example:

ABORT

   This simple ideogram will clear the stack and return to
FORTH so that you can begin again. Your definitions are not
forgotten.

Comment: In some versions of FORTH, this ideogram also
includes a statement of the name of the version and other
information, while in FORTH-79, no indication is made. Since
it is vectored, you may modify its actions however you please.
Normally, ABORT invokes <ABORT>.

ABORT"   flag   ---   C   MVP-FORTH

Used in a colon-definition. If the flag is true, print the
following text, till " . Then execute ABORT.

Form: ABORT" stack empty"

Pronounced: abort-quote

Defined in: FORTH-79(R), STARTING FORTH

Implementation:

: ABORT"   ?COMP COMPILE <ABORT"> 'STREAM
      C@   22 =
    IF 1 >IN +! 0 C,
    ELSE 22 WORD DUP C@ 1+ SWAP OVER
       + C@ 22 = NOT ?STREAM ALLOT
    THEN ; IMMEDIATE

Source usage: Many.

Example:

```
: ?/   DUP  0=  ABORT" DIVISION BY ZERO "  /  ;
```

This example invents a new division operator which works exactly like / unless the divisor is zero.

Comment: A convenient way of providing error messages when aborting a routine.

ABS   n1 --- n2   108   MVP-FORTH

Leave the absolute value of a number.

Pronounced: absolute

Defined in: FORTH-79, fig-FORTH, STARTING FORTH

Implementation:

```
: ABS   DUP  +-  ;
```

Source usage: M/   M*

Example:

-45   ABS

Enter the negative value on the stack and it is converted to a positive value.

Comment: A common ideogram in all versions of FORTH, operates on signed single precision integers. Note that " - 32768 ABS " returns the negative value -32768 because its absolute value cannot be represented as a signed 16 bit number.

AGAIN   I, C MVP-FORTH
       addr n ---   (compiling)
       ---   (run-time)

Effect an unconditional jump back to the start of a BEGIN-AGAIN loop.

Defined in: FORTH-79(R), fig-FORTH

Implementation:

```
: AGAIN   1 ?PAIRS  COMPILE  BRANCH
   HERE  -  ,  ;   IMMEDIATE
```

Source usage: INTERPRET   QUIT   REPEAT

Example:

: TEST   0   BEGIN   1+   DUP   .   AGAIN   ;

   You will have to reboot your system if you try this example - a
good lesson !   Defines an infinite loop to print the number
series beginning with the value 1.

Comment: An ideogram used to implement M V P - F O R T H , but not
part of FORTH-79.

ALLOT   n   ---   154   MVP-FORTH

Add   n   bytes to the parameter field of the   most recently
defined word.

Defined in: FORTH-79, fig-FORTH, STARTING FORTH

Implementation:

: ALLOT   DP   +!   ;

Source usage: ,   C,   CREATE   VARIABLE

Example:

            VARIABLE   NEW-VALUE   20   ALLOT

   After creating an uninitialized variable, NEW-VALUE, 20
bytes are skipped over in the dictionary before a new definition
will be compiled.   These could be used as a small buffer, for
example.

Comment: Allows one to reserve space in the definition of a
new ideogram.   This space can be used in a variety of ways such
as making room for an array.   It is the normal way to reserve
space for arrays, buffers and other data structures.   In this
implementation, there is no security.   If one were to ALLOT
into the data stack, he could crash the system.

AND   n1   n2   ---   n3   183   MVP-FORTH

Leave the bitwise logical 'and' of n1 and n2.

Defined in: FORTH-79, fig-FORTH, STARTING FORTH

Implementation:

8080:

```
CODE AND   D POP  H POP  E A MOV  L ANA
    A L MOV  D A MOV  H ANA  A H MOV
    HPUSH JMP  END-CODE
```

Source usage: BUFFER

Example:

```
: TEST    E5  P@  20  AND  IF  ." READY"  THEN ;
```

   This ideogram is used as a mask to see if bit 6 of an input port
is set and, if it is, to type READY.

Comment: This ideogram allows the masking of the bit pattern
of one number on the stack with the other, an operation which is
common in computing.

APUSH   --- addr   MVP-FORTH

A constant used in 8086/8088 implementations pointing to a
machine code entry point which pushes the contents of the AX
register onto the stack and then falls through to NEXT, the
inner interpreter.

Defined in: MVP-FORTH (8086/8088)

Implementation:

APUSH CONSTANT APUSH

(The cross-compiler takes the label APUSH and makes it a
constant.)

Source usage: Many - in CODE definitions.

Example:

```
CODE  +
    AX POP  BX POP  AX,BX ADD  APUSH JMP  END-CODE
```

   This example is taken from the MVP-FORTH 8086/8088 source
code.

Comment: This is a machine, system, and implementation
dependent location used only at the machine code level. It
allows trimming one byte off CODE definitions which would
otherwise end with AX PUSH NEXT JMP END-CODE.

ASSEMBLER   ---

Sets CONTEXT vocabulary to ASSEMBLER if that vocabulary is
implemented.

Comment: The implementation of this ideogram is left to the
user. It is machine- and implementation- dependent.
Although not a part of the MVP-FORTH implementation, it may
be written and loaded in a high-level source code form.

B/BUF   ---   n

A constant leaving 1024, the number of bytes per block buffer.

Pronounced: bytes-per-buffer

Defined in: FORTH-79(R), fig-FORTH

Implementation:

400 CONSTANT   B/BUF

Source ussage: None.

Example:

B/BUF .

    This ideogram followed by . will print the current size of
the disk buffers.

Comment: An installation dependent primitive which may be
available in other implementations of forth. In many
implementations of fig-FORTH, the value of this constant may
be hex 80. Note that the implementation values are all in
hexadecimal.

B/SCR   ---   n

This constant leaves the number of blocks per editing screen.
By convention, an editing screen is 1024 bytes organized as 16
lines of 64 characters each.

Defined in: fig-FORTH

Implementation:

8 CONSTANT B/SCR

Source usage: None.

Example:

B/SCR   .

This example will print the number of block buffers necessary for a full screen.

Comment: An installation dependent primitive necessary in some versions of FORTH.

BACK   addr ---   NOT USED

Calculate the backward branch offset from   HERE   to addr and compile into the next available dictionary memory address.

Defined in: fig-FORTH

Implementation:

: BACK   HERE - , ;

Source usage: None.

Example:

: UNTIL   1 ?PAIRS COMPILE OBRANCH BACK ;
          IMMEDIATE

This example defines UNTIL in an alternative fashion to the one used to describe the ideogram.

Comment: Not used in the MVP-FORTH implementation.

BASE   --- addr   U, 115   MVP-FORTH

Leave the address of a variable containing the current input-output numeric conversion base.   2..70

Defined in: FORTH-79, fig-FORTH, STARTING FORTH

Implementation:

38 USER BASE

Source usage: # CONVERT   DECIMAL   HEX

Example:

```
: BINARY   2   BASE   !   ;
```

Add the definition of BINARY to your vocabulary.

Comment: The reference variable used to convert numeric input to the binary form in which it is stored on the stack and in memory. It can also be used for coding alphanumeric information by utilizing unusual values.

BEGIN   I, C, 147   MVP-FORTH
         ---   addr   n   (compile time)

Used in a colon definition. BEGIN   marks the start of a word sequence for repetitive execution. A BEGIN-UNTIL loop will be repeated until flag is true.   A   BEGIN-WHILE-REPEAT loop will be repeated until flag is false.   The ideograms after UNTIL or REPEAT will be executed when either loop is finished.   flag is always dropped after being tested.

Form: BEGIN   ...   flag   UNTIL   or
          BEGIN   ...   flag   WHILE   ...   REPEAT

Defined in: FORTH-79, fig-FORTH, STARTING FORTH

Implementation:

```
: BEGIN   ?COMP   HERE   1   ;   IMMEDIATE
```

Source usage: #S   BLOCK   BUFFER   <INTERPRET>
       TRAVERSE

Example:

```
: TEST   0   BEGIN   1+   DUP   .   DUP   10   =   UNTIL
     DROP   ;
```

A definition which will print the values 1 through 10.

Comment: Used in colon definitions to delimit a nestable structure controlling repetitive execution.

BL   ---   c   176   MVP-FORTH

A constant that leaves the ASCII value for "blank".

Defined in: FORTH-79(R), fig-FORTH

Implementation:

20 CONSTANT BL

Source usage: -FIND -TRAILING
    <NUMBER> SPACE

Example:

: SPACE   BL EMIT ;

   A definition which will print a space.

Comment: A useful ideogram allowing one to enter the ASCII value of a "blank" independent of the number system currently in use. Though not always included in implementations, it can be easily added if needed.

BLANK   addr n ---   MVP-FORTH

Fill an area of memory over n bytes with the value for ASCII blank, starting at addr . If n is less than or equal to zero, take no action.

Defined in: MVP-FORTH, STARTING FORTH

Implementation:

: BLANK   BL FILL ;

Source usage: TEXT

Example:

VARIABLE NAME 18 ALLOT
NAME 20 BLANK

   Create a memory location of 20 bytes to store a name and then initialize the field with ASCII spaces.

Comment: This ideogram and its plural do exactly the same thing. There is no reason to have both available. This ideogram does not depend upon knowing the ASCII value of a blank in the current number base. fig-FORTH gives this function the name BLANKS.

BLANKS   addr n ---   NOT USED

This ideogram, in fig-FORTH, has the same function as BLANK in MVP-FORTH.

BLK   --- addr   U, 132   MVP-FORTH

Leave the address of a variable containing the number of the
mass storage block being interpreted as the input stream. If
the content is zero, the input stream is taken from the terminal.
The value of the variable is an unsigned number.

Pronounced: b-l-k

Defined in: FORTH-79, fig-FORTH, STARTING FORTH

Implementation:

3A   USER   BLK

Source usage: ." ?LOADING <LOAD> QUIT WHERE

Example:

BLK @ .

   When entered from the terminal, this user variable will print
the value of 0 indicating that the terminal is being
interpreted.

Comment: A common ideogram in most versions of FORTH.
Together with >IN, it determines the location of the next
character from the input stream.

BLK/DRV   --- addr   MVP-FORTH - DISK I-O

A variable beginning a seven item array containing the number
of blocks of 1024 bytes on a drive of a given density format.

Defined in: MVP-FORTH

Implementation:

VARIABLE BLK/DRV   A0 BLK/DRV !
   FA , 1F4 , 1F4 , 3E8 , 268 , 4D0 ,

Source usage: BPDRV

Example:

: BPDRV   DENSITY @ 6 MIN 2* BLK/DRV + @ ;

   The example is from the source code. Its function is to
leave the number of blocks on a drive according to the present

value of DENSITY.

Comment: An array used to calculate the actual drive to be accessed according to the block number being requested. Early implementations of MVP-FORTH used a similar array, SEC/DR, however, because of variations in formatting, BLK/DRV is more convenient. Note that the actual values in the array are system dependent. For the IBM Personal Computer with single sided 5 inch drives, the correct value of the first element of the array is 0A0 hex. (Each disk will hold 160 blocks.)

BLOCK   n --- addr   191 MVP-FORTH

Leave the address of the first byte in block n. If the block is not already in memory, it is transferred from mass storage into whichever memory buffer has been least recently accessed. If the block occupying that buffer has been UPDATEd (i.e. modified), it is rewritten onto mass storage before block n is read into the buffer. n is an unsigned number. If correct mass storage read or write is not possible, an error condition exists. Only data within the latest block referenced by BLOCK is valid by byte address, due to sharing of the block buffers.

Defined in: FORTH-79, fig-FORTH, STARTING FORTH

Implementation:

: BLOCK   'BLOCK @ EXECUTE ;

Source usage: <LINE> <WORD>

Example:

45 BLOCK

Entering the desired block number followed by the ideogram leaves the address of the beginning of that block on the top of the stack. If it is not already in a buffer, the block will be read in from disk.

Comment: A useful ideogram which speeds access to disk information when it is not modified. The MVP-FORTH has fixed a problem in some earlier implementations of fig-FORTH, which sometimes failed to update the last two lines of a source screen on a disk. In MVP-FORTH, this ideogram is vectored to increase flexibility; it defaults to <BLOCK>.

BLOCK-READ
BLOCK-WRITE

These are the preferred names for the installation dependent code to read and write one block to the disk.

Defined in: fig-FORTH

Implementation:

These ideograms are not implemented in MVP-FORTH.

Comment: Some version of these ideograms may be present to assist in disk I/O. The actual code falls outside the STANDARD and is implementation and hardware dependent.

BMOVE   addr1 addr2 n ---   MVP-FORTH - UTILITY

Move n bytes beginning at address addr1 to addr2 . Perform the operation correctly even if the ranges involved overlap.

Pronounced: b-move

Defined in: MVP-FORTH

Implementation:

```
: BMOVE    ROT  ROT   DDUP  U<
    IF  ROT  <CMOVE
    ELSE  ROT  CMOVE    THEN  ;
```

Source usage: None.

Example:

HERE PAD 20 BMOVE

  Will move the twenty bytes beginning at HERE to PAD.

Comment: Using CMOVE with overlapping source and destination fields may have an annoying or disastrous result. Although <CMOVE may be substituted for an offending CMOVE, the BMOVE chooses the correct move order automatically. This becomes one less worry for the programmer.

BPDRV   --- n   MVP-FORTH - DISK I-0

Find the value in the array BLK/DRV according to the value of DENSITY.

Defined in: MVP-FORTH

Implementation:

: BPDRV   DENSITY @ 6 MIN 2* BLK/DRV + @ ;

Source usage: <R/W>

Example:

SPDRV .

   Get the number of blocks on a drive according to the present
value of DENSITY and print it.

Comment: A factored FORTH utility used in setting up the
system for disk access.

BRANCH   ---   MVP-FORTH

The run-time procedure to unconditionally branch.   An in-line
offset is added to the interpretive pointer IP to branch
ahead or back.   BRANCH is compiled by ELSE , AGAIN ,
REPEAT .

Defined in: fig-FORTH

Implementation:

8080:

```
CODE BRANCH
   HERE LABEL BRAN1   B H MOV   C L MOV
      M E MOV   H INX   M D MOV   H DCX
      D DAD   L C MOV   H B MOV
      NEXT JMP   END-CODE
```

Source usage: AGAIN   ELSE   REPEAT

Example:

```
: AGAIN    1  ?PAIRS
   COMPILE  BRANCH   HERE  -  ,  ;
```

   The definition of the implementation of AGAIN illustrates
the use of this ideogram. " COMPILE BRANCH " generates the
pseudo-opcode to which the clause " HERE - , " supplies
the displacement.

Comment: A primitive which is not available in some

implementations of FORTH. The compilation address of
BRANCH functions as an unconditional branching opcode for the
address interpreter. An in-line branch displacement must
follow any compiled instance .of this ideogram. These
displacements are automatically generated by the control
structures. User defined control structures such as CASE may
be implemented by using BRANCH and 0BRANCH within new
immediate compiling ideograms.

CAUTION: Executing BRANCH directly from the terminal or
screen will crash your system.

BUFFER   n --- addr   130   MVP-FORTH

Obtain the next block buffer, assigning it to block n. The
block is not read from mass storage. If the previous contents
of the buffer has been marked as UPDATEd , it is written to
mass storage. If correct writing to mass storage is not
possible, an error condition exists. The address left is the
first byte within the buffer for data storage. n is an
unsigned number.

Defined in: FORTH-79, fig-FORTH, STARTING FORTH

Implementation:

```
: BUFFER
  ( USE  @  PREV  @  =  )
  ( IF  USE  @  +BUF  DROP  USE  !  THEN  )
    USE  @  DUP  >R
    BEGIN  +BUF  UNTIL
    USE  !  R@  @  0<
    IF  R@  2+  R@  @  7FFF  AND  0  R/W  THEN
    R@  !  R@  PREV  !  R>  2+  ;
```

Note: Some implementation of MVP-FORTH have left out the
commented portion. The buffers rotate in sequence if there are
three or more. Though no problem is apparent to the user, the
commented portion is necessary for only two buffers to rotate in
sequence. A modified definition would be necessary for use of
only one buffer.

Source usage: BLOCK EMPTY-BUFFERS SAVE-BUFFERS

Example:

```
: SAVE-BUFFERS    #BUFF  1+  0
    DO  0  BUFFER  DROP  LOOP  ;
```

The implementation of SAVE-BUFFERS illustrates this

ideogram and is fully described under its discussion.

Comment: Allows one to enter data into a new block for later storage without reading the current content of that block from the disk. If the buffer is marked for update it will be later written to disk.

BYE   ---   MVP-FORTH

Leave FORTH and return to the underlying operating system.

Defined in: MVP-FORTH

Implementation:

```
: BYE    FREEZE    HERE   0   100   U/MOD
     SWAP   DROP   1+   2/   2*
     DECIMAL   CR   .   ." PAGES "   CR   0 GO ;
```

Source usage: None.

Example:

BYE

Entering this ideogram calculates and then prints the space necessary for saving as a CP/M COM file, rounded up to the next even integer value as required, and then exits to CP/M.

Comment: Though not included in the usual FORTH vocabulary it is available in many implementations. It allows one to exit FORTH to an underlying operating system. The size indicates the number of segments which must be included to save FORTH as a load module, in this case by CP/M. The actual implementation is implementation dependent.

C!   n addr ---   219   MVP-FORTH

Store the least significant 8-bits of n at addr .

Pronounced: c-store

Defined in: FORTH-79, fig-FORTH, STARTING FORTH

Implementation:

8080:

```
CODE C!   H POP   D POP   E M MOV
     NEXT JMP   END-CODE
```

Source usage: C, EXPECT HOLD WORD

Example: CAUTION: May corrupt or crash your system.

HEX   41   4AC2   C!   DECIMAL

   Place the ASCII value of the character   A   on the stack
followed by an address.   This ideogram will store that value in
the addressed byte.

Comment: Note that the most significant bits of n are ignored
and lost.   Since C! will store anywhere in your memory space,
take care not to corrupt your dictionary, FORTH nucleus, or
operating system.

C!L   n seg addr ---   MVP-FORTH

In an 8086/8088 system, store the least significant 8-bits of
n (a byte) in segment, seg, at address addr.

Defined in: MVP-FORTH

Implementation:

8086/8088

CODE C!L   BX POP   DS POP   AX POP
     [BX], AL MOV   BX, CS MOV   DS, BX MOV
     NEXT JMP   END-CODE

Example:

HEX
0   40   17   C!L
DECIMAL

   Set the "caps lock" key's flag to 0 for lower case.

Comment: Note that the 'C' implies a character whereas it is a
byte which is stored.   The 'L' connotes long, i.e., out of the
current data segment.

C,   n ---   152   MVP-FORTH

Store the low order 8 bits of   n   at the next byte in the
dictionary, advancing the dictionary pointer.

Pronounced: c-comma

Defined in: FORTH-79(R), fig-FORTH, STARTING FORTH

Implementation:

: C,   HERE C! 1 ALLOT ;

Source usage: DOES>

Example:

00 C,

   Insert the code for an 8080/Z80 NOOP on the top of the
dictionary.

Comment: A convenient byte operator for filling dictionary
space one byte at a time, as when constructing name headers,
machine code sequences, or parameter fields. It may not be
available on some 16-bit machines.

C/L   --- n   MVP-FORTH

Constant leaving the number of characters per line; used by the
editor.

Defined in: fig-FORTH (8080)

Implementation:

40 CONSTANT C/L

Source usage: <LINE> WHERE

Example:

C/L .

   This ideogram places the value of the length of a line on a
screen, and, in the example, the value is printed.

Comment: C/L is used in calculations within the EDITOR. It
is not present in all systems, and its value, normally 64, may be
terminal dependent.

C@   addr --- byte   156 MVP-FORTH

Leave on the stack the contents of the byte at addr (with
higher bits zero, in a 16-bit field).

Pronounced: c-fetch

Defined in: FORTH-79, fig-FORTH, STARTING FORTH

Implementation:

8080:

```
CODE C@   H POP   M L MOV   O H MVI
    HPUSH JMP   END-CODE
```

Source usage: Many.

Example:

```
HEX  4AC2  C@  EMIT  DECIMAL
```

Place an address on the stack and fetch the byte value at that
address. Presuming that it is an ASCII character, then print
it.

Comment: Allows fetching individual bytes in memory for
inspection or output as in text processing.

C@L   seg   addr   ---   b   MVP-FORTH

In an 8086/8088 system, leave on the stack the contents of the
byte in segment seg, at address addr, (with higher bits zero,
in a 16-bit field).

Defined in: MVP-FORTH

Implementation:

8086/8088

```
CODE  C@L   BX POP   DS POP   AL, [BX] MOV
    AH, AH SUB   BX, CS MOV   DS, BX MOV
    APUSH JMP   END-CODE
```

Source usage: None.

Example:

```
HEX
40  17  C@L  .
DECIMAL
```

Check the "caps lock" key's flag on the IBM Personal
Computer and print it. A zero value is lower case and a value
of 40 is upper case.

Comment: This ideogram allows one to examine bytes in memory which are outside of the segments used by FORTH. Though the 'C' connotes character, one is actually fetching the byte. The 'L' connotes long, i.e., outside of the FORTH segments. It is used in the UTILITY for a "dump long", DUMPL.

CFA   pfa --- cfa   MVP-FORTH

Convert the parameter field address of a definition to its code field address.

Defined in: fig-FORTH

Implementation:

: CFA   2- ;

Source usage: Many.>

Example:

' ?CONFIGURE   CFA   EXECUTE

   Find   the   parameter   field   address   of   the   ideogram ?CONFIGURE and convert it to the code field address so that it can be executed.

Comment: A function which is needed in an indirect threaded code implementation of FORTH, to allow execution of ideograms after being found in the dictionary.   This practice, useful in some applications, is implementation dependent and violates the usage constraints of the FORTH-79 STANDARD.

CHANGE   ---   MVP-FORTH

Modify the size of your FORTH image and the number of buffers in use according to the current values of LIMIT and #BUFF.

Defined in: MVP-FORTH

Implementation: Note - the following auxiliary definitions are compiled headerless from source code.   One can add those ideograms to his vocabulary.

: CHANGE   FREEZE   LIMIT   HDBT   #BUFF   *   -
    DUP ' FIRST ! US - DUP RTS -
    DUP INIT-USER !
    [INIT-USER 4 +] LITERAL !
    DUP [INIT-USER 2+] LITERAL !

```
UP   OVER   RPP   ORIGIN   HERE   !
HERE   ROT   ROT   !   ROT   ROT   !   EXECUTE   ;
```

(Note: HDBT is compiled to a hex literal value 404 which is
the number of bytes in a block buffer plus four.   US is compiled
to a hex literal value 52 which is the size of the user area.
RTS is compiled to a hex literal value of A0 which is the offset
below the return stack pointer at which the stack pointer is
located.)

Source usage: None.

Example:

```
HEX
8000   '   LIMIT   !
4   '   #BUFF   !
CHANGE
DECIMAL
```

First set the constants LIMIT and #BUFF to the desired
values, then execute CHANGE.

Comment: This ideogram lets you dynamically alter the number
and location of your block buffers.   Simply modify the values
in the constants LIMIT and #BUFF and enter CHANGE.   All the
other buffer management parameters, including the startup data
in low memory, are adjusted accordingly.   This allows much
greater flexibility in deployment of your available RAM.

CLEAR   n   ---   MVP-FORTH

Clear Screen   n   to all blanks.

Defined in: MVP-FORTH

Implementation:

```
: CLEAR    OFFSET  @  +  BUFFER  400
    BL  FILL  UPDATE  ;
```

Source usage: None.

Example:

```
: WIPE   SCR  @  CLEAR  ;
```

This ideogram could be used to define WIPE for an EDITOR.

Comment: This ideogram performs the function in the original
fig-FORTH EDITOR.   It is included in the MVP-FORTH

implementation so that rudimentary screen editing can be done with the ideogram PP .

CMOVE addr1 addr2 n --- 153 MVP-FORTH

Move n bytes beginning at address addr1 to addr2 . The contents of addr1 is moved first proceeding toward high memory. If n · is zero or negative nothing is moved.

Pronounced: c-move

Defined in: FORTH-79, fig-FORTH, STARTING FORTH

Implementation:

```
: CMOVE   DUP  1 <
   IF  DDROP  DROP  ELSE  <CMOVE>  THEN  ;
```

Source usage: COLD FREEZE WORD TEXT

Example:

```
HEX  4AC2  6AC2  20  CMOVE   DECIMAL
```

Place the source address and then the destination address followed by a count on the stack followed by the ideogram and the move of 20 bytes will be accomplished. Make sure that it won't write over anything important.

Comment: This ideogram will propagate data toward high memory when source and destination fields overlap. Although such an effect may sometimes be desirable, BMOVE averts that phenomenon.

COLD   ---   MVP-FORTH

The cold start procedure to adjust the dictionary pointer to the minimum standard and restart via ABORT . May be called from the terminal to remove application programs and restart.

Defined in: fig-FORTH

Implementation:

```
: COLD   EMPTY-BUFFERS
   INIT-USER  UP  @  6  +  30  CMOVE
   PAGE  ." MVP-FORTH  VERSION 1.xx.03 "  CR
   1  DENSITY  !  FIRST  USE  !  FIRST  PREV  !
   DRO  0  EPRINT  !
   INIT-FORTH  @  '  FORTH  2+  !
```

          DECIMAL   ABORT   ;

Source usage: Used only for start up in the source code.

Example: CAUTION: This will erase all new definitions.

COLD

     This ideogram will cause the version of FORTH in memory to
be reconfigured to its condition on start up.   All source code
and application programs loaded upon the start up image are
lost.

Comment: This ideogram is a start-up primitive present only
in some versions of FORTH.   In other versions other ideograms
may be used to remove application programs from the dictionary.
Some versions of FORTH overwrite the startup information and
it is impossible to restart without rebooting the entire system.
COLD is similar to EMPTY.

COMPILE   ---   C 146   MVP-FORTH

When a word containing COMPILE executes, the 16-bit
value following the compilation address of COMPILE is
copied (compiled) into the dictionary. i.e., COMPILE
DUP will copy the compilation address of DUP.

Form: COMPILE [0 ,]   (will copy a zero).

Defined in: FORTH-79, fig-FORTH, STARTING FORTH

Implementation:

: COMPILE   ?COMP R>   DUP 2+ >R @ , ;

Source usage: +LOOP ; ?COMP <."> AGAIN
DO   DOES> ELSE IF LITERAL   LOOP   UNTIL

Example:

: ITERAL   STATE @
   IF COMPILE LIT , THEN ;
   IMMEDIATE

     The implementation of LITERAL provides an example of this
ideogram.

Comment: COMPILE is usually used within immediate words
such as IF and DOES> .

This ideogram lets you change the number of drives available on your system and the physical sector formatting used on each drive. First, it asks you to key in the total number of drives --- a digit from 1 through 5; any other key will abort the process, changing nothing. Once the number of drives is set, you are prompted to enter a "density code" for each drive starting with drive 0.

```
0 - 5"  Single Sided,  Single Density    (5-SSSD)
1 - 8"  Single Sided,  Single Density    (8-SSSD)
2 - 8"  Double Sided,  Single Density    (8-DSSD)
3 - 8"  Single Sided,  Double Density    (8-SSDD)
4 - 8"  Double Sided,  Double Density    (8-DSDD)
5 - 8"  Single Sided,  Extended Density  (8-SSEXT)
6 - 8"  Double Sided,  Extended Density  (8-DSEXT)
```

No density parameters will be updated until a correct code has been keyed in for every requested drive. Thus, this stage of CONFIGURE may be nondestructively aborted by the user at any time. On successful completion, OFFSET is cleared, directing BLOCK access to drive 0.

Defined in: MVP-FORTH

Implementation:

```
: CONFIGURE    ?CONFIGURE
  CR ." NUMBER OF DRIVES ?  "  KEY  31
  -  DUP  5  U<  NOT
  ABORT" TOO MANY DRIVES"
  DUP  31  +  EMIT  1+  '  MAX-DRV  !
  MAX-DRV  0
  DO  CR ." DRIVE "  I  . ."  ?  "
     KEY  30  -  DUP  7  U<  NOT
     ABORT" OUT OF RANGE"
     DUP  30  +  EMIT  I  2*  DEN  +  !
  LOOP
  DR0  CR  CR  ." DR0 SELECTED "  CR ;
```

Source usage: None.

Example:

CONFIGURE

   The system shows you the current drive settings, and then prompts you to change them. The density codes refer to the order of items in the arrays SEC/TR and BLK/DRV. They can be easily examined with DUMP and modified as necessary.

Comment: This ideogram is designed to be used from the terminal. For program control of drive configuration the array DEN and the alterable constant MAX-DRV may be modified directly. The use of dynamically adjustable disk parameters gives greater flexibility to the MVP-FORTH system. Note that DRG is always re-selected on completion, since the previous value of OFFSET may no longer be correct. The new disk configuration parameters may be permanently stored into the cold-start system image on disk. (See FREEZE)

CONSTANT   n ---   185   MVP-FORTH

A defining word to create a dictionary entry for <name>, leaving n in its parameter field. When <name> is later executed, n will be left on the stack.

Form: n CONSTANT   <name>

Defined in: FORTH-79, fig-FORTH, STARTING FORTH

Implementation:

8080:

: CONSTANT   CREATE , ;CODE D INX   XCHG
    M E MOV   H INX M D MOV   D PUSH
    NEXT JMP END-CODE

Note: ;CODE is defined in the cross compiler's ASSEMBLER and not in the MVP-FORTH nucleus.

Source usage: USER

Example:

HEX 20 CONSTANT   BL DECIMAL

   This example is the implementation of BL, the ASCII value of the space character in hex.

Comment: The use of CONSTANT is more efficient than VARIABLE if the value is not to be changed frequently.

CONTEXT   --- addr   U, 151   MVP-FORTH

Leave the address of a variable specifying the vocabulary in which dictionary searches are to be made, during interpretation of the input stream.

Defined in: FORTH-79, fig-FORTH, STARTING FORTH

Implementation:

3C USER CONTEXT

Source usage: -FIND : BYE DEFINITIONS FORGET

Example:

: DEFINITIONS CONTEXT @ CURRENT ! ;

   The implementation of DEFINITIONS illustrates how this
ideogram is used.

Comment: Some implementations of FORTH will chain multiple
vocabularies for searching while FORTH-79 requires every
vocabulary to chain to the FORTH vocabulary. CONTEXT
contains a pointer to a pointer to the length byte of the first
name to be searched, but this may vary among implementations.

CONVERT   d1 addr1 --- d2 addr2   195   MVP-FORTH

Convert to the equivalent stack number the text beginning at
addr1+1 with regard to BASE . The new value is accumulated
into double number d1 , being left as d2 .   addr2 is the
address of the first non-convertable character.

Defined in: FORTH-79, STARTING FORTH

Implementation:

```
: CONVERT
    BEGIN 1+  DUP  >R  C@  BASE  @  DIGIT  WHILE
        SWAP  BASE  @  U*  DROP  ROT  BASE  @  U*
        D+  DPL  @  1+
        IF  1  DPL  +!  THEN
        R>
    REPEAT  R>  ;
```

Source usage: <NUMBER>

Example:

HEX 0 0 4AC2 CONVERT DECIMAL

   Place a double precision value of 0 on the stack and then an
address in memory at which the ideogram is to begin its
conversion.

Comment: This ideogram replaces the now obsolete

(NUMBER) in the older fig-FORTH. As you might expect, no error message is given if the numeric text converts to a number larger than 32 bits. Any higher bits are lost.

COPY   n1 n2   ---   MVP-FORTH - UTILITY

Copy the contents of screen n1 to screen n2.

Defined in: fig-FORTH (EDITOR), STARTING FORTH

Implementation:

: COPY   SWAP   BLOCK   2- ! UPDATE ;

Source usage: None.

Example:

20 120 COPY

   Copies screen 20 to screen 120 .

Comment: This ideogram is defined in the vocabulary of most editors. However, it is convenient to have it defined in the FORTH vocabulary, too.

COUNT   addr   ---   addr+1 n   159   MVP-FORTH

Leave the address addr+1 and the character count of text beginning at addr . The first byte at addr must contain the character count n . Range of n is 0..255 .

Defined in: FORTH-79, fig-FORTH, STARTING FORTH

Implementation:

: COUNT   DUP 1+ SWAP C@ ;

Source usage: <.">   <ABORT">

Example:

PAD COUNT TYPE

   PAD leaves an address of a byte which contains the number of characters presently in PAD. This byte is placed on the stack on top of an address which increased by one.

Comment: A one-byte count limits string length to 255 characters. Although intended primarily for string handling, this ideogram will work for any kind of data.

CR   ---   160   MVP-FORTH

Cause a carriage-return and line-feed to occur on the current output device.

Defined in: FORTH-79, fig-FORTH, STARTING FORTH

Implementation:

```
: CR   'CR @ EXECUTE ;
```

Source usage: Many.

Example:

```
CR  CR ." HELLO"
```

The two ideograms cause the display to advance two lines and then print HELLO at the left margin of the display.

Comment: Placing the ideogram, CR, in the input stream is not equivalent to pressing the "Return" key on the terminal keyboard. Because of differences among output devices in the inclusion of line-feeds, this ideogram is vectored. This will simplify modification if necessary. Normally, CR vectors to <CR>.

CREATE   ---   239   MVP-FORTH

A defining word used to create a dictionary entry for <name>, without allocating any parameter field memory. When <name> is subsequently executed, the address of the first byte of <name>'s parameter field is left on the stack.

Form: CREATE <name>

Defined in: FORTH-79, fig-FORTH, STARTING FORTH

Implementation:

8080:

```
: CREATE   BL  WORD  DUP  DUP  1+  C@  0 =
    ABORT" ATTEMPTED TO REDEFINE NULL"
    DUP  CONTEXT @  @  <FIND>
    IF  DDROP  WARNING @
        IF  DUP  COUNT  TYPE  SPACE
        ." ISN'T UNIQUE "  THEN
```

```
THEN  C@  WIDTH  @  MIN  1+  ALLOT  DUP  80
TOGGLE  HERE  1-  80  TOGGLE  LATEST  ,
2  ALLOT  CURRENT  @  !  ;CODE
D  INX  D  PUSH  NEXT  JMP  END-CODE
```

Source usage: : CONSTANT VARIABLE VOCABULARY

Example:

: VARIABLE   CREATE 2 ALLOT ;

The implementation of VARIABLE illustrates how this ideogram is used to create a new header for an ideogram in the dictionary.

Comment: Under FORTH-79, CREATE builds a VARIABLE header with no parameter space. In contrast, fig-FORTH's CREATE sets up a CODE definition which will jump into the parameter field and crash unless <;CODE> is used to redirect the code address toward a valid machine language routine. FORTH-79's CREATE now replaces the older <BUILDS ideogram in generating defining words. Care must be taken by those already familiar with this word when they move to different implementations of FORTH. Note: Since the ASCII null is used as an ideogram to terminate interpretation from terminal and disk buffers, it must not be redefined.

CSP   --- addr   U   MVP-FORTH

A user variable temporarily storing the stack pointer position, for compilation error checking.

Defined in: fig-FORTH

Implementation:

3E USER CSP

Source usage: : ?CSP

Example:

: SP   SP@   CSP ! ;

This example comes from fig-FORTH and is not used in MVP-FORTH.

Comment: CSP stands for "check stack position." If the stack position is changed within a colon definition, an error condition is raised. This compiler security is a fig-FORTH feature outside the scope of the FORTH-79 STANDARD.

CURRENT   --- addr   U, 137   MVP-FORTH

Leave the address of a variable specifying the vocabulary into
which new word definitions are to be entered.

Defined in: FORTH-79, fig-FORTH, STARTING FORTH

Implementation:

40 USER CURRENT

Source usage: DEFINITIONS FORGET LATEST

Example:

: LATEST   CURRENT @ @ ;

   The implementation of LATEST illustrates the use of this
variable.

Comment: Early printings of the fig-FORTH Glossary left out
this ideogram. Now it is present in it and most other
implementations of FORTH. CURRENT contains a pointer to a
pointer to the length byte of the latest name in the current
vocabulary, but this may vary among implementations.

D!   d addr ---   MVP-FORTH

Store d as a double precision integer.

Pronounced: d-store

Defined in: MVP-FORTH

Implementation:

8080:

CODE D!   H POP D POP E M MOV H INX
    D M MOV   H INX D POP E M MOV H INX
    D M MOV   NEXT JMP END-CODE

Source usage: None.

Example: CAUTION: May corrupt or crash your system.

HEX 33.33 4AC2 D! DECIMAL

Enter the double precision value on the stack taking four bytes. Then remove these four bytes from the stack and store them in four bytes beginning at memory address 4AC2. FORTH-79 leaves the order of the bytes in each pair unspecified.

Comment: A useful operation whose function is provided in the extended vocabulary of FORTH-79. This ideogram D! is used in MVP-FORTH to avoid the misleading connotations of the numeral 2 .   The synonym 2! may be loaded as an alias for MVP-FORTH Double Number Word Set compatibilty.

D +   d1   d2   ---   d3   241   MVP-FORTH

Leave the arithmetic sum of d1 plus d2 .

Pronounced: d-plus

Defined in: FORTH-79, fig-FORTH, STARTING FORTH

Implementation:

8080:

```
CODE D+    6 H LXI   SP DAD   M E MOV   C M MOV
    H INX   M D MOV   B M MOV   B POP   H POP
    D DAD   XCHG   H POP   L A MOV   C ADC
    A L MOV   H A MOV   B ADC   A H MOV
    B POP   DPUSH JMP   END-CODE
```

Source usage: M +   M*/   CONVERT

Example:

2.2   3.3   D +

Place two double precision values on the stack and add them leaving the sum, 55, as a double precision value on the stack. Note that the location of the decimal point is not maintained.

Comment: A primitive present in most versions of FORTH with which other double precision ideograms can be defined.

D +-   d1   n   ---   d2   MVP-FORTH

Apply the sign of n to the double number d1 , leaving it as d2 .

Pronounced: d-plus-minus

Defined in: fig-FORTH

Implementation:

: D+-   0<   IF   DNEGATE   THEN   ;

Source usage: D.R   DABS   M/   M*

Example:

2.2   -1   D+-

   Place a double precision value on the stack followed by a
single precision negative value and then the ideogram to
convert, in this case, the 22 to -22 . Note that the position of
the decimal point is lost.

Comment: Similar to the ideogram,   +-   , for single precision
numbers and useful for double precision number manipulations.

D-   d1   d2   ---   d3   MVP-FORTH - UTILITY

Subtract d2 from d1 and leave the difference d3 .

Pronounced: d-minus

Defined in: FORTH-79(E), STARTING FORTH

Implementation:

: D-   DNEGATE   D+   ;

Source usage: None.

Example:

3.3   2.2   D-

   Place two double precision values on the stack and subtract
them leaving the difference as the double precision value, 11 .
Note that the location of the decimal point is not maintained.

Comment: This is part of the FORTH-79 Double Number Word
Set which can be defined easily if it is not already present.

D.   d   ---   (129)   MVP-FORTH

Display d converted according to BASE in a free-field
format, with one trailing blank. Display the sign only if

negative.

Pronounced: d-dot

Defined in: FORTH-79(E), fig-FORTH

Implementation:

: D.   0   D.R   SPACE   ;

Source usage: .   U.

Example:

2.2   D.

   Place a double precision value on the stack and then print it. Note that the location of the decimal point is not maintained but the number of significant digits is.

Comment: The counterpart of . with single precision numbers to display double precision numbers. Note: The serial number assigned this ideogram conflicts with that given 2-.

D.R   d n ---   MVP-FORTH

Display d converted according to BASE , right aligned in an n character field. Display the sign only if negative.

Pronounced: d-dot-r

Defined in: FORTH-79(E), fig-FORTH, STARTING FORTH

Implementation:

```
: D.R     DEPTH  3  <
    ABORT" EMPTY STACK"
    >R  SWAP  OVER  DUP  D+-
    <#  #S  ROT  SIGN  #>
    R>  OVER  -  SPACES  TYPE  ;
```

Source usage: .R   D.

Example:

2.2 10 D.R

   Enter a double precision value, 22 , and then a single precision value for the field width, ten. This ideogram then

prints the value 22 as two digits preceded by 8 leading blanks.
Note that the location of the decimal point is lost but that all
of the digits are printed.

Comment: Allows formatting the output of double precision
numbers. It is actually the primitive for many of the other
ideograms which output both single and double precision
numbers in some implementations of FORTH including MVP-
FORTH. Note that it traps an empty stack before garbage is
printed.

DO=   d --- flag   MVP-FORTH - UTILITY

Leave true if d is zero.

Pronounced: d-zero-equal

Defined in: FORTH-79(E), STARTING FORTH

Implementation:

: DO=   OR O= ;

Source usage: None.

Example:

2.2   DO=

    Enter a double precision value and test it.   In this case a   0
flag will be left.

Comment: A logical test for double precision numbers.   The
test destroys the comparand.

D<   d1 d2 --- flag   244   MVP-FORTH

True if d1 is less than d2 .

Pronounced: d-less-than

Defined in: FORTH-79, STARTING FORTH

Implementation:

: D<   ROT DDUP =
   IF ROT ROT DNEGATE D+ O<
   ELSE SWAP < SWAP DROP
   THEN SWAP DROP ;

Source usage: U<

Example:

2.2   3.3   D<

Enter two double precision values on the stack and then compare them. In this case the value of the flag left on the stack is   1 . Note that the location of the decimal point is lost.

Comment: Though not present in many versions of FORTH, it provides a convenient tool when working with double precision numbers. The comparison destroys both double precison comparands.

D =   d1   d2   ---   flag   MVP-FORTH - UTILITY

True if d1 equals d2 .

Pronounced: d-equal

Implementation:

: D =   D -   D 0= ;

Source usage: None.

Example:

2.2   3.3   D =

Enter two double precision values on the stack and compare them. In this case the flag left on the stack is 0.   Note that the location of the decimal point is not considered.

Comment: Though not present in many versions of FORTH, it provided a convenient tool when working with double numbers. The comparison destroys both double precision comparands.

D >   d. d2   ---   f   MVP-FORTH - UTILITY

True if d1 is less than d2 .

Pronounced: d-greater-than

Defined in: MVP-FORTH

Implementation:

: D>   DSWAP   D< ;

Source usage: None.

Example:

22.   2.3   D>

   Enter two double precision values on the stack and compare
them.   In this case, the resulting flag is false.   Note that no
decimal point alignment was performed.

Comment: This simple ideogram hardly needs adding to the
vocabulary.   However, I have often tried it and found it
missing, and therefore, have included it among the UTILITY's
for symmetry.

D@   addr   ---   d   MVP-FORTH - UTILITY

Leave on the stack the contents of the four consecutive bytes
beginning at addr, as for a double number.

Pronounced: d-fetch

Defined in: MVP-FORTH

Implementation:

: D@   DUP   2+   @   SWAP   @ ;

Source usage: None.

Example:

HEX   4AC2   D@   DECIMAL

   Take the four bytes beginning at address 4AC2 and place them
on the stack.   FORTH-79 leaves the storage order within byte
pairs unspecified.

Comment: This operation is provided in MVP-FORTH with the
ideogram, D@ , to avoid misleading connotations of the numeral
2 . The synonym 2@ may be loaded as an alias for FORTH-79
Double Number Word Set compatibility.

DABS   d1   ---   d2   MVP-FORTH

Leave as a positive double number   d2 , the absolute value of a double number, d1 .   Range 0..2,147,483,647 .

Pronounced: d-abs

Defined in: FORTH-79(E), fig-FORTH, STARTING FORTH

Implementation:

: DABS   DUP D+- ;

Source usage: M*/

Example:

2.2 DABS

   Enter a double precision value and then make its value
absolute. In this case it is left unchanged.

Comment: An almost indispensable ideogram when using double
precision arithmetic.

DCONSTANT   d   ---   MVP-FORTH - UTILITY

A defining word used to create a dictionary entry for <name>,
leaving d in its parameter field. When <name> is later
executed, d will be left on the stack.

Pronounced: d-constant

Form: 2   DCONSTANT   <name>

Defined in: MVP-FORTH

Implementation:

: DCONSTANT   CREATE SWAP , ,
   DOES> DUP @ SWAP 2+ @ ;

Source usage: None.

Example:

33.33   DCONSTANT   NEW-VALUE

   Enter the value 33.33, which will be a double precision
number, and store it in an ideogram named NEW-VALUE.
Executing NEW-VALUE will then cause the 3333 to be placed on
the stack, the location of the decimal point being lost.

Comment: In MVP-FORTH, the prefix mnemonic D for

double precision is used in place of 2 which has the
connotation of the numeral value. The synonym 2CONSTANT
may be used as an alias in the system for FORTH-79 double
precision word set compatibility.

DDROP   d ---   MVP-FORTH

Drop the top double number on the stack.

Pronounced: d-drop

Defined in: MVP-FORTH

Implementation:

8080:

CODE DDROP   H POP H POP   NEXT JMP   END-CODE
Source usage: Many.

Example:

DDROP

   This ideogram will cause the top four bytes on the stack to be
removed, which would drop a double precision number or any
other four bytes.

Comment: In MVP-FORTH, the prefix   mnemonic D for
double precision is used in place of 2, which has the
connotation of the numeral value. The synonym 2DROP may be
loaded as an alias for FORTH-79 Double Number Word Set
compatibility.

DDUP   d --- d d   MVP-FORTH

Duplicate the top double number on the stack.

Pronounced: d-dup

Defined in: MVP-FORTH

Implementation:

8080:

CODE DDUP   H POP D POP D PUSH H PUSH
     DPUSH JMP   END-CODE

Source usage: Many.

Example:

33.33   D D U P

   Place the double precision number on the stack and duplicate
it.

Comment: In MVP-FORTH, the prefix mnemonic D for
double precision, is used in place of 2 which has the
connotation of the numeral value.   The synonym 2DUP may be
loaded as an alias for FORTH-79 Double Number Word Set
compatibility.

DECIMAL   ---   197   MVP-FORTH

Set the input-output numeric conversion base to ten.

Defined in: FORTH-79, fig-FORTH, STARTING FORTH

Implementation:

: DECIMAL   0A   BASE   !   ;

Source usage: ABORT   BYE   COLD

Example:

DECIMAL

   Using this ideogram assures you that the present value of
BASE is decimal 10 .

Comment: This ideogram DECIMAL lets you put the value ten
into BASE without having to know its current value.   Note that
" 10 BASE ! " is useless regardless of the base you are currently
using.   Except for the disk interface, all of the implementation
code uses HEX for the number base.

DEFINITIONS   ---   155   MVP-FORTH

Set CURRENT to the CONTEXT vocabulary so that
subsequent definitions will be created in the vocabulary
previously selected as CONTEXT.

Defined in: FORTH-79, fig-FORTH, STARTING FORTH

Implementation:

: DEFINITIONS   CONTEXT @ CURRENT ! ;

Source usage: ABORT FORGET FORTH

Example:

FORTH DEFINITIONS

This sets the necessary pointer so that new definitions will be added to the FORTH vocabulary.

Comment: This ideogram is necessary in starting a new vocabulary or adding to an existing one.

DEN   ---   MVP-FORTH - DISK I-O

An array of variables which stores a value of the variable, DENSITY, for each of the drives up to a maximum of 5.

Defined in: MVP-FORTH

Implementation:

VARIABLE DEN 1 DEN ! 1 , 1 , 1 , 1 ,

Source usage: CONFIGURE   DR-DEN

Example:

1 2* DEN + @ .

To select a value for DENSITY on drive 1, enter a value 1 and then calculate the offset from the address of DEN to the location of the current density code for that drive. Then, fetch and print that value.

Comment: The values are initialized with a COLD start and can be subsequently changed according to the responses to CONFIGURE. The values associated with DENSITY are encoded as integers according to the prompts given when CONFIGURE is executed.

DENSITY   --- addr   MVP-FORTH - DISK I-O

A variable used by the disk interface. It may have a value from 0 to 6 according to the particular drive being selected.

Defined in: MVP-FORTH

Implementation:

VARIABLE DENSITY 1 DENSITY !

Source usage: COLD DR-DEN SET-DRX SPDRV SPT
<T&SCALC>

Example:

DENSITY @ .

The address of the variable DENSITY is placed on the
stack. The value of the variable is then fetched and printed.

Comment: In the MVP-FORTH implementation, the original
values associated with the variable in the 8080 fig-FORTH are
extended to include a number of possible configurations. For
each value a different number of sectors per track and tracks
per disk are taken from the appropriate arrays and used in
T&SCALC in making the necessary calculations to access the
proper physical sector on the disks. The values are modified
from those used by fig-FORTH 8080 to run with the current
interface.

DEPTH   --- n   238 MVP-FORTH

Leave the number of the quantity of 16-bit values contained in
the data stack, before n was added.

Defined in: FORTH-79

Implementation:

: DEPTH SP@ S0 SWAP - 2 / ;

Source usage: D.R

Example:

DEPTH .

Find the number of values on the stack and print it.

Comment: This ideogram is the FORTH-79 higher level
alternative to calculations which can be made with S0 and
SP@. It is more general and less implementation dependent,
but it is not defined in fig-FORTH and some other systems.

```
DIGIT     c  n1  ---  n2  tf                    MVP-FORTH
          c  n1  ---  ff          (bad)
```

Converts the ASCII character c (using base n1) to its
binary equivalent n2 , accompanied by a true flag. If the
conversion is invalid, leaves only a false flag.

Defined in: fig-FORTH

Implementation:

8080:

```
CODE DIGIT    H POP   D POP   E A MOV    30 SUI
      1DIGIT JM   0A CPI   0DIGIT JM   7 SUI   0A CPI
      1DIGIT JM
     HERE LABEL 0DIGIT    L CMP  1DIGIT JP   A E MOV
      1 H LXI   DPUSH JMP
     HERE LABEL 1DIGIT    H L MOV
      HPUSH JMP   END-CODE
```

Source usage: CONVERT

Example:

```
: CONVERT
   BEGIN   1+  DUP  >R  C@  BASE  @  DIGIT
   WHILE  SWAP  BASE  @  U*  DROP  ROT  BASE  @
      U*  D+  DPL  @  1+
      IF  1  DPL  +!  THEN
      R>
   REPEAT  R>  ;
```

   In this example taken for the source code of MVP-FORTH,
CONVERT calls DIGIT to test whether the ASCII character on
the stack is a valid numeric.

Comment: It is a primitive in most versions of FORTH.


```
DISK-ERROR       ---  addr          MVP-FORTH - DISK I-O
```

A variable used by the disk interface, containing the disk
status for the last sector read or written. 0 means no error.

Defined in: fig-FORTH (8080)

Implementation:

```
VARIABLE  DISK-ERROR       0  DISK-ERROR  !
```

Source usage: SEC-READ   SEC-WRITE

Example:

DISK-ERROR @ .

   Check the value of the variable by fetching it and printing it.

Comment: This word makes it possible to check for disk errors from FORTH. After calling CP/M's I/O routines via SEC-READ or SEC-WRITE, this variable contains the byte error code returned by the operating system. See the CP/M MANUAL for details if you wish to implement action based on the error codes.

DLIST --- NOT USED

List the names of the dictionary entries in the CONTEXT vocabulary.

Defined in: fig-FORTH

Implementation:

(This ideogram has not been implemented.)

Comment: This ideogram differs from VLIST by listing only the CONTEXT vocabulary without chaining to FORTH. It is not used in many fig-FORTH implementations.

DLITERAL C, I MVP-FORTH
```
        d  ---  d     (executing )
        d  ---        (compiling)
```

If compiling, compile a stack double number into a literal. Later execution of the definition containing this literal will push it to the stack. If executing, the number will remain on the stack.

Defined in: fig-FORTH

Implementation:

```
: DLITERAL   STATE @
    IF  SWAP [COMPILE] LITERAL
        [COMPILE] LITERAL  THEN ;  IMMEDIATE
```

Source usage: INTERPRET

Example:

```
: INTERPRET
   BEGIN  -FIND
      IF   STATE  @  <
         IF  2-  ,  ELSE  2-  EXECUTE  THEN  ?STACK
      ELSE  HERE  NUMBER  DPL  @  1+
         IF  [COMPILE]  DLITERAL
         ELSE  DROP  [COMPILE]  LITERAL
         THEN   ?STACK
      THEN
   AGAIN  ;
```

This example comes from an earlier version of the MVP-FORTH source code.

Comment: Though not always present in FORTH it is usually necessary for any serious double precision arithmetic.

DMAX   d1 d2 --- d3   MVP-FORTH - UTILITY

Leave the larger of two double numbers.

Pronounced: d-max

Defined in: FORTH-79(E), STARTING FORTH

Implementation:

```
: DMAX   DOVER  DOVER  D<  IF  DSWAP  THEN
   DDROP  ;
```

Source usage: None.

Example:

2.2   3.3   DMAX

Enter the two double precision values and then test them, leaving the larger on the stack.   In this case the value 33 as a double precision, 4 byte value is left.   Note that the decimal point is not considered.

Comment: A convenient double precision operator.

DMIN   d1 d2 --- d3   MVP-FORTH - UTILITY

Leave the smaller of two double numbers.

Pronounced: d-min

Defined in: FORTH-79(E), STARTING FORTH

Implementation:

: DMIN   DOVER   DOVER   D<   NOT
   IF   DSWAP   THEN   DDROP ;

Source usage: None.

Example:

2.2   3.3   DMIN

   Enter two double precision values and then test them, leaving
the smaller on the stack. In this case the double precision
value   22   is left in the top 4 bytes on the stack.   Note that
the decimal point is not considered.

Comment: A convenient double precision operator.

DMINUS   d1   ---   d2   NOT USED

Convert   d1   to its double number two's complement.

Defined in: fig-FORTH

Implementation:

: DMINUS   DNEGATE ;

Source usage: None.

Example:

2.2   DMINUS

   Enter the double precision value on the stack and then change
the sign.   In this case, the double precision value   -22   is
left on the stack.

Comment: This ideogram is now obsolete and its function is
replaced with   DNEGATE .   Furthermore, its pronunciation
would clash with   D- .   It may appear in older programs.

DNEGATE   d1   ---   -d1   245   MVP-FORTH

Leave the two's complement of a double number.

Pronounced: d-negate

Defined in: FORTH-79, STARTING FORTH

Implementation:

```
CODE  DNEGATE    H POP   D POP   A SUB   E SUB
   A E MOV   0 A MVI   D SBB   A D MOV
   0 A MVI   L SBB   A L MOV   0 A MVI
   H SBB   A H MOV   DPUSH JMP   END-CODE
```

Source usage: D+-   D<   NUMBER

Example:

2.2   DNEGATE

   Enter the double precision value on the stack and then leave
the negative of its value. In this case, the double precision
value -22 is left on the stack.

Comment: This ideogram replaces the now obsolete one,
DMINUS .

DO   n1 n2 ---   I, C, 142 MVP-FORTH

Use only in a colon definition.   Begin a loop which will
terminate based on control parameters.   The loop index begins
at   n2 , and terminates based on the limit   n1 . At LOOP
or +LOOP , the index is modified by a positive or negative
value.   The range of a DO-LOOP is determined by the
terminating word.   DO-LOOP may be nested. Capacity for
three levels of nesting is specified as a minimum for standard
systems.

Form: DO ... LOOP
          DO ... n +LOOP

Defined in: FORTH-79, fig-FORTH, STARTING FORTH

Implementation:

: DO   COMPILE <DO>   HERE   3   ;   IMMEDIATE

Source usage: <R/W>   -TRAILING   EMPTY-BUFFERS
                    EXPECT   SAVE-BUFFERS   SPACES

Example:

: TEST   10 1 DO I . LOOP ;

   This definition used the DO structure to print the digits 1

through 9.

Comment: DO-LOOPs are one of the three major control structures (IF, BEGIN, DO) in FORTH. They are more efficient than BEGIN loops when an index must be incremented and compared with a limit. The ideogram LEAVE may be used to terminate a DO-LOOP before the index has run its full course. This implementation keeps the loop limits and indices on the return stack. For indexing on addresses, use a step value with /LOOP.

DOES>   ---   I, C, 168   MVP-FORTH

Define the run-time action of a word created by a high-level defining word. It marks the termination of the defining part of the defining word <name> and begins the definition of the run time action for words that will later be defined by <name>. On execution of <namex> the sequence of words between DOES> and ; will be executed, with the address of <name>'s parameter field on the stack.

Form   : <name> ... CREATE ... DOES> ... ;
           and then   <name> <namex>

Pronounced: does

Defined in: FORTH-79, fig-FORTH, STARTING FORTH

Implementation:

8080:

```
HEX
: DOES>   ?CSP   COMPILE  <;CODE>  CD  C,
    COMPILE  [ HERE  4 + , ] ;
    IMMEDIATE  HEX  ASSEMBLER
       HERE LABEL DODOES   D INX   RPP LHLD
         H DCX   B M MOV   H DCX   C M MOV
         RPP SHLD   B POP   D PUSH
     NEXT JMP   FORTH
DECIMAL
```

Source usage: CONSTANT   VOCABULARY

Example:

```
: DCONSTANT   CREATE  SWAP , ,
    DOES>  DUP @  SWAP  2+ @ ;
```

This example comes from the implementation of MVP-FORTH utilities.

Comment: This implementation uses the FORTH-79 CREATE ...
DOES> technique which differs internally from fig-FORTH's
now obsolete <BUILDS ... DOES> . DOES> is immediate. It
compiles <;CODE> and a machine language call to the low level
routine labeled "DODOES". By embedding that one machine
instruction in the body of the defining word, two bytes are saved
from every one of its generated offspring. But perhaps more
importantly, the FORTH-79 approach makes ' (tick) work on
DOES> products without the inconsistent adjustment by two
required in fig-FORTH.

DOVER   d1 d2 --- d2 d1   MVP-FORTH - UTILITY

Leave a copy of the second double number on the stack.

Pronounced: d-over

Defined in: MVP-FORTH

Implementation:

: DOVER   4 PICK   4 PICK ;

Source usage: None.

Example:

33.33   44.44   DOVER

   Place the two double precision numbers on the stack and then
place a copy of the first one on top.

Comment: The prefix mnemonic D for double precision is
used in place of 2 which has the connotation of the numeral
value. However, its synonym, 2OVER, may be loaded as an
alias for compatibility with the FORTH-79 Double Precision
Number Word Set.

DP   --- addr   U   MVP-FORTH

A user variable, the dictionary pointer, which contains the
address of the next free memory above the dictionary. The
value may be read by HERE and altered by ALLOT .

Defined in: fig-FORTH

Implementation:

12 USER DP

Source usage: ALLOT   FORGET   HERE

Example:

DP   @   U.

   Entering the user variable name leaves the address of the
variable which can then be fetched and printed as an unsigned
number.

Comment: This is a primitive in most implementations of
FORTH even if it is not immediately available to the
programmer. Some implementations may give it the name H .

DPL   ---   addr   U   MVP-FORTH

A user variable containing the number of digits to the right of
the decimal on double integer input. It may also be used to
hold output column location of a decimal point, in user
generated formatting. The default value on single number
input is -1.

Pronounced: d-p-l

Defined in: FORTH-79(R), fig-FORTH

Implementation:

42   USER   DPL

Source usage: CONVERT   INTERPRET   NUMBER

Example:

2.2 DPL @ .

   Entering a double precision value, followed by fetching the
value at this user variable and printing it, will show the number
of digits which were entered to the right of the decimal point; in
this case, 1 .

Comment: This ideogram may save you expense and worry with a
floating point package. User-defined numeric input routines
may inspect the value of DPL and adjust the converted number as
necessary. This makes the use of scaled, fixed point
arithmetic transparent to the user who, for example, need not
type in unnecessary trailing zeros after a decimal point.

A constant used in 8080/Z80 and 8086/8088 implementations pointing to a machine code entry point which pushes the D E or D X register followed by the H L or A X register onto the stack and then falls through to N E X T, the inner interpreter.

Defined in: M V P - F O R T H

Implementation:

D P U S H   C O N S T A N T   D P U S H

(The cross-compiler takes the label D P U S H and makes it a constant.)

Source usage: Several.

Example:

```
C O D E    D D U P
   H  POP   D  POP   D  PUSH   H  PUSH
   D PUSH JMP   END-CODE
```

The example of 8080 code is from the M V P - F O R T H source.

Comment: This is a machine, system and implementation dependent location used only at the machine code level. It allows trimming two bytes off C O D E definitions which would otherwise end with: D PUSH   H PUSH   N E X T JMP.

DR-DEN   n1   ---   n2   MVP-FORTH - DISK I-O

Converts the drive number to the current density code for that drive.

Defined in: M V P - F O R T H

Implementation:

: D R - D E N   2*   D E N   +   @ ;

Source usage: <T&SCALC>   ?CONFIGURE   SET-DRX

Example:

2   D R - D E N

Enter the number for a given drive and the ideogram will convert the value on the stack to the current code value of D E N S I T Y .

Comment: The calculation is made by reference to the array
DEN.   Nothing is actually fetched from or stored into the
variable DENSITY with this ideogram.

DR0   ---   MVP-FORTH - DISK I-0
DR1
DR2
DR3
DR4

Installation dependent commands to select disk drives, by
presetting OFFSET. The contents of OFFSET is added to
the block number in BLOCK to allow for this selection.

Defined in: MVP-FORTH, fig-FORTH

Implementation:

```
: DR0    0  OFFSET  !  ;
: DR1    DR0  0  SET-DRX  ;
: DR2    DR1  1  SET-DRX  ;
: DR3    DR2  2  SET-DRX  ;
: DR4    DR3  3  SET-DRX  ;
```

Source usage: None.

Example:

DR0

   Entering this ideogram sets the value of the variable OFFSET
to 0 .

Comment: These ideograms affect only the value in OFFSET.
Because they use the current disk configuration parameters in
their calculation, they are safer, easier, and more flexible than
storing a value directly into OFFSET.   More than five drives
cannot be accommodated without re-cross-compiling MVP-
FORTH.

DRIVE   --- addr   MVP-FORTH - DISK I-0

A variable used by the disk interface, containing the disk drive
number (0 to MAX-DRV) used on the last sector read or written.

Defined in: fig-FORTH (8080)

Implementation:

VARIABLE   DRIVE   0   DRIVE   !

Source usage: <T&SCALC>   SET-DRIVE

Example:

1   DRIVE   !

Enter the desired drive number, in this case   1 , and store it in the variable designated by this ideogram.

Comment: This ideogram SET-DRIVE passes the value of this variable to the operating system to select a physical drive. Ordinarily, this value should be no greater than the value of the alterable constant, MAX-DRV, less one.

DROP   n ---   233   MVP-FORTH

Drop the top number from the stack.

Defined in: FORTH-79, fig-FORTH, STARTING FORTH

Implementation:

8080:

CODE DROP   H POP   NEXT JMP   END-CODE

Source usage: Many.

Example:

45   DROP

Enter a number and then drop it as though nothing happened.

Comment: A   common   ideogram   used   in   virtually   all implementations of FORTH.

DSWAP   d1   d2   ---   d2   d1   MVP-FORTH - UTILITY

Exchange the top two double numbers on the stack

Pronounced: d-swap

Defined in: MVP-FORTH

Implementation:

```
: DSWAP   4   ROLL   4   ROLL   ;
```

Source usage: None.

Example:

```
33.33   44.44   DSWAP
```

Place two double precision numbers on the stack and then exchange their order. The location of the decimal point is ignored.

Comment: The prefix mnemonic   D   for double precision is used in place of   2, which has the connotation of the numeral value.   However, its synonym, 2SWAP, may be loaded as an alias for compatibility with the FORTH-79 Double Precision Number Word Set.

DU<   ud1 ud2 --- flag   MVP-FORTH - UTILITY

True if   ud1   is less than   ud2.   Both numbers are unsigned.

Pronounced: d-u-less

Defined in: FORTH-79(E), STARTING FORTH

Implementation:

```
: DU<   >R   >R   8000   +
    R>   R>   8000   +   D<   ;
```

Source usage: None.

Example:

```
3.3   2.2   DU<
```

Enter two double precision values and compare them as unsigned numbers, in this case, leaving a false flag of   0   on the stack.   Note that the location of the decimal point is not considered.

Comment: With some double precision operations unsigned numbers are important and this comparison is necessary. Note that both double precision comparands are destroyed by the comparison.

List the contents of n addresses starting at addr . Each
line of values may be preceded by the address of the first value.

Defined in: FORTH-79(R), fig-FORTH, STARTING FORTH

Implementation:

```
: DUMP   0  BASE  @  >R  HEX
    DO  CR  DUP  I  +   DUP  0  6
      D.R  2  SPACES   DUP  8  0
      DO  DUP  I  +   C@  3  .R  LOOP
      DROP  SPACE  DUP  8  +  8  0
      DO  DUP  I  +   C@  3  .R  LOOP
      DROP  3  SPACES  10 0
      DO  DUP  I  +   C@
         DUP  20  <  OVER  7E  >  OR
         IF  DROP  2E  THEN  EMIT
      LOOP  DROP  10
      PAUSE
      ?TERMINAL  IF  LEAVE  THEN
    /LOOP
    DROP  CR  R>  BASE  !  ;
```

Source usage: None.

Example:

```
HEX
100 80 DUMP
DECIMAL
```

   Dump the first 128 bytes starting from the normal origin of
FORTH.

Comment: A variety of implementations of this ideogram
generate various formats. Some of them include printing the
ASCII characters where printable or a dot if they are not. The
MVP-FORTH version incorporates a PAUSE feature, by which
pressing any key will freeze the display. Once suspended, the
DUMP may be resumed by a single keystroke, or aborted by
striking any two keys in rapid succession.

DUP   n --- n n   205 MVP-FORTH

Leave a copy of the top stack number.

Defined in: FORTH-79, fig-FORTH, STARTING FORTH

Implementation:

8080:

CODE   DUP   H POP   H PUSH   HPUSH JMP   END-CODE

Source usage: Many.

Example:

45   DUP

Enter the value 45 on the stack and then duplicate its value on the top of the stack.

Comment: A common ideogram present in virtually all implementations of FORTH.

DVARIABLE   ---   MVP-FORTH - UTILITY

A defining word used to create a dictionary entry of <name> and assign 4 bytes for storage in the parameter field.   When <name> is later executed, it will leave the address of the first byte of its parameter field on the stack.

Form: DVARIABLE   <name>

Defined in: MVP-FORTH
              Implementation:

: DVARIABLE   CREATE   4   ALLOT   ;

Source usage: None.

Example:

DVARIABLE   NEW-VALUE

Make a new ideogram referring to a double precision variable. Its value is not initialized.

Comment: The prefix mnemonic D for double precision is used in place of 2, which has the connotation of the numeral value.   However, its synonym, 2VARIABLE, may be loaded as an alias for compatibility with the FORTH-79 Double Precision Number Word Set.

EDITOR   ---   I, 172 NOT USED

The name of the editor vocabulary. When this name is
executed, EDITOR is established as the CONTEXT
vocabulary.

Defined in: FORTH-79(R), STARTING FORTH

Implementation:

(An editor is not included as a part of the MVP-FORTH source
code; however, the line editor from FORTH DIMENSIONS is
added to the fully configured FORTH binary image.)

Comment: A variety of EDITORS is available. They are of
various degrees of complexity. The INSTALLATION MANUAL
of fig-FORTH includes a simple version. A version which
performs all of the functions as defined in STARTING FORTH is
available in FORTH DIMENSIONS. The latter can be loaded
directly with fig-FORTH and, after minor modifications, with
MVP-FORTH. A Screen Editor has been published in DR.
DOBBS which can be loaded with either fig-FORTH or FORTH-
79 with appropriate changes. The full MVP-FORTH binary file
includes the EDITOR from FORTH DIMENSIONS, Vol III No.
3., which complies with the EDITOR description in STARTING
FORTH.

Note: The EDITOR is a separate vocabulary. It must be
called before trying the EDITOR ideograms as described in
STARTING FORTH.

ELSE   ---   I, C, 167 MVP-FORTH

Used in a colon-definition and executes after the true part
following IF . ELSE forces execution to skip till just
after THEN . It has no effect on the stack. (See IF)

Form: IF ... ELSE ... THEN

Defined in: FORTH-79, fig-FORTH, STARTING FORTH

Implementation:

: ELSE   2 ?PAIRS COMPILE BRANCH   HERE   0 ,
     SWAP 2 [COMPILE] THEN   2 ;   IMMEDIATE

Source usage: Many.

Example:

: TEST   ?DUP IF . ELSE ." zero " THEN ;

This definition will test the value on the top of the stack and if it is 0, will print the word 'zero' in place of the number.

Comment: In keeping with the traditions of structured programming, the ELSE clause is optional, and the IF ... ELSE ... THEN constructs may be nested. Note that IF ... ELSE ... ELSE ... THEN will go untrapped in this implementation.

EMIT   c ---   207 MVP-FORTH

Transmit a character to the current output device.

Defined in: FORTH-79, fig-FORTH, STARTING FORTH

Implementation:

: EMIT   'EMIT @ EXECUTE ;

Example:

65 EMIT

Entering the decimal value 65 followed by this ideogram will cause the character A to be printed.

Comment: All FORTH terminal output is handled through EMIT. Installation dependencies, though unavoidable, are at least confined within this ideogram. MVP-FORTH builds a vector into EMIT so that output may be redirected to printers, alternate terminals, or even operating system files. By default, EMIT vectors to <EMIT>.

EMPTY   ---   MVP-FORTH - SUPPLEMENTAL

Forget all new words added to the dictionary by the user.

Defined in: STARTING FORTH

Implementation:

: EMPTY   INIT-FORTH @ ' FORTH 2+ !
  INIT-USER UP @ 6 + 30 (hex) CMOVE ;

Source usage: None.

Example:

    EMPTY

This ideogram will reconfigure the system to the initial values at the time of start up, or the last FREEZE.

Comment: This ideogram does essentially the same thing as COLD i.e. restarts the FORTH system. The only difference is that the stack is not cleared, and the block buffers are unaffected.

EMPTY-BUFFERS   ---   145   MVP-FORTH

Mark all block buffers as empty, without necessarily affecting their actual contents. UPDATEd blocks are not written to mass storage.

Defined in: FORTH-79, fig-FORTH, STARTING FORTH

Implementation:

```
: EMPTY-BUFFERS    FIRST  LIMIT  OVER - 0  <FILL>
    #BUFF  0
     DO  7FFF  HDBT  I  *  FIRST  +  !  LOOP  ;
```

Note: HDBT is compiled to a hex literal value 404 which is the number of bytes in a block buffer plus four.

Source usage: COLD

Example:

EMPTY-BUFFERS

This ideogram will empty the contents of all buffers in memory so that those marked for UPDATE will also be erased and not written back to disk.

Comment: In this implementation, EMPTY-BUFFERS clears all buffers to nulls.

CAUTION: Think twice before using it, to make sure you aren't destroying irreplaceable data.

ENCLOSE   MVP-FORTH
         addr1   c   ---   addr1   n1   n2   n3

The text scanning primitive used by WORD . From the text address addr1 and an ASCII delimiting character c , is determined the byte offset to the first non-delimiter character n1 , the offset to the first delimiter after the text n2 , and the offset to the first character not included n3 . This procedure will not process past an ASCII 'null' , treating it as an unconditional delimiter.

Defined in: fig-FORTH

Implementation:

8080:

```
CODE ENCLOSE   D POP   H POP   H PUSH   E A MOV
      1 D LXI   H DCX
    HERE LABEL 0ENCLOSE    H INX    D INX
      M CMP   0ENCLOSE JZ   D PUSH   M INR
      M DCR   1ENCLOSE JNZ   D INX   D PUSH
      D DCX   D PUSH   NEXT JMP
    HERE LABEL 1ENCLOSE    H INX    D INX    M CMP
      2ENCLOSE JZ   M INR   M DCR   1ENCLOSE JNZ
      D PUSH   D PUSH   NEXT JMP
    HERE LABEL 2ENCLOSE    D PUSH   D INX   D PUSH
      NEXT JMP   END-CODE
```

Source usage: WORD

Example:

```
: WORD   BLK @
    IF   BLK @   BLOCK   ELSE   TIB @   THEN
    >IN @ +   SWAP   ENCLOSE   DUP 4 PICK  -  FF  >
    IF   WHAT   ." INPUT > 255"   QUIT THEN
    HERE   22 BL   FILL   >IN +!   OVER  -  >R   R@
    HERE   C! +   HERE   1+   R>   CMOVE   HERE   ;
```

   The example comes from an early version of the MVP-FORTH
source code.

Comment: ENCLOSE is a highly specialized ideogram useful
only for implementing WORD. In such usage, the ASCII null
marks the end of the input stream and n3 , the " offset to the
first character not included ," is added directly into >IN.

END   ---   I, C,   NOT USED

A synonym for UNTIL.

Defined in: FORTH-79(R), fig-FORTH

Implementation:

: END   [COMPILE]   UNTIL   ;   IMMEDIATE

Source usage: None.

Example:

: TEST   0   BEGIN   1+ DUP   .   DUP   10   =   END   DROP
;

A definition to print the numbers 1 through 10 ;

Comment: This ideogram is now obsolete and replaced by UNTIL. It may appear in older programs.

ENDIF   C, I,   NOT USED
          addr   n   ---   (compile)

Occurs in a colon-definition. At run-time, ENDIF serves only as the destination of a forward branch from IF   or   ELSE . It marks the conclusion of the conditional structure. THEN is another name for ENDIF. Both names are supported in fig-FORTH. See also IF and ELSE . At compile-time, ENDIF computes the forward branch offset from addr to HERE and stores it at addr .   n is used for error tests.

Defined in: fig-FORTH

Implementation:

: ENDIF   [COMPILE] THEN ;   IMMEDIATE

Source usage: None.

Example:

: TEST   ?DUP IF   .   ENDIF ;

With this new definition, if a value of 0 is on the stack, nothing will be done, otherwise, the value on the stack will be printed.

Comment: This ideogram is now obsolete and has been replaced by THEN. It may appear in older programs.

EPRINT   ---   addr   MVP-FORTH

A variable directing the output of PEMIT through CP/M.   0 = Terminal Device; 1 = List Device.

Defined in: MVP-FORTH

        Implementation:

VARIABLE   EPRINT   0 EPRINT !

Source usage: CPOUT called by PEMIT

Example:

1 EPRINT !

   Change output of PEMIT, and thereby also EMIT, to the CP/M
LIST Device.

Comment: This ideogram is used in most fig-FORTH
implementations, but is usually not available to the
programmer. In MVP-FORTH, it is made available.

ERASE   addr n ---   MVP-FORTH - SUPPLEMENTAL

Clear a region of memory to zero from addr over n
addresses.

Defined in: fig-FORTH, STARTING FORTH

Implementation:

: ERASE   0 FILL ;

Source usage: None.

Example:

PAD 40 ERASE

   Beginning with the address of PAD, fill the next 40 bytes with
nulls.

Comment: Though not present in all implementations of FORTH
it can easily be added with the FILL function.

ERROR   line --- in blk   NOT USED

Execute error notification and restart of system. WARNING
is first examined. If 1, the text of line n, relative to screen
4 of drive 0 is printed. This line number may be positive of
negative, and beyond just screen 4. If WARNING is 0, n is
just printed as a message number (non disk installation). If
WARNING is -1, the definition (ABORT) is executed, which
executes the system ABORT . The user may cautiously
modify this execution by altering (ABORT) . fig-FORTH
saves the contents of IN (now >IN) and BLK to assist in
determining the location of the error. Final action is
execution of QUIT .

Defined in: fig-FORTH

Implementation:

(This ideogram is not implemented)

Comment: Almost all implementations of FORTH have a unique
way of handling error messages. There are no standard
techniques. Instead of using mysterious error numbers or
messages out on disk, MVP-FORTH keeps memory resident
error messages in-line with system code.

EXECUTE   addr   ---   163   MVP-FORTH

Execute the dictionary entry whose compilation address is on
the stack.

Defined in: FORTH-79, fig-FORTH, STARTING FORTH

Implementation:

8080:

CODE EXECUTE   H POP   NEXT1 JMP   END-CODE

Source usages: <INTERPRET>

Example:

: CR   'CR @ EXECUTE ;

   This example comes from the MVP-FORTH source code and
illustrates vectoring.

Comment: This ideogram is most often used with execution
vectors and with the code field addresses stored in variables.
In some systems, EXECUTE takes a parameter field address
instead of the code field address. Though there is only two
bytes' difference, it is sufficient to trigger catastrophe.

CAUTION: Trying to execute a garbage value may crash your
system.

EXIT   ---   C, 117 MVP-FORTH

When compiled within a colon-definition, terminate execution
of that definition, at that point. May not be used within a DO
... LOOP .

Defined in: FORTH-79, STARTING FORTH

Implementation:

```
CODE EXIT   RPP LHLD   M C MOV   H INX
    M B MOV   H INX   RPP SHLD
    NEXT JMP   END-CODE
```

Source usage: ;

Example:

: ;   COMPILE EXIT [COMPILE] [; IMMEDIATE

This is a simplified version of the ideogram ";".   No error
checking or unsmudging is performed.

Comment: This ideogram replaces the now obsolete ;S in
fig-FORTH.   When encountered outside of a colon definition,
it will fool LOAD into thinking the end of the screen has been
reached.   This latter function will save some load time, but
may not work on all systems.

EXPECT   addr n ---   189   MVP-FORTH

Transfer characters from the terminal beginning at addr ,
upward, until a "return" or the count of n has been received.
Take no action for n less than or equal to zero.   One or two
nulls are added at the end of the text.

Defined in: FORTH-79, fig-FORTH, STARTING FORTH

Implementation:

: EXPECT   'EXPECT @ EXECUTE ;

Source usage: QUERY

Example:

: QUERY   TIB @ 50 EXPECT 0 >IN ! ;

This example comes from the MVP-FORTH implementation.

Comment: This ideogram takes a line from the input terminal
and places it anywhere you like. EXPECT includes some
features, such as backspace handling, which may be installation
dependent.   Therefore, in later versions of MVP-FORTH, it's
run-time implementation has been vectored through 'EXPECT.

A user variable containing an address below which
FORGETting is trapped. To forget below this point the user
must alter the contents of FENCE.

Defined in: fig-FORTH

Implementation:

10 USER FENCE

Source usage: FORGET

Example:

' LIST NFA FENCE !

   Change the protected part of the dictionary to the name field
address of LIST.   Subsequently, it will be possible to forget
from the top of the dictionary back to and including LIST.

Comment: This variable is set by a value in low memory at the
time of   system boot or execution of COLD.   By changing its
value the boundary between the full FORTH implementation and
the application definitions can be changed.

Fill memory beginning at address with a sequence of n copies of
byte.   If the quantity is less than or equal to zero, take no
action.

Defined in: FORTH-79, fig-FORTH, STARTING FORTH

Implementation:

: FILL   OVER   0>
    IF <FILL>
    ELSE   DDROP   DROP   THEN   ;

Source usages: <WORD>   BLANK   EMPTY-BUFFERS

Example:

: BLANK   BL FILL ;

   This example is taken from the MVP-FORTH implementation.

Comment: ERASE and BLANKS, if not already in the system,

may easily be defined using this ideogram.

FIND   ---   addr   203   MVP-FORTH

Leave the compilation address of the next word name which is accepted from the input stream. If that word cannot be found in the dictionary after a search of CONTEXT and FORTH leave zero.

Defined in: FORTH-79

Implementation:

: FIND   -FIND   IF   DROP   CFA   ELSE   0   THEN   ;

Source usage: None.

Example:

FIND DUP

   Leaves the code field address of the ideogram, DUP, on the stack.

Comment: This ideogram is closely related to the older -FIND. Note that FIND leaves the code field address while -FIND leaves the parameter field address and a length byte.

FIRST   ---   n   MVP-FORTH

A constant that leaves the address of the first (lowest) block buffer.

Defined in: fig-FORTH

Implementation:

BUF1 CONSTANT FIRST

Source usage: +BUF   COLD   EMPTY-BUFFERS   PREV
                      USE

Example:

FIRST

   This ideogram is a constant which leaves the address on the stack.

Comment: The value of this constant is implementation

dependent. It is not available in all implementations of
FORTH. In MVP-FORTH, its value may be modified
dynamically with CHANGE.

FLD   --- addr   U   MVP-FORTH

A variable pointing to the field length reserved for a number
during output conversion.

Pronounced: f-l-d

Defined in: FORTH-79(R), fig-FORTH

Implementation:

44   USER   FLD

Source usage: None.

Example:

FLD   @   .

   Fetch the value of this variable and print it.

Comment: Though defined in the INSTALLATION MANUAL, it
has not been implemented in fig-FORTH or FORTH-79 but is
included in the FORTH-79 Reference Word Set.

FLUSH   ---   MVP-FORTH - SUPPLEMENTAL

A synonym for SAVE-BUFFERS.

Defined in: FORTH-79(R), STARTING FORTH

Implementation:

: FLUSH   SAVE-BUFFERS ;

Source usage: None.

Example:

FLUSH

   This ideogram, without taking any parameters, causes all
buffers marked for UPDATE to be written back to disk.

Comment: This obsolete synonym for SAVE-BUFFERS may be
included for compatibility with older programs. However, its

use is well established and it is included in the FORTH-79
Reference Word Set.   FLUSH may therefore continue to be used.
It is included in MVP-FORTH.

FORGET   ---   186   MVP-FORTH

Delete from the dictionary <name> (which is in the
CURRENT vocabulary) and all words added to the dictionary
after <name>, regardless of their vocabulary. Failure to
find <name> in CURRENT or FORTH is an error condition.

Form: FORGET   <name>

Defined in: FORTH-79, fig-FORTH, STARTING FORTH

Implementation:

```
: FORGET   BL   WORD   CURRENT   @   @   <FIND>   0=
    ABORT"   NOT IN CURRENT VOCABULARY "
    DROP   NFA   DUP   FENCE   @   U<
    ABORT"   IN PROTECTED DICTIONARY "
    >R   R@   CONTEXT   @   U<
    IF   [COMPILE]   FORTH   THEN
    R@   CURRENT   @   U<
    IF   [COMPILE]   FORTH   DEFINITIONS   THEN
    VOC-LINK   @
    BEGIN   R@   OVER   U<   WHILE   @   REPEAT
    DUP   VOC-LINK   !
    BEGIN   DUP   4   -
      BEGIN   PFA   LFA   @   DUP   R@   U<   UNTIL
    OVER   2-   !   @   ?DUP   0=
    UNTIL   R>   DP   !   ;
```

Source usage: None.

Example:

FORGET TEST

   This ideogram will forget everything from the top of the
dictionary to the most recent definition of TEST.

Comment: This is an implementation of a smart   FORGET   as
discussed in FORTH DIMENSIONS, Vol II, No. 6. With
multiple vocabularies containing ideograms added at various
times, all ends must be properly linked together or the system
will crash.   This implementation, though appearing moderately
complex, is quite safe.   FENCE serves as a movable address
boundary to protect ideograms defined prior to that point.

The name of the primary vocabulary. Execution makes FORTH
the   CONTEXT   vocabulary.   New definitions become a part
of   FORTH   until   a   differing   CURRENT   vocabulary   is
established.   User vocabularies conclude by 'chaining' to
FORTH , so it should be considered that FORTH is
'contained' within each users' vocabulary.

Defined in: FORTH-79, fig-FORTH, STARTING FORTH

Implementation:

VOCABULARY   FORTH   IMMEDIATE

Source usage: <ABORT>   COLD   FORGET

Example:

FORTH

   Set CONTEXT to point to FORTH and leave CURRENT
unchanged.

Comment: MVP-FORTH conforms with FORTH-79. All
vocabularies chain only to FORTH. In fig-FORTH, daughter
vocabularies chain to their parents before FORTH. There is
some ambiguity in the definition of the proper function and not
all implementations of FORTH are the same.

FREEZE   ---   MVP-FORTH

Save the current values of the user variables and the top of the
dictionary in low memory in place of the original values.

Defined in: MVP-FORTH

Implementation:

: FREEZE   UP @ 6 + INIT-USER   30   CMOVE
   ' FORTH 2+ @ INIT-FORTH ! ;

Source usage: None.

Example:

FREEZE

   This ideogram requires no parameters. It sets the start up
values in low memory to the current values of the user
variables.   When COLD is executed later, the system will

return to the configuration at the time of the most recent execution of FREEZE. Nothing is written to disk.

Comment: This ideogram reconfigures low memory, changing the startup parameters. A new startup image can be saved on disk.

GO   addr   ---   MVP-FORTH

Makes the address on the stack the next address in the hardware program counter.

Defined in: MVP-FORTH

Implementation:

8080:

CODE GO   H POP   PCHL   END-CODE

Source usage: BYE

Example:

HEX   100   GO

   Execution of this example is equivalent to COLD.

Comment: The implementation of this ideogram is system dependent. As used in the implementation of BYE, it will return to the operating system.

H   --- addr   MVP-FORTH - SUPPLEMENTAL

A synonym for DP, the dictionary pointer.

Defined in: MVP-FORTH, STARTING FORTH

Implementation:

: H   DP ;

Source usage: None.

Example:

H @ U.

   This ideogram is identical to DP and returns the address of the value returned by HERE which in this case is then printed.

Comment: Though not used in the Forth Interest Group community, this ideogram has been in use for a number of years in the University of Rochester implementation among others.

HERE   --- addr   188   MVP-FORTH

Return the address of the next available dictionary location.

Defined in: FORTH-79, fig-FORTH, STARTING FORTH

Implementation:

: HERE   DP @ ;

Source usage: Many.

Example:

SP@ HERE - .

   This example is implementation dependent. In MVP-FORTH, the address of the top of the stack (actually the bottom) less the address of the top of the dictionary is printed. It is the free space available in memory.

Comment: In MVP-FORTH, the address returned by HERE, is the lower limit of free space between the top of the dictionary and the bottom of the stack. Note that the location of PAD moves in this free space.

HEX   ---   MVP-FORTH

Set the numeric conversion base to sixteen (hexadecimal).

Defined in: FORTH-79(R), fig-FORTH, STARTING FORTH

Implementation:

: HEX   10 BASE ! ;

Source usage: Occasional.

Example:

HEX FF DECIMAL .

   Convert the hex value FF to decimal and print it: 255 .

Comment: This ideogram is not included in FORTH-79. It may be easily defined if you know the current value of BASE.

HLD   --- addr   U   MVP-FORTH

A user variable that holds the address of the latest character of text during numeric output conversion.

Defined in: fig-FORTH

Implementation:

46   USER   HLD

Source usage: #>   <#   HOLD

Example:

HLD   @   U.

   Get the value of the user variable HLD, and print it unsigned.

Comment: In fig-FORTH and MVP-FORTH, this user variable determines the number of characters below PAD which contain the formatted string resulting from a binary number conversion. Not all implementations utilize this method of formatting number conversions.

HOLD   char   ---   175   MVP-FORTH

Insert   char   into a pictured numeric output string.   May only be used between <#   and #> .

Defined in: FORTH-79, fig-FORTH, STARTING FORTH

Implementation:

: HOLD   -1 HLD   +! HLD   @   C! ;

Source usage: # SIGN

Example:

3.33 <# # # 46 HOLD #S #> TYPE

   Enter the double precision value with two digits to the right of the decimal and then print it in the same format.

Comment: The ASCII value for the desired character is used to form the output picture such as   decimal 47 for each slash when

outputting the date as 01/01/81. Note the backward order of
the picture generation.

HPUSH   --- addr   MVP-FORTH

A constant used in 8080/Z80 implementations pointing to a
machine code entry point which pushes the contents of the HL
register onto the stack and then falls through to NEXT, the
inner interpreter.

Defined in: MVP-FORTH

Implementation:

HPUSH   CONSTANT   HPUSH

(The cross-compiler takes the label HPUSH and makes it a
constant.)

Source usage: Many - in CODE definitions.

Example:

CODE +
    D POP   H POP   D DAD   HPUSH JMP   END-CODE

    This example is taken from the MVP-FORTH 8080 source code.

Comment: This is a machine, system, and implementation
dependent location used only at the machine code level. It
allows trimming one byte off CODE definitions which would
otherwise end with H PUSH   NEXT JMP.

I   --- n   C, 136   MVP-FORTH

Copy the loop index onto the data stack. May be only used in
the DO-LOOP control structure.

Form: DO ... I ... LOOP   (or +LOOP)

Defined in: FORTH-79, fig-FORTH, STARTING FORTH

Implementation:

8080:

CODE I   RPP LHLD   M E MOV   H INX   M D MOV
    D PUSH   NEXT JMP   END-CODE

Source usage: Many.

Example:

: TEST 10 0 DO I . LOOP ;

   This new definition will print the values of the digits 0
through 9.

Comment: In this implementation the indices and limits are
held on the return stack. Thus, I is synonymous with R@ .
Some implementations hold the loop parameters in a separate
stack.

I'   --- n   C   MVP-FORTH

Used within a colon-definition executed only from within a DO-
LOOP to return the corresponding loop index.

Pronounced: i-prime

Defined in: FORTH-79(R), STARTING FORTH

Implementation:

8080:

CODE I'   RPP LHLD   2 D LXI   D DAD   M E MOV
     H INX   M D MOV   D PUSH   NEXT JMP   END-CODE

Source usage: None.

Example:

: TEST   10 0
     DO 45 >R I' . R> DROP LOOP ;

   This contrived example will print the digits from 0 through 9.

Comment: This ideogram is useful for accessing the index
when it has been buried one level in the return stack.   The
return stack must be restored at the end of the DO-LOOP.   This
ideogram is not available in all implementations.

ID.   addr ---   MVP-FORTH - UTILITY

Print a definition's name from its name field address.

Defined in: fig-FORTH

Implementation:

`: ID.   COUNT  1F  AND   TYPE  ;`

Source usage: None.

Example:

`'  ID.  @  2+   NFA   ID.`

This example could be used as a factor in a decompiler. Since ID. is a colon definition, its parameter field address contains the code field address of its first ideogram. The 2+ moves to its parameter field address and then NFA to its name field address. Then ID. will print the first ideogram in its definition: COUNT .

Comment: Such poking around the header structure is prohibited in the FORTH-79 STANDARD. However, it can be most useful in a development system. Clearly, its implementation depends on the structure of the header. If the ideogram being decompiled is not a colon definition, ID. as used in the example, will produce garbage. For names truncated to less than their natural WIDTH when defined, ID. will represent the lost character(s) with garbage.

`IF                 flag  ---           I, C, 210   MVP-FORTH`

Used only in a colon definition. If flag is true, the words following IF are executed and the words following ELSE are skipped.   The ELSE part is optional.   If flag is false, words between IF and ELSE , or between IF and THEN (when no ELSE is used), are skipped. IF-ELSE-THEN conditionals may be nested.

Form: IF ... ELSE ... THEN   or
         IF ... THEN

Defined in: FORTH-79, fig-FORTH, STARTING FORTH

Implementation:

`: IF   COMPILE  0BRANCH  HERE  0 , 2 ;`
`IMMEDIATE`

Source usage: Many.

Example:

`: TEST  1  IF  ."  ONE  "  THEN  ;`

This definition will always print the text " ONE " .

Comment: An indispensable control structure. However, in place of extensive nesting, it may be more efficient to define and use one of the several CASE utilities which have been defined in FORTH DIMENSIONS.

IMMEDIATE   ---   103   MVP-FORTH

Mark the most recently made dictionary entry as a word which will be executed when encountered during compilation rather than compiled.

Defined in: FORTH-79, fig-FORTH, STARTING FORTH

Implementation:

: IMMEDIATE   LATEST 40 TOGGLE ;

Source usage: Make the following ideograms immediate:

Example:

: (-1 >IN +! 29 WORD DROP ; IMMEDIATE

   This example comes form the MVP-FORTH implementation.

Comment: This ideogram forces execution during compiling by flipping the precedence bit in the most recently defined name. When the precedence bit is set, the ideogram will execute, regardless of whether the system is compiling or executing.

IN   --- addr   NOT USED

A user variable containing the byte offset within the current input text buffer (terminal or disk) from which the next text will be accepted. WORD uses and moves the value of IN .

Defined in: fig-FORTH

Implementation:

: IN   >IN ;

Source usage: None.

Example:

IN @ .

Get the present value of the offset in the input stream and print it.

Comment: This ideogram is now obsolete having been replaced by >IN in FORTH-79. It may appear in older programs.

INDEX   from   to   ---   MVP-FORTH - UTILITY

Print the first line of each screen over the range from, to. This is used to view the comment lines of an area of text on disk screens.

Defined in: FORTH-79(R), fig-FORTH

Implementation:

```
: INDEX   CR  1+  SWAP
    DO   CR   I  4  .R  4 SPACES  I  .INDEX
      PAUSE  ?TERMINAL  IF LEAVE THEN
    1  /LOOP  ;
```

Source usage: None.

Example:

20 40 INDEX

This will cause the first line of each of the screens 20 through 40, inclusive, to be printed in succession.

Comment: If you adopt the convention of putting a descriptive comment on line 0 of every screen, INDEX will generate something like a table of contents. This MVP-FORTH version incorporates a PAUSE feature, which holds the display still when any key is pressed. Once suspended, the INDEX may be resumed by striking any key once, or aborted by striking any two keys in rapid succession.

INIT-FORTH   ---   addr   MVP-FORTH

A constant locating the bootup parameter used to initialize the FORTH vocabulary.

Defined in: MVP-FORTH

Implementation:

INIT-FORTH CONSTANT INIT-FORTH

(The cross-compiler uses the label INIT-FORTH to define the constant INIT-FORTH).

Source usage: COLD   FREEZE

Example:

INIT-FORTH   @   ID.

   Fetch the name field address of the topmost ideogram in the current cold-start image.   This address is passed, without adjustment, to ID. which types the name at the terminal.

Comment: This   element   within   the   INIT-USER   array   is important enough to deserve its own ideogram.   A COLD start stores this value into the body of the FORTH vocabulary. Executing FREEZE reverses the process, expanding or cutting back the bootup system image to match the current system configuration.

INIT-USER   ---   addr   MVP-FORTH

A constant returning a pointer to the start of the bootup parameter area in low memory.   This area is an array containing cold-start values for the user variables.

Defined in: MVP-FORTH

Implementation:

INIT-USER   CONSTANT   INIT-USER

(The cross-compiler uses the label INIT-USER to define the constant INIT-USER).

Source usage: CHANGE   COLD   FREEZE

Example:

INIT-USER   U.

   Print   the   beginning   address   of   the   low   memory   array containing the initial user variables.

Comment: Access to this array allows one to modify the initial values of some of the user variables, as is done in FREEZE and CHANGE.

INTCALL   ax bx cx dx int# --- n   MVP-FORTH

Pass the parameters to set up the respective registers and the
interrupt number to the ideogram so the 8086/8088 system
interrupt calls can be made directly from high-level FORTH.

Defined in: MVP-FORTH (IBM)

Implementation:

High-level & 8086/8088

```
: INTCALL   INTCA2  1  +  C!
   INTCA1  EXECUTE  ;
ASSEMBLER
   HERE LABEL INTCA1   INTCA1  2+  ,
      DX POP   CX POP  BX POP  AX POP
      SI PUSH  BP PUSH
   HERE LABEL INTCA2   0  INT
      BP POP  SI POP   APUSH JMP
```

(This is a sneaky bit of implementation.)

Source usage: Many of the I/O routine in high-level FORTH.

Example:

```
: PEMIT   ( b --- )
         0  0  0  23  INTCALL  ;
```

Output the ASCII character in byte b to the printer on
the IBM Personal Computer via an interrupt call.

Comment: The implementation of this ideogram is system
dependent. It has been added to the vocabulary for the
convenience of IBM users. For example, with it, new disk
drivers can be written in high-level FORTH and vectored to the
proper functions.

INTERPRET   ---   MVP-FORTH

Begin interpretation at the character indexed by the contents of
>IN relative to the block number contained in BLK, continuing
until the input stream is exhausted. If BLK contains zero,
interpret characters from the terminal input buffer.

Defined in: FORTH-79(R), fig-FORTH, STARTING FORTH

Implementation:

```
: INTERPRET   'INTERPRET  @  EXECUTE  ;
```

Source usage: <LOAD> CONFIGURE QUIT

Example:

```
: <LOAD>    BLK  @  >R  >IN  @  >R  0  >IN  !
    BLK  !  INTERPRET  R>  >IN  !  R>  BLK  !  ;
```

   This example is taken from the MVP-FORTH source code.

Comment: The ideogram used to interpret text source in MVP-FORTH. This ideogram is vectored in MVP-FORTH for the convenience of the programmer. Normally, it calls <INTERPRET>.

J   --- n   C, 225   MVP-FORTH

Return the index of the next outer loop. May be used only within a nested DO- LOOP.

Form: DO ... DO ... J ... LOOP ... LOOP   (or +LOOP)

Defined in: FORTH-79, STARTING FORTH

Implementation:

8080:

```
CODE J    RPP LHLD   4 D LXI   D DAD   M E MOV
    H INX   M D MOV   D PUSH   NEXT JMP   END-CODE
```

Source usage: None.

Example:

```
: TEST    3  0  DO  CR    10  0
                DO  J  .  LOOP
            LOOP  ;
```

   This definition will print a row of 10 0's, 10 1's, and 10 2's.

Comment: This utility allows reference to both loops from within the inner one as may be required for some two dimensional array applications.

KEY   --- char   100 MVP-FORTH

Leave the ASCII value of the next available character from the current input device.

Defined in: FORTH-79, fig-FORTH, STARTING FORTH

Implementation:

: KEY   'KEY @ EXECUTE ;

Source usage: EXPECT

Example:

KEY

Execution of this ideogram causes the program to wait for any single input from the keyboard and upon receiving it places the ASCII value of the input on the stack.

Comment: The ideogram provides a way of finding out the ASCII value of characters without reference to a chart. It may also be used in selecting from a menu requiring only a single character input or for a wait until any character is input from the terminal. The internal details of KEY are installation dependent. Therefore, KEY has been vectored in MVP-FORTH, defaulting to <KEY>.

LATEST   --- addr   MVP-FORTH

Leave the name field address of the topmost word in the CURRENT vocabulary.

Defined in: fig-FORTH

Implementation:

: LATEST   CURRENT @ @ ;

Source usage: <;CODE> CREATE   IMMEDIATE
                 SMUDGE

Example:

LATEST ID.

This example causes the name of the topmost ideogram in the CURRENT vocabulary to be printed.

Comment: Though not included in FORTH-79 it is usually available in most systems. Note that switching vocabularies for new definitions will change the address left by LATEST . Through the name field address at LATEST, one can find the code field address and write recursive routines.

Force termination of a DO-LOOP at the next LOOP or +LOOP by setting the loop limit equal to the current value of the index. The index itself remains unchanged, and execution proceeds normally until the loop terminating word is encountered.

Defined in: FORTH-79, fig-FORTH, STARTING FORTH

Implementation:

8080:

```
CODE LEAVE    RPP LHLD   M E MOV  H INX
    M D MOV   H INX  E M MOV  H INX   D M MOV
    NEXT JMP   END-CODE
```

Source usage: <T&SCALC> -TRAILING EXPECT

Example:

```
: TEST  20000  0  DO  I  .  ?TERMINAL
    IF  LEAVE  THEN  LOOP ;
```

This definition starts printing digits which can be stopped by typing any key.

Comment: Using LEAVE within a conditional structure within a DO-LOOP makes it function somewhat like a BEGIN-UNTIL with an escape clause.

CAUTION: Executing LEAVE outside of a colon definition may crash your system.

LFA   pfa --- lfa   MVP-FORTH

Convert the parameter field address of a dictionary definition to its link field address.

Defined in: fig-FORTH

Implementation:

: LFA 4 - ;

Source usage: FORGET

Example:

'   U*   LFA   U.

   Find and print the link field address of   U* , perhaps in
anticipation of sealing the dictionary at that point.

Comment: Although this activity is forbidden by FORTH-79
STANDARD, it is a convenient utility for moving around the
header structure in a FORTH development system. Its
definition is dependent upon the implementation of the header
structure.

LIMIT   ---   n   MVP-FORTH

A constant leaving the address just above the highest memory
available for a disk buffer.   Usually this is the highest system
memory.

Defined in: fig-FORTH

Implementation:

EM   CONSTANT   LIMIT

Source usage: +BUF   EMPTY-BUFFERS

Example:

LIMIT   U.

   Examine the first location in memory not currently used by
FORTH.

Comment: Really, this is the limit for the FORTH program in
memory.   In some implementations, this limit may not include
all of RAM available. FORTH can access all existing RAM
addresses even if they are not within the confines of the FORTH
program.   Such areas can be used for buffers by FORTH.   In
MVP-FORTH, modifying the value in LIMIT and then executing
CHANGE will change the upper bound of the FORTH image in
memory.   In MVP-FORTH, its value may be altered and then
CHANGE will dynamically reconfigure memory to the new value
of LIMIT.

LIST   n   ---   109   MVP-FORTH

List the ASCII symbolic contents of screen   n   on the current
output device, setting SCR   to contain   n .

Defined in: FORTH-79, fig-FORTH, STARTING FORTH

Implementation:

```
: LIST   CR   DUP  SCR  !
   ." SCR #" U.  10  0
   DO  CR  I  3  .R  SPACE  I  SCR  @
      .LINE  ?TERMINAL
      IF  LEAVE  THEN
   LOOP  CR  ;
```

Source usage: None.

Example:

45 LIST

   This causes Screen 45 to be printed.

Comment: This utility allows one to view the text contents in
the selected screen.

LIT   --- n   C   MVP-FORTH

Within a colon-definition, LIT is automatically compiled
before each 16 bit literal number encountered in input text.
Later execution of LIT causes the contents of the next
dictionary address to be pushed to the stack.

Defined in: fig-FORTH

Implementation:

8080:

```
CODE LIT   B LDAX  B INX  A L MOV  B LDAX  B INX
   A H MOV  HPUSH JMP  END-CODE
```

Source usage: LITERAL

Example:

```
: LITERAL   STATE @
   IF  COMPILE  LIT  ,  THEN  ;  IMMEDIATE
```

   This example comes from the MVP-FORTH implementation.

Comment: An ideogram which tells the address interpreter
that the next two bytes in the compiled definition are not an
address to be executed but rather a numeric value to be pushed.

LITERAL   n ---   I, 215   MVP-FORTH

If compiling, then compile the stack value n as a 16-bit
literal, which when later executed, will leave n on the
stack.

Defined in: FORTH-79, fig-FORTH, STARTING FORTH

Implementation:

```
: LITERAL    STATE  @
   IF  COMPILE  LIT  ,  THEN  ;  IMMEDIATE
```

Source usage: ' DLITERAL

Example:

```
: ADD-RECORDLENGTH   [ BLOCKSIZE
   RECORDS-PER-BLOCK  / ] LITERAL + ;
```

A time-consuming calculation using constants is done once at
compile time and placed into the definition by LITERAL. Note
that BLOCKSIZE and RECORDS- PER-BLOCK used in the
example must also be defined.

Comment: LITERAL, while harder to spell than LIT, is
transportable, implementation independent and FORTH-79
STANDARD.

LOAD   n ---   202   MVP-FORTH

Begin interpretation of screen n by making it the input
stream; preserve the locators of the present input stream (
from >IN and BLK). If interpretation is not terminated
explicitly it will be terminated when the input stream is
exhausted. Control then returns to the input stream
containing LOAD , determined by the input stream locators
>IN and BLK.

Defined in: FORTH-79, fig-FORTH, STARTING FORTH

Implementation:

```
: LOAD   'LOAD  @ EXECUTE  ;
```

Source usage: None.

Example:

45 LOAD

This example will start loading the contents of Screen 45.

Comment: Screens which end with several blank lines will load faster if the ideogram, EXIT, appears following the last definition or operation. Also, one can avoid loading the whole screen without erasing the undesired contents by terminating the desired source with this ideogram. This technique is not sanctioned by FORTH-79 and is implementation dependent. This ideogram is vectored in MVP-FORTH for the benefit of the programmer. Normally, it invokes <LOAD>. Note that Screen zero is unloadable.

LOOP   ---   I, C, 124   MVP-FORTH

Increment the DO-LOOP index by one, terminating the loop if the new index is equal to or greater than the limit. The limit and index are signed numbers in the range -32,768..32,767 .

Defined in: FORTH-79, fig-FORTH, STARTING FORTH

Implementation:

: LOOP   3 ?PAIRS COMPILE <LOOP>
  HERE - , ; IMMEDIATE

Source usage: -TRAILING CONFIGURE
          LIST <R/W> SAVE-BUFFERS SPACES
          <T&SCALC>

Example:

: TEST   10 0 DO I . LOOP ;

This definition will cause the digits 0 through 9 to be printed.

Comment: This ideogram completes a DO-LOOP control structure. In the FORTH-79 STANDARD and MVP-FORTH, the comparison uses signed arithmetic which may lead to problems if addresses are used as the parameters. The DO-LOOP structure can also be terminated with +LOOP or /LOOP. Both of these take an explicit increment from the stack; the latter uses unsigned arithmetic.

M*   n1 n2 --- d   MVP-FORTH

A mixed magnitude math operation which leaves the double number signed product to two signed numbers.

Defined in: fig-FORTH, STARTING FORTH

Implementation:

```
: M*    DDUP  XOR  >R  ABS  SWAP  ABS
    U*  R>  D+-  ;
```

Source usage: */MOD

Example:

45 2 M* D.

   The two single precision values are placed on the stack and operated upon to leave a double precision value which is then printed.

Comment: With this ideogram, overflow is impossible. Use U* for full precision unsigned multiplication.

M*/   d1 n1 n2 --- d2   MVP-FORTH

Multiplies d1 by n1 and divides the triple precision product by n2 leaving the quotient d2. All values are signed.

Defined in: MVP-FORTH, STARTING FORTH

Implementation:

```
: M*/   DDUP  XOR  SWAP  ABS  >R  SWAP
    ABS  >R  OVER  XOR  ROT  ROT  DABS
    SWAP  R@  U*  ROT  R>  U*  ROT  0  D+
    R@  U/MOD  ROT  ROT  R>  U/MOD
    SWAP  DROP  SWAP  ROT  D+-  ;
```

Source usage: None.

Example:

: IN>CM   254 100 M*/ ;

   This example converts inches in double precision to centimeters, also in double precision. The result is rounded toward zero.

Comment: This ideogram is most useful in maintaining precision in double number arithmetic. Its scaling capagilities frequently avert the expense of a full floating point math package. The notation in the book, STARTING FORTH, showing the divisor to be unsigned is in error.

M+   d1 n --- d2   MVP-FORTH

Add d1 to n and return d2. Note all values are signed.

Defined in: MVP-FORTH, STARTING FORTH

Implementation:

: M+   S->D   D+ ;

Source usage: None.

Example:

3456. 4 M+ D.

    The integer value 3456 is entered as a double precision
number by appending a decimal point, and then the single
precision value of 4 is entered.   The latter is converted to a
double precision value and summed by the operator, leaving the
double precision value on the stack to be printed.

Comment: This ideogram relieves some of the inconvenience of
double precision arithmetic.   Note that carry and overflow are
ignored.

M/   d n1 --- n2 n3   MVP-FORTH

A mixed magnitude math operator which leaves the signed
remainder n2 and signed quotient n3 , from a double number
dividend and divisor n1 .   The remainder takes its sign from the
dividend.

Defined in: fig-FORTH, STARTING FORTH

Implementation:

: M/   OVER >R   >R   DUP   D+-   R@   ABS   U/MOD
    R>   R@   XOR   +-   SWAP   R>   +-   SWAP ;

Source usage: /MOD   */MOD

Example:

45. 7 M/ . .

    Enter a double precision integer by ending the value with a
decimal point, and then the single precision value   followed by

the operator. Then print the quotient followed by the remainder.

Comment: An integer operator which permits greater precision than simple integer division. Note that the remainder is left on the stack according to the definition though it is not implied in the ideogram. Overflow if it occurs is ignored, as is division by zero. Note that the implementation used in MVP-FORTH is taken from fig-FORTH and differs from that given in STARTING FORTH.

M/MOD   ud1 u2   --- u3 ud4   MVP-FORTH

An unsigned mixed magnitude math operation which leaves a double quotient ud4 and remainder u3, from a double dividend ud1 and single precision divisor u2 .

Defined in: fig-FORTH

Implementation:

```
: M/MOD   >R  0  R@  U/MOD  R>  SWAP  >R
    U/MOD  R>  ;
```

Source usage: #

Example:

45. 7 M/MOD   <# #S #> TYPE SPACE U.

   Enter a double precision integer by ending the value with a decimal point and follow it by a single precision value. The quotient is then printed followed by the remainder. In the absence of a double precision unsigned output operator, numerical conversion is used in the example.

Comment: This fig-FORTH function does not conform with the convention for the prefix " M " which implies the use of signed values. In this case, the input values are unsigned. Note that this ideogram is very similar to M/ -- both leave the remainder and quotient, but one is signed and the other is not.

MAX   n1 n2 --- n3   218   MVP-FORTH

Leave the greater of two numbers.

Pronounced: max

Defined in: FORTH-79, fig-FORTH, STARTING FORTH

Implementation:

```
: MAX    DDUP  <
  IF  SWAP  THEN  DROP  ;
```

Source usage: SPACES MOVE

Example:

4   3   MAX   .

Enter two single precision values on the stack, leave only the maximum value, and print it.

Comment: Provides a simple way of putting a lower limit on numbers. A signed comparison is used.

MAX-DRV   --- n   MVP-FORTH - DISK I-O

A constant which returns the current maximum number of drives.

Defined in: MVP-FORTH

Implementation:

2   CONSTANT   MAX-DRV

Source usage: <T&SCALC>   ?CONFIGURE   CONFIGURE

Example:

MAX-DRV   .

This example will print the maximum number of drives for which the system is presently configured.

Comment: In some implementations of FORTH this value is fixed and not available to the programmer.   However, in other implementations the value may be changed from time to time.   It therefore needs to be placed in the FORTH vocabulary.   In MVP-FORTH provisions are made for up to 5 drives.   More than five drives cannot be accomodated without re-cross-compiling your system.   It will require extending the array, DEN.

MESSAGE   n ---   NOT USED

Print on the selected output device the text of line n relative to screen 4 of drive 0. n may be positive or negative. MESSAGE   may be used to print incidental text such as report headers. If WARNING is zero, the message will simply be printed as a number (disk un- available).

Defined in: fig-FORTH

Implementation:

(This ideogram is not implemented in MVP-FORTH.)

Comment: This provides one method of accessing error and warning messages without having the text reside in memory. However, it is often more efficient and really takes little more space to place the required error messages in line as in MVP-FORTH. The convention in fig-FORTH of having the text of messages on screen 4, often overlaps binary code used to boot up the system on drive 0 .

MIN   n1 n2 --- n3   127   MVP-FORTH

Leave the lesser of two numbers.

Pronounced: min

Defined in: FORTH-79, fig-FORTH, STARTING FORTH

Implementation:

: MIN   DDUP >
   IF SWAP THEN DROP ;

Source usage: CREATE SPDRV SPT

Example:

4 2 MIN .

Enter two single precision integers and leave only the minimum value on the stack which is then printed.

Comment: Provides a way of placing a ceiling on a number, such as the maximum number of drives. A signed comparison is used.

MINUS   n1 --- n2   NOT USED

Leave the two's complement of a number.

Defined in: fig-FORTH

Implementation:

: MINUS   NEGATE ;

Source usage: None.

Example:

45 MINUS .

Enter an integer and then negate it and print the negative value.

Comment: This now obsolete fig-FORTH ideogram has been replaced by NEGATE in FORTH-79. Note that its pronunciation could be confused with the ideogram which does a subtract operation. It may appear in older programs.

MOD   n1 n2 --- n3   104   MVP-FORTH

Divide n1 by n2, leaving the remainder n3, with the same sign as n1.

Pronounced: mod

Defined in: FORTH-79, fig-FORTH, STARTING FORTH

Implementation:

: MOD   /MOD DROP ;

Source usage: None.

Example:

45 7 MOD .

Enter two integers, divide them leaving the remainder which is then printed.

Comment: A signed integer arithmetic operator. Note that division by zero is ignored; its result is unpredictable.

MON   ---   NOT USED

Exit to the system monitor, leaving a re-entry to FORTH, if possible.

Defined in: fig-FORTH

Implementation:

(This ideogram has not been implemented in the MVP-FORTH.
The ideogram BYE is similar but returns to the operating system
rather than the monitor.)

Comment: Though defined in the INSTALLATION MANUAL, it
is usually not implemented in fig-FORTH. BYE will
usually exit fig-FORTH to the underlying operating system
from which FORTH's current image may be saved.

MOVE   addr1 addr2 n ---   113   MVP-FORTH

Move the specified quantity n of 16-bit memory cells
beginning at addr1 into addr2 . The contents of addr1 is
moved first. If n is negative or zero, nothing is moved.

Defined in: FORTH-79, fig-FORTH, STARTING FORTH

Implementation:

: MOVE   0 MAX 2* <CMOVE> ;

Source usage: None.

Example:

HERE   PAD   20   MOVE

   This example will move 40 bytes from the address of HERE to
the address of PAD .

Comment: This ideogram moves two bytes at a time but otherwise
is similar to CMOVE . Nothing is said about overlapping
source and destination fields. It is probably best reserved
for implementation on 16-bit machines where word boundaries
may be important.

NEGATE   n --- -n   177   MVP-FORTH

Leave the two's complement of a number, i.e., the difference of
0 less n .

Defined in: FORTH-79, fig-FORTH, STARTING FORTH

Implementation:

8080:

CODE NEGATE   H POP   L A MOV   CMA   A L MOV

```
H A MOV  CMA  A H MOV  H INX
HPUSH JMP  END-CODE
```

Source usage: +-

Example:

45 NEGATE .

Enter an integer and then convert to its negative value which is printed.

Comment: This FORTH-79 ideogram replaces MINUS in fig-FORTH. Note that HEX -8000, when negated, has a value outside the range of signed single precision integers. No error condition is raised.

NEXT   ---   MVP-FORTH

A constant used in 8080/Z80 implementations pointing to the machine code entry point of the inner interpreter.

Defined in: MVP-FORTH

Implementation:

NEXT CONSTANT NEXT

(The cross-compiler uses the label NEXT to define the constant NEXT.)

Source usage: Many.

Example:

CODE DROP H POP NEXT JMP END-CODE

This example is taken from the MVP-FORTH 8080 source code.

Comment: A memory location unique to the system implementation, whose execution enters the inner interpreter. The machine code instruction NEXT JMP is the usual exit from a CODE definition.

NEXT1   ---   MVP-FORTH

A constant used in 8080/Z80 implementations, pointing to the entry point within the NEXT routine to be used by EXECUTE.

Defined in: MVP-FORTH

Implementation:

NEXT1 CONSTANT NEXT1

(The cross-compiler uses the label NEXT1 to define the constant NEXT1.)

Source usage: EXECUTE

Example:

CODE EXECUTE   H POP   NEXT1 JMP   END-CODE

This example comes from the MVP-FORTH 8080 source code.

Comment: A memory location unique to the system implementation, which causes the function of EXECUTE to begin.

NFA   pfa --- nfa   MVP-FORTH

Convert the parameter field address of a definition to its name field.

Defined in: fig-FORTH

Implementation:

: NFA 5 - -1 TRAVERSE ;

Source usage: FORGET

Example:

' FORGET NFA ID.

   In this contrived example, get the parameter field address of FORGET and then the name field address and print the name: FORGET.

Comment: This manipulation, though prohibited by FORTH-79, is most convenient in development systems. It sets up the address for ID. .

NOOP   ---   NOT USED

A FORTH 'no operation' .

Defined in: fig-FORTH (8080)
        Implementation:

NOOP ;

Source usage: None.

Example:

NOOP

   Entering this ideogram does nothing but return the prompt.

Comment: This is just a word which does nothing except take
up time and space which, in fact, is sometimes useful.

NOT   flag1   ---   flag2   165   MVP-FORTH

Reverse the boolean value of   flag1 . This is identical to   0= .

Defined in: FORTH-79, STARTING FORTH

Implementation:

8080:

```
CODE NOT   H POP  L A MOV   H ORA   0 H LXI
    0=  IF  H INX   THEN
    HPUSH JMP   END-CODE
```

Source usage: Many.

Example:

0   NOT .

   Enter a false flag   0 , make it true and print it.

Comment: NOT and 0= have the same function; however,
depending on the context, one may be more readable than the
other. Note: NOT is not the bitwise one's complement which
has the FORTH-79 reference word set ideogram COM, (not
implemented in MVP-FORTH) .

NUMBER   addr   ---   d   MVP-FORTH

Convert the count and character string at   addr , to a signed
32-bit integer, using the current base.   If numeric conversion
is not possible, an error condition exists.   The string may

contain a preceding negative sign.

Defined in: FORTH-79(R), fig-FORTH, STARTING FORTH

Implementation:

: NUMBER   'NUMBER @ EXECUTE ;

Source usage: <INTERPRET>

Example:

: ?VALUE ." INPUT A VALUE --- "
    QUERY BL WORD NUMBER QUIT ;

   This example prompts for a value, then converts the value to a
double precision number.

Comment: The version and implementation of this ideogram in
MVP-FORTH conforms with that in the FORTH-79 reference
word set and fig-FORTH. It will recognize two non-numeric
characters: a decimal point and a leading negative sign. The
position of the decimal point is recorded in the user variable
DPL. This feature enables a user program to scale or adjust
the converted value as desired. It will give an error message
if any other special character is used. Note that the
definition given in STARTING FORTH is different. Because
of the possible variations, this ideogram utilizes an execution
vector which will permit easy redefinition. It defaults to
<NUMBER>.

OCTAL   ---   MVP-FORTH - SUPPLEMENTAL

Set the number conversion base to decimal 8.

Defined in: FORTH-79(R), STARTING FORTH

Implementation:

: OCTAL   8 BASE ! ;

Source usage: None.

Example:

HEX   FF   OCTAL .

   Input the hex value FF and print its octal equivalent.

Comment: If octal values are to be used this is the ideogram to
use to set the appropriate value of BASE .

A variable that contains the offset added to the block number on the stack by BLOCK to determine the actual physical block number. The user must add any desired offset when utilizing BUFFER.

Defined in: FORTH-79(R), fig-FORTH, STARTING FORTH

Implementation:

48 USER OFFSET

Source usage: BLOCK   DR0   SET-DRX

Example:

: DR0   0 OFFSET ! ;

   This definition sets the value of the user variable, OFFSET, to 0, such that subsequent Screen accesses will be to drive 0.

Comment: This variable is available in a variety of implementations of FORTH and is convenient not only for accessing different disk drives but for setting a base BLOCK from which data can be read for purposes of drive selection. However, using the ideograms DR0, DR1, etc. is safer, easier and more convenient.

OR   n1 n2 --- n3   223   MVP-FORTH

Leave the bitwise inclusive-or of two numbers.

Defined in: FORTH-79, fig-FORTH, STARTING FORTH

Implementation:

8080:

CODE OR   D POP H POP E A MOV L ORA A L MOV
     D A MOV H ORA A H MOV HPUSH JMP END-CODE

Source usage: #S EXPECT UPDATE

Example:

HEX
20 30 OR

DECIMAL

The bit pattern associated with 20 and 30 will be logically
OR'ed together and left on the stack: 30 .

Comment: An ideogram which performs a logical operation
common in computing.

OUT   --- addr   MVP-FORTH

A user variable that contains a value incremented by EMIT.
The user may alter and examine OUT to control display
formatting.

Defined in: fig-FORTH

Implementation:

4A   USER   OUT

Source usage: <EMIT>   <CR>

Example:

OUT @ .

Examine the present value in the user variable, OUT, and
print it.

Comment: This ideogram, though not present in all
implementations, is useful for checking space remaining on a
line of output. EMIT always increments it by one, even for
nonprinting control characters.

OVER   n1 n2 --- n1 n2 n1   170   MVP-FORTH

Leave a copy of the second number on the stack.

Defined in: FORTH-79, fig-FORTH, STARTING FORTH

Implementation:

8080:

CODE OVER   D POP   H POP   H PUSH
    DPUSH JMP   END-CODE

Source usage: TRAVERSE   M/   D.R   TYPE

Example:

45 7 OVER

Enter two integers and then make a copy of the first one entered on the top of the stack leaving three values on the stack.

Comment: This is one of the most common stack operators.

P!   b n ---   MVP-FORTH

Output byte b to port n on an 8080 or Z80 system.

Pronounced: port store

Defined in: fig-FORTH 8080
        Implementation:

8080:

```
CODE P!   D POP   P!PORT  H LXI   E M MOV
      H POP   L A MOV
   HERE 1+ LABEL P!PORT    0  OUT
      NEXT JMP   END-CODE
```

Source usage: None.

Example:

HEX 41 E0 P! DECIMAL

Go to hex and output the ASCII value of the character, A, on port E0 and return to decimal.

Comment: Gives access to any port of an 8080 or Z80 system. Thus it is possible to write any value to any port. The use of this is obviously hardware dependent.

P@   n --- b   MVP-FORTH

Inputs byte b from port n on an 8080 or Z80 system.

Pronounced: port fetch

Defined in: fig-FORTH (8080)

Implementation:

8080:

```
CODE P@    D POP    P@PORT H LXI E M MOV
    HERE 1+ LABEL P@PORT    0 IN A L MOV
    0 H MVI  HPUSH JMP  END-CODE
```

Source usage: None.

Example:

HEX   E0   P@   DECIMAL   .

   Go to hex and get the value presently on port E0 and return to
decimal and print that value.

Comment: Gives access to any port of an 8080 or Z80 system.
Any port on an 8080 or Z80 CPU is read and its content placed on
the top of the stack.

PAD   ---   addr   226   MVP-FORTH

The address of a scratch area used to hold character strings for
intermediate processing.   The minimum capacity of PAD   is
64 characters. (addr through addr+63)

Defined in: FORTH-79, fig-FORTH, STARTING FORTH

Implementation:

: PAD   HERE   44   +   ;

Source usage: #>   <#

Example:

HERE   PAD   20   CMOVE

   From the address of HERE   to the address of PAD, move 20
bytes.

Comment: The location of PAD changes as the dictionary
grows.   Text strings build up from PAD while numbers are
formatted downward.

PAGE   ---   MVP-FORTH

Clear the terminal screen or perform an action suitable to the
output device currently active.

Defined in: FORTH-79(R), STARTING FORTH

Implementation:

: PAGE   'PAGE @ EXECUTE ;

Source usage: None.

Example:

PAGE

Entering this ideogram will clear the terminal screen by vectoring to <PAGE>.

Comment: There are many different terminals.   Therefore, a new definition must be written and vectored into 'PAGE, before this ideogram will function properly.   It should allow one to start with a clear screen and the cursor at home.

PAUSE   ---   MVP-FORTH - UTILITY

Test the terminal keyboard for actuation of any key.   If true, wait until a key has been pressed again.

Defined in: MVP-FORTH

Implementation:

```
: PAUSE   ?TERMINAL
    IF   KEY   DROP   1000 0 DO LOOP
        BEGIN   ?TERMINAL   UNTIL   KEY   DROP
        2000 0   DO LOOP
    THEN  ;
```

Source usage: None.

Example:

```
: INDEX   CR  1+   SWAP
    DO  CR   I   R   .R   R SPACES  I  .INDEX
    PAUSE  ?TERMINAL   IF   LEAVE   THEN  1 /LOOP ;
```

This example allows one to interrupt the INDEX listing by striking any key.

Comment: When PAUSE is followed by ?TERMINAL as in the example, striking any key once will continue the listing and striking any key twice in rapid succession will terminate the listing.   The delay loops may have to be adjusted for individual systems and user preferences.

PFA   nfa --- pfa   MVP-FORTH

Convert the name field address of a compiled definition to its parameter field address.

Defined in: fig-FORTH

Implementation:

: PFA   1 TRAVERSE   5 + ;

Source usage: <;CODE>   FORGET

Example:

HEX   4AC2   PFA   DECIMAL

   Go to HEX and, presuming that the value, 4AC2, is a name field address, it will be replaced with its parameter field address.

Comment: Allows one to move around in the header of a definition. Although FORTH-79 forbids this, you sometimes have no alternative. See ID. .

PICK   n1 --- n2   240   MVP-FORTH

Return the contents of the n1-th stack value, not counting   n1 itself. An error condition results for n less than one.   2 PICK is equivalent to OVER.   1 .. n

Defined in: FORTH-79

Implementation:

: PICK   DUP 1 <
   ABORT" PICK ARGUMENT < 1"   2*   SP@   +   @   ;

Source usage: ROLL   WORD

Example:

2   PICK

   This example is equivalent to OVER, although OVER is much faster.

Comment: Allows one to pick out of the stack any item and push a copy of it onto the top. In contrast with ROLL, PICK increases the stack depth by one, not counting the parameter eaten by PICK.

POP   ---   NOT USED

The code sequence to remove a stack value and return to NEXT . POP is not directly executable, but is a FORTH re-entry point after machine code.

Defined in: fig-FORTH

Implementation:

(This ideogram is not implemented in MVP-FORTH)

Comment: Though given in the INSTALLATION MANUAL, it is not available in FORTH implemented on an 8080 or Z80 CPU.

PP   n --- <text>   MVP-FORTH

On the latest screen listed, put <text> on line n.

Defined in: MVP-FORTH

Implementation:

```
: PP    DUP  FFF0  AND
    ABORT" OFF SCREEN "
    0  TEXT  PAD  1+  SWAP
    SCR  @  <LINE>  CMOVE  UPDATE ;
```

Source usage: None.

Example:

```
99  LIST  99  CLEAR  99  LIST
0 PP ( THIS IS A NEW SCREEN )
99  LIST
```

After listing the screen, it is cleared with CLEAR and "(THIS IS A NEW SCREEN)" is put in line 0.

Comment: This implementation is adapted from the EDITOR included in the fig-FORTH INSTALLATION MANUAL. Before loading an EDITOR, this ideogram makes it possible to enter new source text on a screen for loading. Without such an ideogram it is difficult to get started unless you are fortunate enough to have a disk already containing the source screens for an EDITOR. Note that this function is different from that described in STARTING FORTH.

PREV   ---   addr   MVP-FORTH

A variable containing the address of the disk buffer most recently referenced. The UPDATE command marks this buffer to be later written to disk.

Defined in: fig-FORTH

Implementation:

VARIABLE PREV   FIRST PREV !

Source usage: +BUF   BLOCK   BUFFER   COLD   UPDATE

Example:

PREV @ U.

   Get the value of this variable and print it.

Comment: The buffer management routines use PREV to monitor the most recently referenced buffer. It is seldom useful in applications.

PUSH   ---   NOT USED

This code sequence stores machine registers to the computation stack and returns to NEXT. It is not directly executable, but is a FORTH re-entry point after machine code.

Defined in: fig-FORTH

Implementation:

(This ideogram is not implemented in MVP-FORTH.)

Comment: This ideogram is not usually a part of an 8080 or Z80 implementation of FORTH. It is usually a part of the ASSEMBLER vocabulary. In MVP-FORTH, the equivalent entry point is named HPUSH, which should not be confused with DPUSH.

PUT   ---   NOT USED

This code sequence stores machine register contents over the topmost computation stack value and returns to NEXT. It is not directly executable, but is a FORTH reentry point after machine code.

Defined in: fig-FORTH

Implementation:

(This ideogram is not implemented in MVP-FORTH.)

Comment: This ideogram is not used on an 8080 or Z80 CPU
implementation of FORTH.

PW!   n1 n2 ---   MVP-FORTH

Output word n1 to port n2 on an 8086/8088 system.

Defined in: MVP-FORTH

Implementation:

8086/8088

CODE PW!   DX POP   AX POP   DS, AX OUT
     NEXT JMP   END-CODE

Example:

4567 PORT PW!

    Output the 16-bit data word to a previously defined PORT.

Comment: Systems with 16-bit data busses may put out all 16
bits to one port. Since the ideogram P! as used in many 8-bit
systems has the connotation of 8 bits already established, a new
ideogram PW! has been added in MVP-FORTH. Other
implementations of FORTH on 16-bit systems have changed the
functional definition of P! to output 16 bits and added PC!
to output 8 bits. The character connotation of 'C' seems wrong
because a byte value is actually output. Furthermore, it seems
better not to change established functional definitions.

PW@ .   n1 --- n2   MVP-FORTH

Input word n2 from port n1 on an 8086/8088 system.

Defined in: MVP-FORTH

Implementation:

8086/8088

CODE PW@   DX POP   AX, DX IN   A PUSH JMP   END-CODE

Source usage: None.

Example:

PORT   PW@   .

   Input the 16 data bits on the previously defined PORT and
print the value.

Comment: Systems with 16-bit data busses may input all 16
bits to one port. Since the ideogram P@   as used in many 8-
bit systems has the connotation of 8 bits already established, a
new ideogram PW@   has been added in MVP-FORTH.   Other
implementations of FORTH on 16-bit systems have changed the
functional definition of P@   to input 16 bits and added PC@
to input 8 bits.   The character connotation of 'C' seems wrong
because a byte value is actually input.   Furthermore, it seems
better not to change established functional definitions.

QUERY   ---   235   MVP-FORTH

Accept input of up to 80 characters (or until a 'return') from the
operator's terminal, into the terminal input buffer.   WORD
may be used to accept text from this buffer as the input stream,
by setting >IN and BLK to zero.

Defined in: FORTH-79, fig-FORTH

Implementation:

: QUERY   TIB @ 50 EXPECT 0 >IN ! ;

Source usage: QUIT

Example:

: TEST   ." Input value --- "   QUERY BL WORD
   NUMBER   ;

   This definition will print a prompt, then wait for an input
value and place it on the stack.

Comment: Places a line of input in the terminal input buffer,
where it may be processed by WORD , NUMBER , INTERPRET ,
or any user-defined routine.

Clear the return stack, setting execution mode, and return control to the terminal. No message is given.

Defined in: FORTH-79, fig-FORTH, STARTING FORTH

Implementation:

```
: QUIT   0  BLK  !  [COMPILE]  [
   BEGIN  CR  RP!  QUERY  INTERPRET
      STATE  @  NOT
      IF  ." OK"  THEN
   AGAIN  ;
```

Source usage: <ABORT> <ABORT">

Example:

." HELLO" QUIT

   Print the text, HELLO, and then return to FORTH without the usual prompt, OK.

Comment: Makes it possible to end the execution of a definition without having the ever-present OK produced. QUIT is also useful for user defined error message routines and application specific prompts.

R   --- n   C   NOT USED

Copy the top of the return stack to the computation stack.

Defined in: fig-FORTH

Implementation:
(This ideogram is not implemented in MVP-FORTH.)

Comment: This ideogram is now obsolete having been replaced by R@ in FORTH-79.

R#   --- addr   U   MVP-FORTH

A user variable which may contain the location of an editing cursor, or other file related function.

Defined in: fig-FORTH, STARTING FORTH

Implementation:

4C   USER   R#

Source usage: None.

Example:

R#   @   .

   Get the address of this user variable, fetch its value and
print it.

Comment: This ideogram is generally only used when in the
EDITOR   vocabulary.   If it is not in the range of 0 .. 1023 , an
error message of out of bounds is sometimes given.

R/W   addr   blk   f   ---   MVP-FORTH

The fig-FORTH standard disk read-write linkage.   addr
specifies the source or destination buffer (not a FORTH-79
block buffer),   blk   is the sequential number of the referenced
block; and   f   is a flag for f = 0 write and   f = 1 read.   R/W
determines the location on mass storage, performs the read or
write and performs any error checking.

Defined in: fig-FORTH

Implementation:

: R/W   'R/W   @   EXECUTE   ;

Source usage: <BLOCK>   BUFFER

Example:

: BUFFER   USE   @   DUP   >R
   BEGIN   +BUF   UNTIL
   USE   !   R@   @   0<
   IF   R@   2+   R@   @   7FFF   AND   0   R/W   THEN
   R@   !   R@   PREV   !   R>   2+   ;

   This definition is one of the principal uses of the ideogram,
R/W.

Comment: This   ideogram   is   a   primitive   in   many
implementations of FORTH.   If it is available, it is possible
to read and write from disk to any area in memory such as a
special buffer, without going through the regular block buffers.
Of course such a procedure is installation dependent and
prohibited by FORTH-79.   It is vectored for the benefit of the

programmer, defaulting to the routine <R/W>.

RO   --- addr   U   MVP-FORTH

A user variable containing the initial location of the return
stack. See   RP!.

Pronounced: r-zero

Defined in: fig-FORTH

Implementation:

08 USER RO

Source usage: None.

Example:

RO @ U.

   Get the address of this user variable, fetch its value and
print it.

Comment: Though it is in MVP-FORTH and may be present in
other implementations, it is not a part of FORTH-79
vocabulary.

R>   --- n   C, 110   MVP-FORTH

Transfer n from the return stack to the data stack.

Pronounced: r-from

Defined in: FORTH-79, fig-FORTH, STARTING FORTH

Implementation:

8080:

```
CODE R>    RPP LHLD  M E MOV  H INX  M D MOV
    H INX  RPP SHLD  D PUSH
    NEXT JMP  END-CODE
```

Source usage: Many.

Example:

: TRY   >R . R> ;

This example accomplishes the same thing as " SWAP . ". Though it illustrates the ideogram, it would be poor programming practice.

Comment: An ideogram allowing manipulations of the return stack. Occasionally values from the data stack can be temporarily stored in the return stack and returned with this ideogram. However, this is a potentially dangerous procedure. Be careful to leave the return stack as you found it before exiting your definition, otherwise you will certainly crash the system.

R@   --- n   C, 228   MVP-FORTH

Copy the number on the top of the return stack to the data stack.

Pronounced: r-fetch

Defined in: FORTH-79

Implementation:

8080:

CODE R@   RPP LHLD   M E MOV   H INX   M D MOV
     D PUSH   NEXT JMP   END-CODE

Source usage: Many.

Example:

R@   .

Get the value present value on top of the return stack and print it.

Comment: This ideogram fetches the value on top of the return stack without changing it, and places it on the data stack. It is useful when using the return stack for temporary storage but be careful to finally leave the return stack as you found it. Otherwise, you will crash the system.

REPEAT   ---   I, C, 120   MVP-FORTH

Used in a colon-definition. At run-time, REPEAT returns to just after the corresponding BEGIN .

Form: BEGIN ... WHILE ... REPEAT

Defined in: FORTH-79, fig-FORTH, STARTING FORTH

Implementation:

```
: REPEAT   >R  >R  [COMPILE]  AGAIN   R>  R>
  2-  [COMPILE]  THEN  ;  IMMEDIATE
```

Source usage: <NUMBER> CONVERT FORGET

Example:

```
: TEST   0  BEGIN  DUP  .  9  <
         WHILE  1+
         REPEAT  ;
```

This definition illustrates another way of printing the digits 0 through 9.

Comment: REPEAT is a closing delimiter for a BEGIN control structure.   Since it compiles an unconditional branch, the structure may be exited only at the corresponding WHILE.

ROLL   n ---   236   MVP-FORTH

Extract the n-th stack value to the top of the stack, not counting n itself, moving the remaining values into the vacated position. An error condition results for n less than one.   1 .. n

Form: 3   ROLL   =   ROT
            1   ROLL   =   null operation

Defined in: FORTH-79

Implementation:

```
: ROLL   DUP  1  <
  ABORT" ROLL ARGUMENT < 1"
  1+  DUP  PICK  SWAP  2*  SP@  +
  BEGIN  DUP  2-  @  OVER  !  2-  SP@
     U<  NOT
  UNTIL  DDROP  ;
```

Source usage: None.

Example:

2   ROLL

This example is the equivalent of the ideogram, SWAP.

Comment: This ideogram is the companion of PICK. While PICK copies its victim onto the top of the stack, ROLL moves it. PICK increases the stack depth by one while ROLL leaves it unchanged -- not counting the parameter eaten by ROLL.

ROT   n1 n2 n3 --- n2 n3 n1   212   MVP-FORTH

Rotate the top three values, bringing the deepest to the top.

Pronounced: rote

Defined in: FORTH-79, fig-FORTH, STARTING FORTH

Implementation:

8080:

CODE ROT   D POP   H POP   XTHL
    DPUSH JMP   END-CODE

Source usage: # CONVERT   D.R   D<   M*/   NUMBER

Example:

45 73 89   ROT

    Enter three values and then take the first one in, 45, and move it to the top of the stack.

Comment: This ideogram performs the function of 3   ROLL, but rather more quickly.

RP!   ---   MVP-FORTH

A computer dependent procedure to initialize the return stack pointer from user variable R0 .

Defined in: fig-FORTH

Implementation:

8080:

CODE RP!   UP LHLD   8 D LXI   D DAD   M E MOV
    H INX   M D MOV   XCHG   RPP SHLD
    NEXT JMP   END-CODE

Source usage: QUIT

Example:

```
: QUIT   0  BLK  !  [COMPILE]  [
    BEGIN  CR  RP!  QUERY  INTERPRET  STATE @  NOT
      IF ." OK"  THEN
    AGAIN  ;
```

This example is taken from the MVP-FORTH implementation.

Comment: This ideogram is not a part of FORTH-79, but may remain in the primitives.

RP@   --- addr   MVP-FORTH

Leaves the current value in the return stack pointer register.

Defined in: fig-FORTH (8080)

Implementation:

8080:

CODE RP@   RPP LHLD   HPUSH JMP   END-CODE

Source usage: None.

Example:

RP@ @ U.

   Nondestructively fetch and print the top item on the return stack.

Comment: Provides more general access to the insides of FORTH, which is, of course, prohibited by FORTH-79 STANDARD.

RPP   --- addr   MVP-FORTH

A constant returning a pointer to the cell in low memory which holds the FORTH return stack pointer. It is used in the 8080/Z80 implementation.

Defined in: MVP-FORTH

Implementation:

RPP CONSTANT RPP

(The cross-compiler uses the label RPP to define the constant
RPP.)

Source usage: RP!   RP@

Example:

RPP @ @ U.

This example achieves the same result as R@.

Comment: The cell at address RPP is a pseudo register for the
simulated FORTH machine. Since the 8080/Z80 version needs
its internal registers for more time-critical activities, the
return stack pointer resides at this fixed location in RAM.

S->D   n --- d   MVP-FORTH

Sign extend a single number to form a double number.

Defined in: fig-FORTH

Implementation:

8080:

CODE S->D   D POP   C H LXI   D A MOV   80 ANI
      0#   IF   H DCX   THEN   DPUSH JMP   END-CODE

Source usage: .   .R   /MOD

Example:

22 S->D

     Enter a single precision number on the stack and sign extend
it to a double precision value. It is equivalent to entering
twenty-two with a terminating decimal point (22.).

Comment: A convenient operation with integer arithmetic
which maintains the correct value of the sign in the extension.

S0   --- addr   MVP-FORTH

Returns the address of the bottom of the stack, when empty.

Pronounced: s-zero

Defined in: FORTH-79(R), fig-FORTH, STARTING FORTH

Implementation:

: S0   SP0   @ ;

Source usage: None.

Example:

S0   U .

   Get the address of the bottom of the stack and print it
unsigned.

Comment: Allows one to reference the empty position of the
data stack. It can be used to implement a nondestructive stack
display such as .S . In fig-FORTH, S0 is defined as a user
variable to which MVP-FORTH has assigned the ideogram SP0,
in order to free the use of S0 in accordance with FORTH-79(R).
STARTING FORTH appears to use the fig-FORTH definition.

SAVE-BUFFERS   ---   221   MVP-FORTH

Write all blocks to mass-storage that have been flagged as
UPDATEd.   An error condition results if mass-storage writing
is not completed.

Defined in: FORTH-79

Implementation:

Source usage: None.

: SAVE-BUFFERS   #BUFF 1+ 0 DO 7FFF
   BUFFER   DROP   LOOP ;

Example:

SAVE-BUFFERS

   Write all buffers marked by UPDATE back to the disks.

Comment: This ideogram replaces the older one FLUSH .
Often the older ideogram is continued as at least an alias
because it is so deeply embedded in FORTH.

SAVE-FORTH   ---   MVP-FORTH - UTILITY

Save the current image of FORTH as a replacement for the
original FORTH.COM file on the default drive.

Defined in: MVP-FORTH

Implementation:

```
DECIMAL
: SAVE-FORTH      FREEZE
  13  0  SYSCALL   DROP          ( RESET DISK SYSTEM)
  14  0  SYSCALL   DROP          ( SELECT DISK )
  CR CR ." FILE NAME ? ---"
  PAD  33  0  FILL  PAD  1+  11  BLANK
  QUERY                          ( MAKE PAD FCB )
  46  WORD COUNT & MIN PAD 1+ SWAP CMOVE
  BL  WORD COUNT 3 MIN PAD 9 + SWAP CMOVE
  19 PAD SYSCALL DROP            ( DELETE FILE )
  22 PAD SYSCALL DROP            ( MAKE FILE )
  256 HERE 0 256 U/MOD SWAP DROP 1+ 2/ 2* 2*
  0 DO DUP 26 SWAP SYSCALL DROP  ( SET DMA ADDRESS)
     21 PAD SYSCALL DROP 128 + ( WRITE SEQUENTIAL)
  LOOP DROP
  16 PAD SYSCALL DROP ;          ( CLOSE FILE )
```

Source usage: None.

Example: CAUTION: This could destroy your present COM
file.

SAVE-FORTH

    Execution of this ideogram will prompt for the desired CP/M
file name and erase it if it is present.   It will then write the
FORTH image in memory to the file you selected.   Drive 0 is
selected.

Comment: This ideogram makes it possible to save a binary
image of FORTH at any time.   It makes a rapid restart after a
system crash possible.   In this implementation all error
messages from CP/M are discarded.   You may wish to modify the
code to better suit your needs.   It is particularly useful in
turnkey systems which submit your FORTH binary image upon
booting up.

SCR   --- addr   U, 217   MVP-FORTH

Leave the address of a variable containing the number of the
screen most recently listed.   The value of the variable is
unsigned.

Pronounced: s-c-r

Defined in: FORTH-79, fig-FORTH, STARTING FORTH

4E USER SCR

Source usage: LIST PP

Example:

: L SCR @ LIST ;

This definition re-lists the last screen listed.

Comment: Using ! or +! to alter the contents of SCR is permitted. Some editors do this in commands which step forward or backward in a series of screens.

SEC   --- addr   MVP-FORTH - DISK I-0

A variable used by the disk interface, containing the sector number last read or written relative to the last drive used.

Defined in: fig-FORTH (8080)

VARIABLE SEC   0 SEC !

Source usage: <T&SCALC> SET-IO

Example:

SEC @ U.

Get the address of this variable, then fetch its contents and print it.

Comment: Used together with TRACK in the calculations and setting up of the calls to the operating system.

SEC-READ   ---   MVP-FORTH - DISK I-0

Reads a disk sector (128 bytes) into memory. All parameters must have been set by SET-DRIVE and SET-IO. The status on completion is stored in DISK-ERROR.

Defined in: fig-FORTH (8080)

Implementation:

8080:

CODE SEC-READ   B PUSH RDSEC D LXI IOS CALL
    DISK-ERROR STA B POP NEXT JMP END-CODE

Source usage: <R/W>

Example:

```
: <R/W>    USE  @  >R   ROT   USE ! SWAP  MAX-DRV  0
    DO  I   DR-DEN   DENSITY   !
        DUP   BPDRV   -  -1  >
        IF  BPDRV   -   I  1+  MAX-DRV  =
            IF  R>  R>  DDROP   R>  USE  !
                1  ABORT" BLOCK OUT OF RANGE"  THEN
        ELSE  I   DRIVE  !  SET-DRIVE  LEAVE
        THEN
    LOOP   SPBLK  *  SPBLK   0
    DO   DDUP  T&SCALC  SET-IO
        IF  SEC-READ
        ELSE  SEC-WRITE
        THEN  1+  HDBT  4  -  SPBLK  /  USE  +!
    LOOP
    DDROP   R>  USE ! ;
```

The definition illustrates the use of this ideogram.

Comment: One of the basic disk read/write operators. With this it is possible to read any physical sector on a disk to any 128 byte segment of memory. It is highly hardware dependent, but it belongs in a good FORTH development system.

SEC-WRITE   ---   MVP-FORTH - DISK I-O

Writes a disk-sector (128 bytes) from memory. All parameters must have been set by SET-DRIVE and SET-IO. The status on completion is stored in DISK-ERROR.

Defined in: fig-FORTH (8080)

Implementation:

8080:

```
CODE SEC-WRITE   B PUSH   RITSEC D LXI  IOS CALL
    DISK-ERROR STA   B POP   NEXT JMP   END-CODE
```

Source usage: <R/W>

Example:

```
: <R/W>    USE  @  >R   ROT   USE ! SWAP  MAX-DRV  0
    DO  I   DR-DEN   DENSITY   !
        DUP   BPDRV   -  -1  >
        IF  BPDRV   -   I  1+  MAX-DRV  =
            IF  R>  R>  DDROP   R>  USE  !
```

```
        1  ABORT" BLOCK OUT OF RANGE"  THEN
     ELSE  I  DRIVE  !  SET-DRIVE  LEAVE
     THEN
  LOOP   SPBLK  *  SPBLK  0
  DO   DDUP  T&SCALC  SET-IO
     IF  SEC-READ
     ELSE  SEC-WRITE
     THEN  1+  HDBT  4  -  SPBLK  /  USE  +!
  LOOP
  DDROP  R> USE ! ;
```

The definition illustrates the use of this ideogram.

Comment: One of the basic disk read/write operators. With this it is possible to write any sector on a disk from any location in memory. It is highly hardware dependent, but it belongs in a good FORTH development system.

SEC/BLK   --- addr   MVP-FORTH - DISK I-O

A variable beginning a seven item array containing the number of sectors on a drive of a give density format.

Defined in: MVP-FORTH

Implementation:

```
VARIABLE  SEC/BLK   2  SEC/BLK !
   8 , 8 , 8 , 8 , 8 , 8 ,
```

Source usage: SPBLK

Example:

```
: SPBLK   DENSITY @ 6 MIN 2* SEC/BLK + @ ;
```

The definition leaves the value of the sectors per block according to the present value of DENSITY.

Comment: Not all systems are formatted with 128 bytes per sector. The IBM Personal Computer under MDOS, formats 512 bytes per sector. Thus for the IBM implementation, the first value in the array was changed to 2. The earler versions of MVP-FORTH had the function of this ideogram a constant with the value of 8.

SEC/DR   --- addr   MVP-FORTH - DISK I-O

A variable beginning a seven item array containing the number of sectors on a drive of a given density format.

Defined in: MVP-FORTH

Implementation:

```
DECIMAL
VARIABLE  SEC/DR    SEC/DR  800  !  2000 ,  4000 ,
   4000 ,  8000 ,  4928 ,  9856 ,
HEX
```

Source usage: SPDRV

Example:

```
: SPDRV   DENSITY @ 6 MIN 2 * SEC/DR + @ ;
```

The definition leaves the value of the sectors on a drive according to the present value of DENSITY.

Comment: An array used to calculate the actual drive being accessed according to the block number being requested. Some systems may require changing these values. If so, it will be necessary to poke the correct values in the proper places, and reselect your drive.

SEC/TR   --- addr   MVP-FORTH - DISK I-O

A variable beginning a seven item array containing the number of sectors on each track on a drive of a given density format.

Defined in: MVP-FORTH

Implementation:

```
DECIMAL
VARIABLE  SEC/TR    20  SEC/TR  !  26 ,  26 ,
   52 ,  52 ,  64 ,  64 ,
HEX
```

Source usage: SPT

Example:

```
: SPT   DENSITY @ 6 MIN 2 * SEC/TR + @ ;
```

The definition leaves the number of sectors per track on a drive according to its current density.

Comment: An array used to calculate the actual drive being accessed according to the block number being requested. Some systems may require changing these values. If so, it will be necessary to poke the correct values in the proper places.

SET-DRIVE   ---   MVP-FORTH - DISK I-O

A CP/M service call which makes subsequent disk reads and
writes use the drive designated in DRIVE. T&SCALC is
usually used to set DRIVE and calls SET-DRIVE. Drive
numbers range from 0 through MAX-DRV less one.

Defined in: fig-FORTH (8080)

Implementation:

8080:

```
CODE SET-DRIVE    B PUSH   DRIVE LDA
    A C MOV   SETDSK   D LXI   IOS CALL
    B POP   NEXT JMP   END-CODE
```

Source usage: <T&SCALC>

Example:

SET-DRIVE

  Issue a command to the CP/M operating system to set a value
for drive access according to the value presently in the
variable DRIVE.

Comment: A utility which interlinks FORTH to CP/M .

SET-DRX   n ---   MVP-FORTH - DISK I-O

For drive number n , calculates and adds the necessary value
to OFFSET.

Defined in: MVP-FORTH

Implementation:

```
: SET-DRX    DR-DEN   DENSITY   !  BPDRV  /
    OFFSET  +!  ;
```

Source usage: DR1   DR2   DR3   DR4

Example:

```
: DR1    DR0   0  SET-DRX  ;
```

  The definition calculates the necessary value for the

variable OFFSET according to the present values established
by CONFIGURE.

Comment: SET-DRX dynamically monitors changes in the value
of MAX-DRV and the array DEN, but only when you execute it.
When CONFIGURE is used to change the density on the various
drives it is necessary to recalculate the values for OFFSET
according to the selected drive.

SET-IO   ---   MVP-FORTH - DISK I-O

A CP/M service call which makes subsequent disk reads and
writes use the drive last set by SET-DRIVE, not part of this
ideogram. The memory address in variable USE, the sector
number in SEC, and the track number in TRACK, must be set first.
T&SCALC is usually used to set these variables.

Defined in: fig-FORTH (8080)

Implementation:

8080:

```
CODE SET-IO   B PUSH
  '  USE    LHLD  H B MOV  L C MOV
     SETDMA D LXI   IOS CALL
  '  SEC    LHLD  H B MOV  L C MOV
     SETSEC D LXI   IOS CALL
  '  TRACK LHLD  H B MOV  L C MOV
     SETTRK D LXI   IOS CALL
  B POP   NEXT JMP   END-CODE
```

Source usage: <R/W>

Example:

```
: <R/W>    USE  @  >R   ROT   USE !  SWAP   MAX-DRV  0
   DO  I   DR-DEN   DENSITY  !
      DUP  BPDRV  -  -1  >
      IF  BPDRV  -  I  1+  MAX-DRV  =
         IF  R>  R>  DDROP   R>  USE  !
            1  ABORT" BLOCK OUT OF RANGE"  THEN
      ELSE  I   DRIVE !  SET-DRIVE  LEAVE
      THEN
   LOOP   SPBLK  *  SPBLK  0
   DO   DDUP  T&SCALC  SET-IO
      IF  SEC-READ
      ELSE  SEC-WRITE
      THEN  1+  HDBT  4  -  SPBLK  /  USE  +!
   LOOP
   DDROP  R>  USE ! ;
```

This example comes from the MVP-FORTH implementation.

Comment: A utility used to interface FORTH with the CP/M operating system.

SIGN   n ---   140   MVP-FORTH

Insert the ASCII   "-"   (minus sign) into the pictured numeric output string, if   n   is negative.

Defined in: FORTH-79, fig-FORTH, STARTING FORTH

Implementation:

: SIGN   0<
    IF   2D   HOLD   THEN   ;

Source usage: D.R

Example:

-22.   DUP   ROT   ROT   DABS   <# #S ROT SIGN #> TYPE

   Enter a double precision negative value by ending with a decimal point and then format and type the value.

Comment: This ideogram will only function between   <#   and   #> . The publication, FORTH-79, flags SIGN as a "compile-only" ideogram; it is, however, generally conceded that was a typographical error.

SMUDGE   ---   MVP-FORTH

Used during word definition to toggle the   "smudge bit" in a definition's   name   field.   This   prevents   an   uncompleted definition from being found during dictionary searches,   until compiling is completed without error.

Defined in: fig-FORTH

Implementation:

: SMUDGE   LATEST   20   TOGGLE   ;

Source usage: :   ;

Example:

: ;   ?CSP   COMPILE   EXIT   SMUDGE   [COMPILE]   [;

This example comes from the MVP-FORTH implementation.

Comment: The closing smudge in " ; " cancels out the initial smudge performed by " : ". If, because of an error, a colon definition is terminated before completion, its smudge bit will hide it from any dictionary searches. Although you will see it in your VLIST, trying to FORGET it will return an error with the message " NOT IN CURRENT VOCABULARY ". If the offending ideogram is at the top of the dictionary, executing SMUDGE will expose it for removal.

SP!   ---   MVP-FORTH

A computer dependent procedure to initialize the stack pointer from S0 .

Defined in: fig-FORTH

Implementation:

8080:

```
CODE SP!    UP LHLD   6 D LXI   D DAD   M E MOV
     H INX   M D MOV   XCHG   SPHL
     NEXT JMP   END-CODE
```

Source usage: <ABORT>   <ABORT">

Example:

```
: <ABORT>   SP! ?STACK   [COMPILE]
    FORTH DEFINITIONS   QUIT ;
```

The definition is used in conjunction with an error routine to reset the stack to its empty position.

Comment: Only the data stack is cleared. The return stack and everything else remain intact.

SP0   --- addr   U MVP-FORTH

A user variable that contains the initial value of the stack pointer. (See S0).

Pronounced: s-p-zero

Defined in: MVP-FORTH

Implementation:

06 USER SP0

Source usage: S0

Example:

: S0   SP0 @ ;

The example is from the MVP-FORTH source code.

Comment: Although this user variable is given a different name in fig-FORTH and STARTING FORTH, its MVP-FORTH identifier makes the ideogram S0 available to function according to FORTH-79(R).

SP@   --- addr   214   MVP-FORTH

Return the address of the top of the stack, just before SP@ was executed.

Pronounced: s-p-fetch

Defined in: FORTH-79(R), fig-FORTH

Implementation:

8080:

CODE SP@   0 H LXI   SP DAD   HPUSH JMP   END-CODE

Source usage: ?CSP ?STACK DEPTH PICK ROLL

Example:

: DEPTH   SP@ S0 SWAP - 2 / ;

This example is taken from the MVP-FORTH implementation.

Comment: The FORTH-79 STANDARD prefers you to use the ideogram DEPTH in place of the implementation dependent SP@.

SPACE   ---   232   MVP-FORTH

Transmit an ASCII blank to the current output device.

Defined in: FORTH-79, fig-FORTH, STARTING FORTH

Implementation:

: SPACE   BL   EMIT   ;

Source usage: D.   LIST   SPACES

Example:

333   3   .R   SPACE   444   3   .R

   This example illustrates the formatted output of two 3-digit
numbers separated by one space.

Comment: This ideogram will place the proper ASCII value
regardless of the current number base.

SPACES   n ---   231   MVP-FORTH

Transmit   n   spaces to the current output device.   Take no
action for   n   of zero or less.

Defined in: FORTH-79, fig-FORTH, STARTING FORTH

Implementation:

: SPACES   0   MAX   ?DUP
      IF   0
        DO   SPACE   LOOP
      THEN   ;

Source usage: D.R   ?CONFIGURE   TRIAD

Example:

33   4   .R   20   SPACES   44   4   .R

   This example illustrates the formatted output of two 4-digit
numeric fields separated by twenty spaces.

Comment: The usefulness of this somewhat trivial ideogram
justifies its inclusion in FORTH-79 and MVP-FORTH.

SPBLK   ---   n   MVP-FORTH - DISK I-0

Find the value in the array   SEC/BLK   according to the value
of DENSITY.

Defined in: MVP-FORTH

Implementation:

: SPBLK   DENSITY   @ 6 MIN 2* SEC/BLK   +   @   ;

    Source usage: SPDRV

Example:

: SPDRV   BPDRV   SPBLK   *   ;

    The example is taken from the source code.

Comment: The ideogram is used to accommodate drives
formatted with various numbers of sectors per block rather than
the 8 sectors per block used in most CP/M systems.

SPDRV   --- n   MVP-FORTH - DISK I-O

Find the value in the array SEC/DR according to the value of
DENSITY.

Defined in: MVP-FORTH

Implementation:

: SPDRV   BPDRV   SPBLK   *   ;

Source usage: <T&SCALC>   SET-DRV

Example:

SPDRV   .

    Get the number of sectors on a drive according the the present
value of DENSITY and print it.

Comment: A factored FORTH utility used in setting up CP/M
for disk access.

SPT   --- n   MVP-FORTH - DISK I-O

Find the value in the array SEC/TR according to the value of
DENSITY.

Defined in: MVP-FORTH

Implementation:

: SPT   DENSITY   @ 6 MIN 2* SEC/TR   +   @   ;

Source usage: <T&SCALC>

Example:

SPT   .

   Get the number of sectors per track according to the value
present value of DENSITY and print it.

Comment: A factored FORTH utility used in setting up CP/M
for disk access.

STATE   --- addr   U, 164   MVP-FORTH

Leave the address of the variable containing the compilation
state. A non-zero content indicates compilation is
occurring, but the value itself may be installation dependent.

Defined in: FORTH-79, fig-FORTH

Implementation:

50 USER STATE

Source usage: ." <INTERPRET> ?COMP DLITERAL
   LITERAL QUIT [ ]

Example:

:]   C0 STATE ! ;

   This example comes from the MVP-FORTH implementation.

Comment: Although STATE is widely used and is part of the
FORTH-79 STANDARD, it is not indispensable. STARTING
FORTH seems to manage quite well without it.

SWAP   n1 n2 --- n2 n1   230   MVP-FORTH

Exchange the top two stack values.

Defined in: FORTH-79, fig-FORTH, STARTING FORTH

Implementation:

8080:

CODE SWAP   H POP   XTHL   HPUSH JMP   END-CODE

Source usage: Many.

Example:

33 44 SWAP

Enter two values on the stack and then exchange them.

Comment: This ideogram is one of the fundamental stack operators.

SYSCALL   n1 n2 --- n3   MVP-FORTH

Setup and execute CP/M function calls. n1 is the function code number and n2 is the parameter value to be placed in the DE register. CP/M BDOS is then called and the error code in register A, if any, is placed on the stack.

Defined in: MVP-FORTH

Implementation:

8080:

```
CODE SYSCALL   D POP   H POP   B PUSH   L C MOV
     BDOS CALL   B POP   0 H MVI   A L MOV
     HPUSH JMP   END-CODE
```

Source usage: None.

Example:

2 65 SYSCALL   DROP

The character A will be printed at the terminal and, since this function returns no error, a meaningless value returned on the stack is dropped.

Comment: This ideogram gives the user access to most of the CP/M functions. It is used to implement SAVE-FORTH.

T&SCALC   n ---   MVP-FORTH - DISK I-O

Track & Sector and drive calculations for disk IO.   n is the total sector displacement from the first logical drive to the desired sector. The corresponding drive, track, and sector numbers are calculated. If the drive number is different from the contents of DRIVE, the new drive number is stored in DRIVE and SET-DRIVE is executed. The track number is stored in TRACK; the sector number is stored in SEC. T&SCALC is usually executed before SET-DRIVE.

Defined in: fig-FORTH (8080)

Implementation:

: T&SCALC   'T&SCALC @ EXECUTE ;

Source usage: <R/W>

Example:

```
: <R/W>    USE  @  >R  ROT   USE !  SWAP  MAX-DRV  0
    DO  I   DR-DEN   DENSITY   !
      DUP  BPDRV  -  -1  >
      IF  BPDRV  -  I  1+  MAX-DRV  =
        IF  R>  R>  DDROP  R>  USE  !
            1  ABORT" BLOCK OUT OF RANGE"  THEN
      ELSE  I   DRIVE  !  SET-DRIVE  LEAVE
      THEN
    LOOP  SPBLK  *  SPBLK  0
    DO   DDUP  T&SCALC  SET-IO
      IF  SEC-READ
      ELSE  SEC-WRITE
      THEN  1+  HDBT  4  -  SPBLK  /  USE  +!
    LOOP
    DDROP  R>  USE  !  ;
```

This example comes from the MVP-FORTH source code.

Comment: This is a revised implementation from that in fig-FORTH; it takes into account the number of sectors which are present on each disk in making the calculation. If T&SCALC cannot map n onto a physical sector, no error message is given and the values of DRIVE, TRACK, and SEC are not altered. In MVP-FORTH, this ideogram is vectored for the convenience of the programmer, defaulting to <T&SCALC>.

TASK   ---   NOT USED

A no-operation word which can mark the boundary between applications. By forgetting TASK and re-compiling, an application can be discarded in its entirety.

Defined in: fig-FORTH

Implementation: (Not implemented in MVP-FORTH.)

: TASK ;

Source usage: None.

Example:

FORGET TASK   : TASK   ;

The example first forgets the ideograms in the dictionary
through TASK, frequently the end of the boot up version, and
then replaces it.

Comment: Regardless of the ideogram you use for this purpose,
remember to redefine it after forgetting it. The name you
choose is secondary to the technique. TASK is simply a dummy
placeholder marking a certain point in the dictionary.

TEXT   c   ---   MVP-FORTH

Accept characters from the input stream, as for WORD, into
PAD, blank filling the remainder of PAD to 64 characters.

Defined in: FORTH-79(R), STARTING FORTH

Implementation:

: TEXT   HERE C/L 1+ BLANK   WORD   BL   OVER
     DUP C@   + 1+ C! PAD   C/L 1+ CMOVE ;

Source usage: PP

Example:

: DELIMIT   BL TEXT ;

DELIMIT, when executed, will take the next word from the
input stream and place it with a preceding length byte, at PAD.

Comment: Though this ideogram is usually present only in the
EDITOR   vocabulary,   it   can   be   convenient   to   have   it
available along with a few others in FORTH when the EDITOR
vocabulary is not loaded.

THEN   ---   I, C, 161   MVP-FORTH

Used in a colon-definition. THEN is the point where
execution resumes after ELSE or IF (when no ELSE is
present).

Defined in: FORTH-79, fig-FORTH, STARTING FORTH

Implementation:

: THEN   ?COMP 2 ?PAIRS   HERE   OVER

- SWAP ! ; IMMEDIATE

Source usage: Many.

Example:

: TEST 1 IF ." ONE " THEN ;

   The definition will always print 'ONE'.

Comment: ENDIF, an obsolete alias for THEN, may appear in older programs.

THRU   n1 n2 ---   MVP-FORTH - UTILITY

Load consecutively the blocks from n1 through n2.

Defined in: FORTH-79(R)

Implementation:

: THRU   1+ SWAP
     DO I U. I LOAD LOOP ;

Source usage: None.

Example:

10 20 THRU

This example will load screens 10 through 20, printing the number of each screen as it is loaded.

Comment: This ideogram is the preferred alternative to "-->" for loading a contiguous series of screens. By typing each screen's number as it is loading, this version lets one monitor the progress of a lengthy compilation.

TIB   --- addr   U   MVP-FORTH

A user variable containing the address of the terminal input buffer.

Defined in: fig-FORTH

Implementation:

0A USER TIB

Source usage: 'STREAM   QUERY

Example:

TIB @ U.

Get the address of this user variable, fetch its contents and print it unsigned.

Comment: Although FORTH-79 requires a terminal input buffer, the means of locating it is left up to the implementation. The MVP-FORTH implementation uses the fig-FORTH approach.

TITLE   ---   MVP-FORTH - UTILITY

Print a fixed message, " MOUNTAIN VIEW PRESS FORTH VERSION 1.xx.03," followed by a carriage return.

Defined in: MVP-FORTH

Implementation:

```
: TITLE   CR  10 SPACES
          ." MOUNTAIN VIEW PRESS FORTH"
          ."    VERSION 1.xx.03 " CR ;
```

Source usage: None.

Example:

FIND TITLE 'TITLE !

This example resets TRIAD to print its default message.

Comment: This default message is printed at the bottom of each page by TRIAD using the vector 'TITLE. Any other ideogram may be defined and used to replace TITLE. The ideogram then vectored by 'TITLE will be invoked by TRIAD.

TOGGLE   addr b ---   MVP-FORTH

Complement the contents of addr by the bit pattern b.

Defined in: fig-FORTH

Implementation:

8080:

```
CODE TOGGLE   D POP  H POP  M A MOV
     E XRA  A M MOV  NEXT JMP  END-CODE
```

Source usage: CREATE   IMMEDIATE   SMUDGE

Example:

: SMUDGE   LATEST   2C   TOGGLE   ;

The definition, taken from the MVP-FORTH implementation, utilizes this ideogram to complement the value of bit 6 in the byte at LATEST.

Comment: Only the byte at   addr   is affected.

TRACK   --- addr   MVP-FORTH - DISK I-O

A variable used by disk I-O.   Contains the track number last read or written relative to the current drive.

Defined in: fig-FORTH (8080)

Implementation:

VARIABLE TRACK   0 TRACK   !

Source usage: <T&SCALC>

Example:

TRACK   @   .

Get the address of the variable, fetch its contents and print it.

Comment: A variable used in interfacing FORTH with CP/M.

TRAVERSE   addr1 n --- addr2   MVP-FORTH

Move across the name field of a fig-FORTH variable length dictionary header.   addr1 is the address of either the length byte or the last letter. If   n = 1, the motion is toward high memory;   if n = -1, the motion is toward low memory.   The addr2 resulting is the address of the other end of the name.

Defined in: fig-FORTH

Implementation:

: TRAVERSE   SWAP
    BEGIN   OVER   +   07F   OVER   C@   <   UNTIL
    SWAP   DROP   ;

Source usage: NFA   PFA

Example:

: NFA   5 - -1 TRAVERSE ;

   The definition is used to find the name field address, given
the parameter field address.

Comment: This ideogram is necessary in implementations of
FORTH with fig-FORTH style name headers. However,
FORTH-79 STANDARD prohibits such poking around with the
header and the operation would remain headerless in a "pure"
implementation. On the other hand, a good FORTH development
system should have it available.

TRIAD   scr   ---   MVP-FORTH - UTILITY

Display on the selected output device the three screens which
include that numbered scr, beginning with a screen evenly
divisible by three.   Output is suitable for source text records
and includes an alterable bottom title.

Defined in: fig-FORTH

Implementation:

: TRIAD   0 3 U/MOD SWAP DROP
    3 * 3 OVER + SWAP
     DO CR I LIST ?TERMINAL
        IF LEAVE THEN
    1 /LOOP 'TITLE @ EXECUTE ;

Source usage: None.

Example:

31   TRIAD

   The example will print three screens beginning with screen
30.

Comment: By making each page evenly divisible by three,
screen listings may be maintained in a loose-leaf notebook.
This version of TRIAD prints a vectored bottom title.
Substituting a different title text is possible by defining a new
message routine and storing its compilation address in 'TITLE.

Transmit n characters beginning at address to the current
output device. No action takes place for n less than or
equal to zero.

Defined in: FORTH-79, fig-FORTH, STARTING FORTH

Implementation:

```
: TYPE    DUP  0>
     IF  OVER  +  SWAP
         DO  I  C@  EMIT  1  /LOOP
     ELSE  DDROP  THEN  ;
```

Source usage: <."> D.R .LINE

Example:

PAD   COUNT   TYPE

   Get the address of PAD, then get the length of the text at PAD
and advance the address by 1, and then type out the contents.

Comment: The definitions vary slightly but for most work they
function identically. Note that you should expect trouble if
your implementation will not handle fields crossing the
addresses 0 or decimal 32768 -- the transition from positive to
negative signed integers.

U*   un1 un2 --- ud3   242   MVP-FORTH

Perform an unsigned multiplication of un1 by un2 , leaving
the double number product ud3. All values are unsigned.

Pronounced: u-times

Defined in: FORTH-79, fig-FORTH, STARTING FORTH

Implementation:

8080:

```
ASSEMBLER
   HERE LABEL MPYX    0 H LXI  8 C MVI
   HERE LABEL MPYX1   H DAD  RAL
       MPYX2 JNC  D DAD  0 ACI
   HERE LABEL MPYX2   C DCR  MPYX1 JNZ  RET
FORTH
   CODE U*   D POP  H POP  B PUSH  H B MOV  L A MOV
       MPYX CALL  H PUSH  A H MOV  B A MOV  H B MOV
```

```
           MPYX CALL  D POP  D C MOV  B DAD  O ACI
           L D MOV  H L MOV  A H MOV  B POP  D PUSH
           HPUSH JMP  END-CODE
```

Source usage: CONVERT M*

Example:

333 444 U* <# #S #> TYPE

   Enter two unsigned single precision values, return the 32 bit
unsigned product to the stack and print it.

Comment: Allows working with unsigned numbers and provides
full precision in the double precision result. No data is lost
and no overflow is possible. U* can be the basis for all other
multipilcations.

U.   un   ---   106   MVP-FORTH

Display un converted according to BASE as an unsigned
number, in a free-field format, with one trailing blank.

Pronounced: u-dot

Defined in: FORTH-79, STARTING FORTH

Implementation:

: U.   0 D. ;

Source usage: None.

Example:

HEX BCAD DECIMAL U.

   Enter a hex value greater than 8000, return to decimal and
print it unsigned. If simply . were used, the value printed
would be negative.

Comment: This ideogram permits the output of an address
which might otherwise appear as a negative number. It is
defined in many implementations of FORTH including fig-
FORTH even though it is not included in the INSTALLATION
MANUAL.

U.R   un1   n2   ---   216 MVP-FORTH - SUPPLEMENTAL

Output un1   as an unsigned number right justified in a field
n2 characters wide. If n2 is smaller than the characters

required for   n1 , no leading spaces are given.

Pronounced: u-dot-r

Defined in: FORTH-79(R), STARTING FORTH

Implementation:

U.R   U SWAP D.R ;

Source usage: None.

Example:

HEX   BCDA   DECIMAL   6   U.R

Enter a hex value greater than 8000, return to decimal and print the value in a field right justified to six spaces.

Comment: This allows the output of addresses or block numbers in a formatted field.

U/   ud   u1   ---   u2   u3   NOT USED

Leave the unsigned remainder   u2   and unsigned quotient   u3   from the unsigned double dividend   ud   and unsigned divisor   u1 .

Defined in: fig-FORTH

Implementation:

: U/   U/MOD ;

Source usage: None.

Example:

45000.   36000   U/

Divide the double dividend by the single divisor, printing the quotient and remainder.   U/ treats all quantities as unsigned. A signed division would return different results for the same inputs.

Comment: This obsolete synonym for U/MOD may appear in older programs.

Perform the unsigned division of double number   ud1   by   un2
, leaving the remainder   un3 , and quotient   un4 .   All values
are unsigned.

Pronounced: u-divide-mod

Defined in: FORTH-79, STARTING FORTH

Implementation:

8080:

```
CODE U/MOD    4 H LXI   SP DAD   M E MOV   C M MOV
        H INX   M D MOV   B M MOV   B POP   H POP
        L A MOV   C SUB   H A MOV   B SBB   USLA1   JC
        FFFF H LXI   FFFF D LXI   USLA7 JMP
    HERE LABEL USLA1   10 A MVI
    HERE LABEL USLA2   H DAD   RAL   XCHG
        H DAD   USLA3 JNC   D INX   A ANA
    HERE LABEL USLA3   XCHG   RAR   PSW PUSH
        USLA4 JNC   L A MOV   C SUB   A L MOV
        H A MOV   B SBB   A H MOV   USLA5 JMP
    HERE LABEL USLA4   L A MOV   C SUB   A L MOV
        H A MOV   B SBB   A H MOV   USLA5 JNC   B DAD
        D DCX
    HERE LABEL USLA5   D INX
    HERE LABEL USLA6   PSW POP   A DCR   USLA2 JNZ
    HERE LABEL USLA7   B POP   H PUSH   D PUSH
        NEXT JMP   END-CODE
```

Source usage: M/   M/MOD

Example:

45000. 36000   U/MOD   . .

   Divide the double dividend by the single divisor, printing the
quotient   and   remainder.   U/MOD   treats   all   quantities   as
unsigned.   A   signed   division   such   as   M/   would   return
different results for the same inputs.

Comment: All division, signed and unsigned, may be expressed
in terms of   U/MOD .

U<   un1   un2   ---   flag   150   MVP-FORTH

Leave the flag representing the magnitude comparison of   un1
<   un2   where   un1   and   un2   are treated as 16 bit unsigned
integers.

Pronounced: u-less-than

Defined in: FORTH-79, STARTING FORTH

Implementation:

: U<   0 SWAP 0 D< ;

Source usage: ?STACK   FORGET   ROLL

Example:

45000   35000   U<

   Enter two large values which if signed would be negative, and
compare them leaving a flag on the stack, in this case a   0   for
false.

Comment: This ideogram is useful when dealing with addresses
which may otherwise confuse negative values.

UNTIL   I, C, 237   MVP-FORTH
          addr n ---   (compiling)
                fl ---   (executing)

Within a colon-definition, mark the end of a   BEGIN-UNTIL
loop, which will terminate based on a flag. If   flag   is true,
the loop is terminated.   If   flag   is false, execution returns
to the first word after   BEGIN .   BEGIN-UNTIL   structures
may be nested.

Defined in: FORTH-79, fig-FORTH, STARTING FORTH

Implementation:

: UNTIL   1   ?PAIRS
    COMPILE   0BRANCH   HERE - , ;
IMMEDIATE

Source usage: Many.

Example:

: TEST   -1   BEGIN   1+   DUP   .   DUP   9 =
              UNTIL   DROP ;

The definition will print the digits 0 through 9.

Comment: Older versions of FORTH use the obsolete synonym,
END.

UP   --- addr   MVP-FORTH

A constant returning a pointer to the cell in low memory which
holds the pointer to the user area. It is used in the 8080/Z80
implementation and some others.

Defined in: MVP-FORTH

Implementation:

UP   CONSTANT   UP

(The cross-compiler uses the label UP to define the constant
UP.)

Source usage: None.

Example:

' SP0   @ UP @ + @ U.

   This contrived example will print the value in the user
variable SP0.

Comment: Multi-user FORTH systems maintain a separate set
of user variables for each terminal task. Switching between
tasks involves saving and restoring CPU registers and
selecting a new user area. In 8080/Z80 systems, a user area is
activated by storing its starting addres into the cell at UP.

UPDATE   ---   229 MVP-FORTH

Mark the most recently referenced block as modified. The
block will subsequently be automatically transferred to mass
storage should its memory buffer be needed for storage of a
different block, or upon execution of SAVE- BUFFERS.

Defined in: FORTH-79, fig-FORTH, STARTING FORTH

Implementation:

: UPDATE   PREV @ @ 8000 OR PREV @ ! ;

Source usage: CLEAR

Example:

50 BLOCK   UPDATE

Enter a block number and then BLOCK followed by this ideogram, ensuring that this block will be written back to disk when the buffer's space is needed. The buffer address from BLOCK remains on the stack unchanged.

Comment: This ideogram is particularly useful when blocks are accessed for the addition or modification of data rather than as source screens.

USE   --- addr   MVP-FORTH

A variable containing the address of the block buffer to use next, as the least recently written.

Defined in: fig-FORTH

Implementation:

VARIABLE USE   FIRST USE !

Source usage: ?LOADING   BUFFER   COLD   <R/W>
                 SET-IO

Example:

```
: <R/W>    USE  @  >R   ROT   USE  !  SWAP   MAX-DRV   0
   DO   I   DR-DEN   DENSITY   !
        DUP   BPDRV   -  -1  >
        IF   BPDRV  -  I  1+   MAX-DRV   =
            IF   R>  R>   DDROP   R>   USE  !
               1  ABORT" BLOCK OUT OF RANGE"   THEN
        ELSE   I   DRIVE   !  SET-DRIVE   LEAVE
        THEN
   LOOP   SPBLK   *   SPBLK   0
   DO    DDUP   T&SCALC   SET-IO
      IF   SEC-READ
      ELSE   SEC-WRITE
      THEN   1+   HDBT   4   -   SPBLK   /   USE   +!
   LOOP
   DDROP   R>  USE  !  ;
```

This definition is from the MVP-FORTH implementation.

Comment: This ideogram is important to the implementation dependent block I/O and buffer management routines, but it is of little value to applications.

USER   n ---   MVP-FORTH

A defining word which creates a user variable <name>.   n is

the cell offset within the user area where the value for   <name>
is stored. Execution of   <name>   leaves its absolute user
area storage address.

Form: n   USER   <name>

Defined in: FORTH-79(R), fig-FORTH

Implementation:

8080:

```
: USER    CONSTANT   ;CODE
   D  INX   XCHG   M  E  MOV   0  D  MVI    UP  LHLD
   D  DAD    HPUSH  JMP    END-CODE
```

Source usage: Many.

Example:

08   USER   SP0

   Enter the offset from the beginning of the user field, followed
by the ideogram and then the name being assigned to that
location.

Comment: A number of variables present in FORTH-79 could be
defined with this construction, though the ideogram is not a
part of the 79-STANDARD vocabulary.   It is, however, in the
Reference Word Set and is customarily utilized, headerless if
necessary.   A group of them is usually initialized with data
from low memory when FORTH is started.   In MVP-FORTH and
in most implementations of fig-FORTH, a block of 64 bytes is
reserved for the user area.   The use of cells in the FORTH-
79(R) definition is interpreted to mean two bytes but not that
word boundaries are required.   The unused portion of this area
is available to the programmer.

VARIABLE   ---   227   MVP-FORTH

A defining word to create a dictionary entry for   <name> and
allot two bytes for storage in the parameter field.   The
application must initialize the stored value.   When   <name>
is later executed, it will place the storage address on the
stack.

Form: VARIABLE   <name>

Defined in: FORTH-79, fig-FORTH, STARTING FORTH

Implementation:

```
: VARIABLE   CREATE  2  ALLOT  ;
```

Source usage: Many.

Example:

```
VARIABLE  NEW-VALUE   0  NEW-VALUE  !
```

This ideogram will define the name of a new variable which is then initialized.

Comment: There is a significant difference between the current FORTH-79 function of this ideogram and that used by fig-FORTH. The MVP-FORTH implementation conforms with FORTH-79. The current function of this ideogram is to create a dictionary space for a variable and leave its contents undetermined. Thus all variables must be initialized after being defined. This differs from fig-FORTH in which the defined function of VARIABLE used the top value on the stack to initialize the variable at creation time.

VLIST   ---   MVP-FORTH - UTILITY

List the word names of the CONTEXT vocabulary starting with the most recent definition.

Defined in: FORTH-79(R), fig-FORTH

Implementation:

```
: VLIST   C/L   OUT  !  CONTEXT  @  @
    BEGIN   C/L   OUT  @  -  OVER  C@
    1F   AND  4  +  <
    IF   CR  0  OUT  !  THEN
    DUP  ID.  SPACE  SPACE  PFA  4  -  @  DUP
    NOT  PAUSE  ?TERMINAL  OR
  UNTIL   DROP ;
```

Source usage: None.

Example:

VLIST

This ideogram will start a printing of the CONTEXT vocabulary.

Comment: In most fig-FORTH based implementations, pressing any key will terminate the listing. The MVP-FORTH

version incorporates a PAUSE feature, by which pressing any
key will freeze the display. Once suspended, the VLIST may be
resumed by a single keystroke, or aborted by striking any two
keys in rapid succession.

VOC-LINK   --- addr   U   MVP-FORTH

A user variable containing the address of a field in the
definition of the most recently created vocabulary. All
vocabulary names are linked by these fields to allow control for
FORGETting through multiple vocabularies.

Defined in: fig-FORTH

Implementation:

14 USER VOC-LINK

Source usage: FORGET VOCABULARY

Example:

VOC-LINK   @   U.

   Get the address of the user variable, fetch its value and print
it.

Comment: An implementation dependent variable not available
in all versions of FORTH.

VOCABULARY   ---   MVP-FORTH

A defining word to create (in the CURRENT vocabulary) a
dictionary entry for <name>, which specifies a new ordered list
of word definitions. Subsequent execution of <name> will make
it the CONTEXT vocabulary. When <name> becomes the
CURRENT vocabulary (see DEFINITIONS), new definitions
will be created in that list. In lieu of any further
specifications, new vocabularies 'chain' to FORTH. That is,
when a dictionary search through a vocabulary is exhausted,
FORTH will be searched.

Form: VOCABULARY <name>

Defined in: FORTH-79, fig-FORTH, STARTING FORTH

Implementation:

: VOCABULARY   'VOCABULARY @ EXECUTE ;

Source usage: None.

Example:

VOCABULARY   EDITOR

   Create a new vocabulary name in FORTH forth the EDITOR.

Comment: Though in fig-FORTH daughter vocabularies may be
chained to parent vocabularies before finally chaining to
FORTH, the common interpretation of FORTH-79 is that all
vocabularies must chain only to FORTH.   Although there are
some applications in which multiple daughter vocabularies
might be desirable, in general the consensus of many FORTH
programmers is that the number of vocabularies should be kept a
minimum.
      For convenience VOCABULARY is vectored.   The strict
FORTH-79 implementation has the code field address of the
run-time   routine   <VOCABULARY79>   in   the   variable
'VOCABULARY. Those   desiring   a   different   functional
definition may write their own and place that code field address
in 'VOCABULARY.   The function in fig-FORTH may be easily
substituted   by   placing   the   code   field   address   of
<VOCABULARYFIG> which is implemented in MVP-FORTH, into
'VOCABULARY.

WARM   ---   NOT USED

Restart FORTH with EMPTY-BUFFERS .

Defined in: fig-FORTH (8080)
Implementation:

: WARM   EMPTY-BUFFERS   ABORT ;

Source usage: None.

Example:

WARM

   This ideogram will simply clear the buffers and restart
FORTH.

Comment: As implemented in the 8080 version of fig-FORTH,
this ideogram simply empties the buffers and clears the stack.
Nothing in the dictionary is changed.

A user variable containing a flag which enables the output of selected non-fatal error messages.

Defined in: MVP-FORTH

Implementation:

OE   USER   WARNING

Source usage: CREATE

Example:

0   WARNING   !

   Suppress the printing of system warning messages.

(This ideogram is not implemented in MVP-FORTH)

Comment: Within the MVP-FORTH nucleus, this flag controls the "ISN'T UNIQUE" message. It is available for the programmer's use. Note that fig-FORTH uses this user variable in a completely different manner: to control the source of all message texts.

Display the last character string parsed by the text interpreter, along with the line containing it. If loading, the screen and line numbers are printed.

Defined in: MVP-FORTH

Implementation:

```
: WHERE    BLK  @
    IF   BLK   @  DUP  SCR  !  CR   CR   ." SCR# "
        DUP  .  >IN  @  3FF  MIN  C/L  /MOD  DUP
        ." LINE# "  .  C/L  *  ROT  BLOCK  +
        CR   CR   C/L  -TRAILING  TYPE
        >IN  @  3FF  >  +
    ELSE    >IN  @
    THEN  CR  HERE  C@  DUP  >R  -  HERE  R@  +
    1+  C@  20  =
    IF   1-  THEN  SPACES  R>  0
    DO   5E  EMIT  LOOP  ;
```

Source usage: <ABORT">

Example:

```
: <ABORT">
   IF  WHERE  CR  R@  COUNT  TYPE  SP!  QUIT
   ELSE  R>  DUP C@  +  1+  >R  THEN  ;
```

This example from the MVP-FORTH source code shows how ABORT" tells you exactly where the text interpreter encountered an error.

Comment: WHERE makes use of the count and character string stored at HERE, to identify the last ideogram interpreted. It is useful for locating the source of common errors during LOADing or terminal interpretation, but is no substitute for good debugging skills.

WHILE   flag   ---   I, C, 149   MVP-FORTH

Used in a colon-definition to select conditional execution based on the flag. On a true flag, continue execution through to REPEAT, which then returns back to just after BEGIN. On a false flag, skip execution to just after REPEAT, exiting the structure.

Form: BEGIN ... flag WHILE ... REPEAT

Defined in: FORTH-79, fig-FORTH, STARTING FORTH

Implementation:

```
: WHILE   [COMPILE]
   IF  2+  ;  IMMEDIATE
```

Source usage: CONVERT FORGET

Example:

```
: TEST    0  BEGIN  DUP  10  <
   WHILE  DUP  .  1+  REPEAT  DROP  ;
```

The definition illustrates this ideogram in another BEGIN construct which will type the digits 0 through 9.

Comment: WHILE makes its exit decision in the middle of the loop. Thus the test can be made and the loop exited before passing through the body of the loop at all. Compare this with the DO-LOOP and BEGIN-UNTIL loops which always make at least one complete pass through the body of the loop before testing the exit criterion.

WIDTH   --- addr   MVP-FORTH

In fig-FORTH, a user variable containing the maximum number
of letters saved in the compilation of a definition's name. It
must be 1 through 31, with a default value of 31. The name
character count and its natural characters are saved, up to the
value in WIDTH. The value may be changed at any time within
the above limits.

Defined in: fig-FORTH

Implementation:

0C   USER   WIDTH

Source usage: CREATE

Example:

        WIDTH   @   .

    Get the address of this user variable, then fetch its value and
print it to show the present maximum size of a name in the
dictionary header.

Comment: Though ideograms may have up to 31 characters in
FORTH-79, the MVP-FORTH implementation gives you the
option of truncating them to the length specified in this user
variable.

WORD   char --- addr   181   MVP-FORTH

Receive characters from the input stream until the non-zero
delimiting character is encountered or the input stream is
exhausted, ignoring leading delimiters. The characters are
stored as a packed string with the character count in the first
character position. The actual delimiter encountered (char or
null) is stored at the end of the text but not included in the
count. If the input stream was exhausted as WORD is
called, then a zero length will result. The address of the
beginning of this packed string is left on the stack.

Defined in: FORTH-79, fig-FORTH, STARTING FORTH

Implementation:

: WORD   'WORD   @   EXECUTE   ;

Source usage: (."   -FIND   CREATE   FORGET

Example:

```
: INPUT  ." Input an integer  -- "
  QUERY  BL  WORD  NUMBER  DROP  ;
```

The definition provides for a prompt and then a pause for the
operator to input the requested integer. Then the input
character stream is parsed with this ideogram, converted to a
double precision value and reduced to a single precision value
left on the stack.

Comment: Care must be taken in moving source code from fig-
FORTH to FORTH-79 which includes the ideogram WORD. In
FORTH-79, WORD leaves the address of HERE on the top of the
stack. Also, while in fig-FORTH the string is stored at
HERE, in FORTH-79 another buffer may be used. Because of
the possible variations, this ideogram utilizes an execution
vector which will permit easy redefinition. It defaults to
<WORD>.

X   ---   MVP-FORTH

This is a pseudonym for the "null" or dictionary entry for a name
of one character of ASCII null. It is the execution procedure
to terminate interpretation of a line of text from the terminal or
within a disk buffer, as both buffers always have a null at the
end.

Defined in: fig-FORTH

Implementation:

```
: X    BLK @
  IF  STATE @  ?STREAM  THEN
  R>  DROP  ;  IMMEDIATE  IS-X
```

Source usage: None.

Example:

This ideogram is not available to the programmer.

Comment: This somewhat confusing word is defined in the
INSTALLATION MANUAL but is not included in FORTH-79.
Defining the null character as an ideogram is a clever trick for
telling <INTERPRET> that the end of a buffer has been reached.
Note the intentionally unbalanced use of R> . This ideogram
IS-X, is part of the CROSS-COMPILER. It locates the " X "
in the latest definition's dictionary and overwrites it with a
null. The sequence " 0 ' X NFA 1+ C! " would
accomplish the same thing.

XOR   n1 n2 --- n3   174   MVP-FORTH

Leave the bitwise exclusive-or of two numbers.

Pronounced: x-or

Defined in: FORTH-79, fig-FORTH

Implementation:

8080:

```
CODE XOR    D POP   H POP   E A MOV   L XRA
    A L MOV   D A MOV   H XRA   A H MOV
    HPUSH JMP   END-CODE
```

Source usage: M/ M*

Example:

HEX   20 10   XOR   DECIMAL

   The example does a logical exclusive-or operation on the bit
patterns which are perhaps more easily recognized when in hex.
The two values are replaced by the result on the stack.

Comment: This ideogram is a common logical operator.

[---   I, 125   MVP-FORTH

End the compilation mode.   The text from the input stream is
subsequently executed.   See   ]

Pronounced: left-bracket

Defined in: FORTH-79, fig-FORTH, STARTING FORTH

Implementation:

: [0 STATE ! ;   IMMEDIATE

Source usage: ;   QUIT

Example:

: ADD-RECORDLENGTH   [BLOCKSIZE
    RECORDS-PER-BLOCK   /] LITERAL + ;

   This ideogram   [suspends compilation so that the division of two constants is done, only once, at compile time. Of course, the constants will have been defined earlier.

Comment: Allows switching out of the compile mode within a definition. It can be used for compile-time calculation, SMUDGE-ing the name of a recursive definition, or anything else. Take care, however not to interfere with the compiler's use of the stack, as inside IF or BEGIN constructs.

[']   ---   I, C,   MVP-FORTH - SUPPLEMENTAL

Used in a colon definition to compile the parameter field address of the next word in the input stream as a literal.

Form: ---   (compile time)
         --- adr   (run time)

Pronounced: bracket-tick-bracket

Defined in: STARTING FORTH

Implementation:

: ['] ?COMP [COMPILE] ' ;   IMMEDIATE

Source usage: None.

Example:

: TEST   ['] B/BUF ;

The parameter field address of B/BUF is compiled as a literal into the definition of TEST. TEST will behave like a constant, always pushing the same literal value onto the stack.

Comment: This form of ' is used in colon definitions apparently to keep things straight in poly-FORTH. Note that the address returned by ['] should not be EXECUTEd in this version until it has been adjusted by the operator CFA.

[COMPILE]   ---   I, C, 179   MVP-FORTH

Used in a colon-definition to force compilation of the following word. This allows compilation of an IMMEDIATE word when it would otherwise be executed.

Form: [COMPILE]   <name>

Pronounced: bracket-compile

Defined in: FORTH-79, fig-FORTH, STARTING FORTH

Implementation:

```
: [COMPILE]   ?COMP  -FIND  NOT
   ABORT" NOT FOUND" DROP  CFA  ,  ;
IMMEDIATE
```

Source usage: Many.

Example:

```
: ENDIF   [COMPILE]  THEN  ;  IMMEDIATE
```

The example illustrates the renaming of an ideogram which is marked immediate.

Comment: This is another ideogram which gives versatility to the defining ideograms in FORTH. It overrides an ideogram's precedence bit.

\   ---   MVP-FORTH - UTILITY
Ignore all subsequent characters on this line. Begin interpretation with the next line. May be used only while loading.

Pronounced: back-slash

Implementation:

```
: \    ?LOADING  >IN  @  C/L  /  1+
   C/L  *  >IN  !  ;
IMMEDIATE
```

Source usage: None.

Example:

```
\   THIS IS A COMMENT
```

The interpreter will ignore this text.

Comment: This ideogram offers an alternative method for commenting a source program. While it has the advantage of not requiring a closing delimiter, it is non-standard and works only for the 16 x 64 screen format.

]   ---   126   MVP-FORTH

Set the compilation mode. The text from the input stream is subsequently compiled.   See [.

Pronounced: right-bracket

Defined in: FORTH-79, fig-FORTH, STARTING FORTH

Implementation:

:]   CO STATE ! ;

Source usage: :

Example:

: ADD-RECORDLENGTH   [BLOCKSIZE
    RECORDS-PER-BLOCK   /] LITERAL + ;

    This ideogram,] , resumes compilation after a compile-time
calculation has been performed.

Comment: This ideogram works with [to allow access to
FORTH's execution-time functions within a colon definition.
Take care not to disturb stack data being used by the compiler,
as in IF, BEGIN and DO-LOOP conditional constructs.

FORTH-79 STANDARD

A PUBLICATION OF THE FORTH STANDARDS TEAM

0.   FOREWORD

The computer language FORTH was created by Mr. Charles Moore, as an
extensible, multi-level environment containing elements of an operating system,
a machine monitor, and facilities for program development and testing.

This Standard is a direct descendant of FORTH-77, a work of the FORTH
Users Group (Europe). The constituency of the Standards Team has steadily
broadened, to include users of an increasing variety of host computers.

1.   PURPOSE

The purpose of this FORTH Standard is to allow transportability of standard
FORTH programs in source form among standard FORTH systems. A standard program
shall execute equivalently on all standard FORTH systems.

2.   SCOPE

This standard shall apply to any Standard FORTH program executing on any
Standard FORTH system, provided sufficient computer resources (memory, mass
storage) are available.

3.   ORGANIZATION

This standard consists of:

1)   General Text
2)   Definitions of Terms
3)   Required Word Set
4)   Extension Word Sets

Word sets may be subdivided for conceptual purposes by function:

      Nucleus
      Interpreter
      Compiler
      Devices

Tradeoffs

When conflicting choices must be made, the following order shall guide the Standards Team.

1) Functional correctness
   - known bounds, non-ambiguous.

2) Portability
   - repeatable results when transported among Standard systems.

3) Simplicity.

4) Naming clarity
   - uniformity of expression. Descriptive names are preferred over procedural. (i.e., [COMPILE] rather than 'C, and ALLOT rather than DP+! .)

5) Generality.

6) Execution speed.

7) Memory compactness.

8) Compilation speed.

9) Historical continuity.

10) Pronounceability.

11) Teachability.

4. DEFINITIONS OF TERMS

These definitions, when in lower case, are terms used within this Standard. They present terms as specifically used within FORTH.

address, byte

An unsigned number that locates an 8-bit byte in a standard FORTH address space over {0..65,535}. It may be a native machine address or a representation on a virtual machine, locating the 'addr-th' byte within the virtual byte address space. Address arithmetic is modulo 65,536 without overflow.

address, compilation

The numerical value equivalent to a FORTH word definition, which is compiled for that definition. The address interpreter uses this value to locate the machine code corresponding to each definition. (May also be called the code field address.)

address, native machine

The natural address representation of the host computer.

address, parameter field

The address of the first byte of memory associated with a word definition for the storage of compilation addresses (in a colon-definition), numeric data and text characters.

arithmetic

All integer arithmetic is performed with signed 16 or 32 bit two's complement results, unless noted.

block

The unit of data from mass storage, referenced by block number. A block must contain 1024 bytes regardless of the minimum data unit read/written from mass storage. The translation from block number to device and physical record is a function of the implementation.

block buffer

A memory area where a mass storage block is maintained.

byte

An assembly of 8 bits. In reference to memory, it is the storage capacity for 8 bits.

cell

A 16-bit memory location. The n-th cell contains the 2n-th and (2n+1)-th byte of the FORTH address space. The byte order is presently unspecified.

character

A 7-bit number which represents a terminal character. The ASCII character set is considered standard. When contained in a larger field, the higher order bits are zero.

compilation

The action of accepting text words from the input stream and placing corresponding compilation addresses in a new dictionary entry.

defining word

A word that, when executed, creates a new dictionary entry. The new word name is taken from the input stream. If the input stream is exhausted before the new name is available, an error condition exists. Common defining words are:

    : CONSTANT CREATE

definition

See 'word definition'.

dictionary

A structure of word definitions in a computer memory. In systems with a text interpreter, the dictionary entries are organized in vocabularies to enable location by name. The dictionary is extensible, growing toward high memory.

equivalent execution

For the execution of a standard program, a set of non-time dependent inputs will produce the same non-time dependent outputs on any FORTH Standard System with sufficient resources to execute the program. Only standard source code will be transportable.

error condition

An exceptional condition which requires action by the system other than the expected function. Actions may be:

1. ignore, and continue

2. display a message

3. execute a particular word

4. interpret a block

5. return control to the text interpreter

A Standard System shall be provided with a tabulation of the action taken for all specified error conditions.
General error conditions:

1. input stream exhausted before a required <name>.

2. empty stack and full stack for the text interpreter.

3. an unknown word, not a valid number for the text interpreter.

4. compilation of incorrectly nested conditionals.

5. interpretation of words restricted to compilation.

6. FORGETing within the system to a point that removes a word required for correct execution.

7. insufficient space remaining in the dictionary.

false

A zero number represents the false condition flag.

flag

A number that may have two logical states, zero and non-zero. These are named 'true' = non-zero, and 'false' = zero. Standard word definitions leave 1 for true, 0 for false.

glossary

A set of word definitions given in a natural language describing the corresponding computer execution action.

immediate word

A word defined to automatically execute when encountered during compilation, which handles exception cases to the usual compilation. See IF LITERAL ." etc.

input stream

A sequence of characters available to the system, for processing by the text interpreter. The input stream conventionally may be taken from a terminal (via the terminal input buffer) and mass storage (via a block buffer). >IN and BLK specify the input stream. Words using or altering >IN and BLK are responsible for maintaining and restoring control of the input stream.

interpreter, address

The (set of) word definitions which interprets (sequences of) FORTH compilation addresses by executing the word definition specified for each one.

interpreter, text

The (set of) word definitions that repeatedly accepts a word name from the input stream, locates the corresponding dictionary entry, and starts the address interpreter to execute it. Text in the input stream interpreted as a number leaves the corresponding value on the data stack. When in the compile mode, the addresses of FORTH words are compiled into the dictionary for later interpretation by the address interpreter. In this case, numbers are compiled, to be placed on the data stack when later interpreted. Numbers shall be accepted unsigned or negatively signed, according to BASE.

load

The acceptance of text from a mass storage device and execution of the dictionary definition of the words encountered. This is the general method for compilation of new definitions into the dictionary.

mass storage

Data is read from mass storage in the form of 1024 byte blocks. This data is held in block buffers. When indicated as UPDATEd (modified) data will be ultimately written to mass storage.

number

When values exist within a larger field, the high order bits are zero. When stored in memory the byte order of a number is unspecified.

type	range	minimum field
bit	0..1	1
character	0..127	7
byte	0..255	8
number	-32,768..32,767	16
positive number	0..32,767	16
unsigned number	0..65,535	16
double number	-2,147,483,648.. 2,147,483,647	32
positive double number	0..2,147,483,647	32
unsigned double number	0..4,294,967,295	32

When represented on the stack, the higher 16-bits (with sign) of a double number are most accessible. When in memory the higher 16-bits are at the lower address. Storage extends over four bytes toward high memory. The byte order within each 16-bit field is unspecified.

output, pictured

The use of numeric output primitives, which convert numerical values into text strings. The operators are used in a sequence which resembles a symbolic 'picture' of the desired text format. Conversion proceeds from low digit to high, from high memory to low.

program

A complete specification of execution to achieve a specific function (application task) expressed in FORTH source code form.

return

The means of terminating text from the input stream. (Conventionally a null (ASCII 0) indicates end of text in the input stream. This character is left by the 'return' key actuation of the operator's terminal, as an absolute stopper to text interpretation.)

screen

Textual data arranged for editing. By convention, a screen consists of 16 lines (numbered 0 thru 15) of 64 characters each. Screens usually contain program source text, but may be used to view mass storage data. The first byte of a screen occupies the first byte of a mass storage block, which is the beginning point for text interpretation during a load.

source definition

Text consisting of word names suitable for execution by the text interpreter. Such text is usually arranged in screens and maintained on a mass storage device.

stack, data

A last in, first out list consisting of 16-bit binary values. This stack is primarily used to hold intermediate values during execution of word definitions. Stack values may represent numbers, characters, addresses, boolean values, etc.

When the name 'stack' is used, it implies the data stack.

stack, return

A last in, first out list which contains the machine addresses of word definitions whose execution has not been completed by the address interpreter. As a word definition passes control to another definition, the return point is placed on the return stack.

The return stack may cautiously be used for other values, such as loop control parameters, and for pointers for interpretation of text.

string

A sequence of 8-bit bytes containing ASCII characters, located in memory by an initial byte address and byte count.

transportability

This term indicates that equivalent execution results when a program is executed on other than the system on which it was created. See 'equivalent execution'.

true

A non-zero value represents the true condition flag. Any non-zero value will be accepted by a standard word as 'true'; all standard words return one when leaving a 'true' flag.

user area

An area in memory which contains the storage for user variables.

variables, user

So that the words of the FORTH vocabulary may be re-entrant (to different users), a copy of each system variable is maintained in the user area.

vocabulary

An ordered list of word definitions. Vocabulary lists are an advantage in reducing dictionary search time and in separating different word definitions that may carry the same name.

word

A sequence of characters terminated by at least one blank (or 'return'). Words are usually obtained via the input stream, from a terminal or mass storage device.

word definition

A named FORTH execution procedure compiled into the dictionary. Its execution may be defined in terms of machine code, as a sequence of compilation addresses or other compiled words. If named, it may be located by specifying this name and the vocabulary in which it is located.

word name

The name of a word definition. Standard names must be distinguished by their length and first thirty-one characters, and may not contain an ASCII null, blank, or 'return'.

word set

A group of FORTH word definitions listed by common characteristics. The standard word sets consist of:

        Required Word Set
            Nucleus Words
            Interpreter Words
            Compiler Words
            Device Words

        Extension Word Sets
            32-bit Word Set
            Assembler Word Set

    Included as reference material only:
        Reference Word Set

word set, compiler

Words which add new procedures to the dictionary or aid compilation by adding compilation addresses or data structures to the dictionary.

word set, devices

Words which allow access to mass storage and computer peripheral devices.

word set, interpreter

Words which support interpretation of text input from a terminal or mass storage by execution of corresponding dictionary entries, vocabularies, and terminal output.

word set, nucleus

The FORTH words generally defined in machine code that create the stacks and fundamental stack operators (virtual FORTH machine).

word set, reference

This set of words is provided as a reference document only, as a set of formerly standardized words and candidate words for standardization.

word set, required

The minimum words needed to compile and execute all Standard Programs.

word, standard

A named FORTH procedure definition, formally reviewed and accepted by the Standards Team. A serial number identifier {100..999} indicates a Standard Word. A functional alteration of a Standard Word will require assignment of a new serial number identifier.

The serial number identifier has no required use, other than to correlate the definition name with its unique Standard definition.

5.   REFERENCES

The following documents are considered to be a portion of this Standard:

American Standard Code for Information Interchange, American National Standards Institute, X3.4-1968

Webster's Collegiate Dictionary shall be used to resolve conflicts in spelling and English word usage.

The following documents are noted as pertinent to the FORTH-79 Standard, but are not part of this Standard.

FORTH-77, FORTH Users Group, FST-780314

FORTH-78, FORTH International Standards Team

6.   REQUIREMENTS

6.1   Documentation Requirements

Each Standard System and Standard Program shall be accompanied by a statement of the minimum (byte) requirements for:

1.   System dictionary space

2.   Application dictionary space

3.   Data stack

4.   Return stack

5.   Mass storage contiguous block quantity required

6.   An operator's terminal.

Each Standard System shall be provided with a statement of the system action upon each of the error conditions as identified in this Standard.

6.2   Testing Requirements

The following host computer configuration is specified as a minimum environment for testing against this Standard. Applications may require different capacities.

1.   2000 bytes of memory for application dictionary

2.   Data stack of 64 bytes

3.   Return stack of 48 bytes

4.   Mass storage capacity of 32 blocks, numbered 0 through 31

5.   One ASCII input/output device acting as an operator's terminal.

7. COMPLIANCE AND LABELING

The FORTH Standards Team hereby specifies the requirements for labeling of systems and applications so that the conditions for program portability may be established.

A system may use the specified labeling if it complies with the terms of this Standard, and meets the particular Word Set definitions.

A Standard Program (application) may use the specified labeling if it utilizes the specified standard system according to this Standard, and executes equivalently on any such system.

FORTH Standard

A system may be labeled 'FORTH-79 Standard' if it includes all of the Required Word Set in either source or object form, and complies with the text of this Standard. After executing "79-STANDARD" the dictionary must contain all of the Required Word Set in the vocabulary FORTH, as specified in this Standard.

Standard Sub-set

A system may be labeled 'FORTH-79 Standard Sub-set' if it includes a portion of the Required Word Set, and complies with the remaining text of this standard. However, no Required Word may be present with a non-standard definition.

Standard with Extensions

A system may be labeled 'FORTH-79 Standard with <name> Standard Extension(s)' if it comprises a FORTH-79 Standard System and one or more Standard Extension Word Set(s). The designation would be in the form:

'FORTH-79 Standard with Double-Number Standard Extensions'

A FORTH Standard program may reference only the definitions of the Required Word Set, and definitions which are subsequently defined in terms of these words.   Furthermore, a FORTH Standard program must use the standard words as required by any conventions of this Standard.   Equivalent execution must result from Standard programs.

The FORTH system may share the dictionary space with the user's application, and the native addressing protocol of the host computer is beyond the scope of this Standard.

Therefore, in a Standard program, the user may only operate on data which was stored by the application.   No exceptions!

A Standard Program may address:

1.   parameter fields of variables, constants and DOES> words.   A DOES> word's parameter field may only be addressed with respect to the address left by DOES> , itself.

2.   dictionary space ALLOTed.

3.   data in mass storage block buffers.   (Note restriction in BLOCK on latest buffer addressing.)

4.   the user area and PAD.

A Standard Program may NOT address:

1.   directly into the data or return stacks.

2.   into a definition's name field, link field, or code field.

3.   into a definition's parameter field if not stored by the application.

Further usage requirements are expected to be added for transporting programs between standard systems.

FORTH Standard definitions have a serial number assigned, in the range 100 thru 999.   Neither a Standard System nor Standard Program may redefine these word names, within the FORTH vocabulary.

9. GLOSSARY NOTATION

Order

The Glossary definitions are listed in ASCII alphabetical order.

Stack Notation

The first line of each entry describes the execution of the definition:

> stack parameters before execution
> ─── showing point of execution
> stack parameters after execution
>
> i.e., before ─── after

In this notation, the top of the stack is to the right. Words may also be shown in context, when appropriate.

Attributes

Capitalized symbols indicate attributes of the defined words:

C   The word may only be used within a colon-definition.

I   Indicates that the word is IMMEDIATE and will execute during compilation, unless special action is taken.

U   A user variable.

Capitalization

Word names as used within the dictionary are conventionally written in upper case characters. Within this Standard lower case will be used when reference is made to the run-time machine code, not directly accessible, i.e., VARIABLE is the user word to create a variable. Each use of that variable makes use of a code sequence 'variable' which executes the function of the particular variable.

Pronunciation

The natural language pronunciation of FORTH names is given in double quotes (").

Stack Parameters

Unless otherwise stated, all references to numbers apply to 16-bit signed integers.

The implied range of values is shown as {from..to}. The content of an address is shown by double curly brackets, particularly for the contents of variables. i.e., BASE {{2..70}}

addr   {0..65,535}

A value representing the address of a byte, within the FORTH standard memory space. This addressed byte may represent the first byte of a larger data field in memory.

byte   {0..255}

A value representing an 8 bit byte. When in a larger field, the higher bits are zero.

char   {0..127}

A value representing a 7 bit ASCII character code. When in a larger field, the higher bits are zero.

d   {-2,147,483,648..2,147,483,647}

32 bit signed 'double' number. The most significant 16-bits, with sign, is most accessible on the stack.

flag

A numerical value with two logical states; 0= false, non-zero = true.

n   {-32,768..32,767}

16 bit signed integer number.

Any other symbol refers to an arbitrary signed 16-bit integer in the range {-32,768..32,767}, unless otherwise noted.

Input Text

<name>

An arbitrary FORTH word accepted from the input stream. This notation refers to text from the input stream, not to values on the data stack. If the input stream is exhausted before encountering <name>, an error condition exists.

10. REQUIRED WORD SET

The words of the Required Word Set are grouped to show like character-istics. No implementation requirements should be inferred from this grouping.

Nucleus Words

```
!  *  */  */MOD  +  +!  +loop  -  /
/MOD  0<  0=  0>  1+  1-  2+  2-  <
=  >  >R  ?DUP  @  ABS  AND  begin  C!
C@  colon  CMOVE  constant  create  D+
D<  DEPTH  DNEGATE  do  does>
DROP  DUP  else  EXECUTE  EXIT  FILL  I
if  J  LEAVE  literal  loop  MAX  MIN
MOD  MOVE  NEGATE  NOT  OR  OVER  PICK
R>  R@  repeat  ROLL  ROT  semicolon
SWAP  then  U*  U/  U<  until  variable
while  XOR
```

(note that the lower case entries refer to just the run-time code corresponding to a compiling word.)

Interpreter Words

```
#  #>  #S  '  (  -TRAILING  .
79-STANDARD  <#  >IN  ?  ABORT  BASE  BLK
CONTEXT  CONVERT  COUNT  CR  CURRENT
DECIMAL  EMIT  EXPECT  FIND  FORTH  HERE
HOLD  KEY  PAD  QUERY  QUIT  SIGN  SPACE
SPACES  TYPE  U.  WORD
```

Compiler Words

```
+LOOP  ,  ."  :  ;  ALLOT  BEGIN
COMPILE  CONSTANT  CREATE  DEFINITIONS  DO
DOES>  ELSE  FORGET  IF  IMMEDIATE
LITERAL  LOOP  REPEAT  STATE  THEN  UNTIL
VARIABLE  VOCABULARY  WHILE  [  [COMPILE]  ]
```

Device Words

```
BLOCK  BUFFER  EMPTY-BUFFERS  LIST
LOAD  SAVE-BUFFERS  SCR  UPDATE
```

* In CP/M MVP-FORTH Kernel
++ Added in CP/M FORTH+++.COM

ALL ABOUT FORTH

ALL ABOUT FORTH

FORTH-79 HANDY REFERENCE

Stack inputs and outputs are shown; top of stack on right. See operand key at bottom.

STACK MANIPULATION

DUP	(n → n n)	Duplicate top of stack.
DROP	(n →)	Discard top of stack.
SWAP	(n1 n2 → n2 n1)	Exchange top two stack items.
OVER	(n1 n2 → n1 n2 n1)	Make copy of second item on top.
ROT	(n1 n2 n3 → n2 n3 n1)	Rotate third item to top. "rote"
PICK	(n1 → n2)	Copy n1-th item to top. (Thus 1 PICK = DUP , 2 PICK = OVER)
ROLL	(n →)	Rotate n-th item to top. (Thus 2 ROLL = SWAP , 3 ROLL = ROT)
?DUP	(n → n (n))	Duplicate only if non-zero. "query-dup"
>R	(n →)	Move top item to "return stack" for temporary storage (use caution). "to-r"
R>	(→ n)	Retrieve item from return stack. "r-from"
R@	(→ n)	Copy top of return stack onto stack. "r-fetch"
DEPTH	(→ n)	Count number of items on stack.

COMPARISON

<	(n1 n2 → flag)	True if n1 less than n2. "less-than"
=	(n1 n2 → flag)	True if top two numbers are equal. "equals"
>	(n1 n2 → flag)	True if n1 greater than n2. "greater-than"
0<	(n → flag)	True if top number negative. "zero-less"
0=	(n → flag)	True if top number zero. (Equivalent to NOT) "zero-equals"
0>	(n → flag)	True if top number greater than zero. "zero-greater"
D<	(d1 d2 → flag)	True if d1 less than d2. "d-less-than"
U<	(un1 un2 → flag)	Compare top two items as unsigned integers. "u-less-than"
NOT	(flag → ¬flag)	Reverse truth value. (Equivalent to 0=)

ALL ABOUT FORTH

ARITHMETIC AND LOGICAL

+	(n1 n2 → sum)	Add. "plus"
D+	(d1 d2 → sum)	Add double-precision numbers. "d-plus"
-	(n1 n2 → diff)	Subtract (n1−n2). "minus"
1+	(n → n+1)	Add 1 to top number. "one-plus"
1-	(n → n−1)	Subtract 1 from top number. "one-minus"
2+	(n → n+2)	Add 2 to top number. "two-plus"
2-	(n → n−2)	Subtract 2 from top number. "two-minus"
*	(n1 n2 → prod)	Multiply. "times"
/	(n1 n2 → quot)	Divide (n1/n2). (Quotient rounded toward zero) "divide"
MOD	(n1 n2 → rem)	Modulo (i.e., remainder from division n1/n2). Remainder has same sign as n1. "mod"
/MOD	(n1 n2 n3 → rem quot)	Divide, giving remainder and quotient. "divide-mod"
*/MOD	(n1 n2 n3 → rem quot)	Multiply, then divide (n1*n2/n3), with double-precision intermediate. "times-divide-mod"
*/	(n1 n2 n3 → quot)	Like */MOD, but give quotient only, rounded toward zero. "times-divide"
U*	(un1 un2 → ud)	Multiply unsigned numbers, leaving unsigned double-precision result. "u-times"
U/MOD	(ud un → urem uquot)	Divide double number by single, giving remainder and quotient, all unsigned. "u-divide-mod"
MAX	(n1 n2 → max)	Leave greater of two numbers. "max"
MIN	(n1 n2 → min)	Leave lesser of two numbers. "min"
ABS	(n → |n|)	Absolute value. "absolute"
NEGATE	(n → −n)	Leave two's complement.
DNEGATE	(d → −d)	Leave two's complement of double-precision number. "d-negate"
AND	(n1 n2 → and)	Bitwise logical AND.
OR	(n1 n2 → or)	Bitwise logical OR.
XOR	(n1 n2 → xor)	Bitwise logical exclusive-OR. "x-or"

MEMORY

@	(addr → n)	Replace address by number at address. "fetch"
!	(n addr →)	Store n at addr. "store"
C@	(addr → byte)	Fetch least significant byte only. "c-fetch"
C!	(n addr →)	Store least significant byte only. "c-store"
?	(addr →)	Display number at address. "question-mark"
+!	(n addr →)	Add n to number at addr. "plus-store"
MOVE	(addr1 addr2 n →)	Move n numbers starting at addr1 to memory starting at addr2, if n>0.
CMOVE	(addr1 addr2 n →)	Move n bytes starting at addr1 to memory starting at addr2, if n>0. "c-move"
FILL	(addr n byte →)	Fill n bytes in memory with byte beginning at addr, if n>0.

CONTROL STRUCTURES

DO . . . LOOP	do: (end+1 start →)	Set up loop, given index range.
I	(→ index)	Place current loop index on data stack.
J	(→ index)	Return index of next outer loop in same definition.
LEAVE	(→)	Terminate loop at next LOOP or +LOOP, by setting limit equal to index.
DO . . . +LOOP	do: (limit start →) +loop: (n →)	Like DO . . . LOOP, but adds stack value (instead of always 1) to index. Loop terminates when index is greater than or equal to limit (n>0), or when index is less than limit (n<0). "plus-loop"
IF . . . (true) . . . THEN	if: (flag →)	If top of stack true, execute.
IF . . . (true) . . . ELSE . . . (false) . . . THEN	if: (flag →)	Same, but if false, execute ELSE clause.
BEGIN . . . UNTIL	until: (flag →)	Loop back to BEGIN until true at UNTIL.
BEGIN . . . WHILE . . . REPEAT	while: (flag →)	Loop while true at WHILE; REPEAT loops unconditionally to BEGIN. When false, continue after REPEAT.
EXIT	(→)	Terminate execution of colon definition. (May not be used within DO . . . LOOP)
EXECUTE	(addr →)	Execute dictionary entry at compilation address on stack (e.g., address returned by FIND).

Operand key:

n, n1, . . . 16-bit signed numbers	d, d1, . . . 32-bit signed numbers	addr, addr1, . . . addresses	char	7-bit ascii character value
	u unsigned	byte 8-bit byte	flag	boolean flag

ALL ABOUT FORTH 275

TERMINAL INPUT-OUTPUT

CR	(→)	Do a carriage return and line feed. "c-r"
EMIT	(char →)	Type ascii value from stack.
SPACE	(→)	Type one space.
SPACES	(n →)	Type n spaces, if n>0.
TYPE	(addr n →)	Type string of n characters beginning at addr, if n>0.
COUNT	(addr → addr+1 n)	Change address of string (prefixed by length byte at addr) to TYPE form.
−TRAILING	(addr n1 → addr n2)	Reduce character count of string at addr to omit trailing blanks. "dash-trailing"
KEY	(→ char)	Read key and leave ascii value on stack.
EXPECT	(addr n →)	Read n characters (or until carriage return) from terminal to address, with null(s) at end.
QUERY	(→)	Read line of up to 80 characters from terminal to input buffer.
WORD	(char → addr)	Read next word from input stream using char as delimiter, or until null. Leave addr of length byte.

NUMERIC CONVERSION

BASE	(→ addr)	System variable containing radix for numeric conversion.
DECIMAL	(→)	Set decimal number base.
.	(n →)	Print number with one trailing blank and sign if negative. "dot"
U.	(un →)	Print top of stack as unsigned number with one trailing blank. "u-dot"
CONVERT	(d1 addr1 → d2 addr2)	Convert string at addr1+1 to double number. Add to d1 leaving sum d2 and addr2 of first non-digit.
<#	(→)	Start numeric output string conversion. "less-sharp"
#	(ud1 → ud2)	Convert next digit of unsigned double number and add character to output string. "sharp"
#S	(ud → 0 0)	Convert all significant digits of unsigned double number to output string. "sharp-s"
HOLD	(char →)	Add ascii char to output string.
SIGN	(n →)	Add minus sign to output string if n<0.
#>	(d → addr n)	Drop d and terminate numeric output string, leaving addr and count for TYPE. "sharp-greater"

ALL ABOUT FORTH

MASS STORAGE INPUT/OUTPUT

LIST	(n →)	List screen n and set SCR to contain n.
LOAD	(n →)	Interpret screen n, then resume interpretation of the current input stream.
SCR	(→ addr)	System variable containing screen number most recently listed.
BLOCK	(n → addr)	Leave memory address of block, reading from mass storage if necessary.
UPDATE	(↑ → addr)	Mark last block referenced as modified.
BUFFER	(n → addr)	Leave addr of a free buffer, assigned to block n; write previous contents to mass storage if UPDATEd.
SAVE-BUFFERS	(↑ →)	Write all UPDATEd blocks to mass storage.
EMPTY-BUFFERS	(↑)	Mark all block buffers as empty, without writing UPDATEd blocks to mass storage.

DEFINING WORDS

: xxx	(↑ ↑)	Begin colon definition of xxx . "colon"
;	(↑ ↑)	End colon definition. "semi-colon"
VARIABLE xxx	xxx: (→ addr)	Create a two-byte variable named xxx ; returns address when executed.
CONSTANT xxx	(n →) xxx: (→ n)	Create a constant named xxx with value n; returns value when executed.
VOCABULARY xxx	(↑ ↑)	Create a vocabulary named xxx : becomes CONTEXT vocabulary when executed.
CREATE ... DOES>	does: (→ addr)	Used to create a new defining word, with execution-time routine in high-level FORTH. "does"

VOCABULARIES

CONTEXT	(→ addr)	System variable pointing to vocabulary where word names are searched for.
CURRENT	(→ addr)	System variable pointing to vocabulary where new definitions are put.
FORTH	(↑ ↑)	Main vocabulary, contained in all other vocabularies. Execution of FORTH sets context vocabulary.
DEFINITIONS	(↑ ↑)	Sets CURRENT vocabulary to CONTEXT.
' xxx	(↑ → addr)	Find address of xxx in dictionary; if used in definition, compile address. "tick"
FIND	(↑ → addr)	Leave compilation address of next word in input stream. If not found in CONTEXT or FORTH, leave 0.
FORGET xxx	(↑)	Forget all definitions back to and including xxx , which must be in CURRENT or FORTH.

COMPILER

Word	Stack	Description
,	(n →)	Compile a number into the dictionary. "comma"
ALLOT	(n →)	Add two bytes to the parameter field of the most recently-defined word.
."	(→)	Print message (terminated by "). If used in definition, print when executed. "dot-quote"
IMMEDIATE		Mark last-defined word to be executed when encountered in a definition, rather than compiled.
LITERAL	(n →)	If compiling, save n in dictionary, to be returned to stack when definition is executed.
STATE	(→ addr)	System variable whose value is non-zero when compilation is occurring.
[		Stop compiling input text and begin executing. "left-bracket"
]		Stop executing input text and begin compiling. "right-bracket"
COMPILE		Compile the address of the next non-IMMEDIATE word into the dictionary.
[COMPILE]		Compile the following word, even if IMMEDIATE. "bracket-compile"

MISCELLANEOUS

Word	Stack	Description
(	(→)	Begin comment, terminated by) on same line or screen; space after (. "paren", "close-paren"
HERE	(→ addr)	Leave address of next available dictionary location.
PAD	(→ addr)	Leave address of a scratch area of at least 64 bytes.
>IN	(→ addr)	System variable containing character offset into input buffer, used, e.g., by WORD. "to-in"
BLK	(→ addr)	System variable containing block number currently being interpreted, or 0 if from terminal. "b-l-k"
ABORT	(→)	Clear data and return stacks, set execution mode, return control to terminal.
QUIT	(→)	Like ABORT, except does not clear data stack or print any message.
79-STANDARD	(→)	Verify that system conforms to FORTH-79 Standard.

FORTH INTEREST GROUP, P.O. Box 1105, San Carlos, CA 94070, USA

ALL ABOUT FORTH